How to Measure
Anything

How to Measure Anything

Finding the Value of "Intangibles" in Business

Douglas W. Hubbard

BICENTENNIAL

1807

WILEY

2007

BICENTENNIAL

John Wiley & Sons, Inc.

Library of Congress Cataloging-in-Publication Data:

Hubbard, Douglas W., 1962-

How to measure anything : finding the value of "intangibles" in business / Douglas W. Hubbard.

p. cm.

Includes index.

ISBN 978-0-470-11012-6 (cloth)

1. Intangible property—valuation.   I. Title.

HF5681.I55H83 2007

657'.7–dc22

2007004998

Printed in the United States of America

10 9 8 7 6 5

I dedicate this book to the people who are my inspirations for so many things: my wife Janet and to our children Evan, Madeleine, and Steven who show every potential for being renaissance people.

I also would like to dedicate this book to the military men and women of the United States, so many of whom I know personally. I've been out of the Army National Guard for many years, but I hope my efforts at improving battlefield logistics for the U.S. Marines by using better measurements have improved their effectiveness and safety.

Contents

Preface

I wrote this book to correct a costly myth that permeates many organizations today: that certain things can't be measured. The widely held belief must be a significant drain on the economy, public welfare, the environment, and even national security. "Intangibles" such as the value of quality, employee morale, or the economic impact of cleaner water are frequently part of some critical business or government policy decision. Often, an important decision requires better knowledge of the alleged intangible but when an executive believes something to be immeasurable, attempts to measure it will not even be considered.

As a result, decisions are less informed than they could be. The chance of error increases. Resources are misallocated, good ideas are rejected, and bad ideas are accepted. Money is wasted. In some cases life and health are put in jeopardy. The belief that some things—even very important things—might be impossible to measure is sand in the gears of the entire economy.

Any important decision maker could benefit from learning that anything they really need to know is measurable. On the other hand, in a democracy and a free enterprise economy, voters and consumers count among these "important decision makers." Chances are, your decisions in some part of your life or your professional responsibilities would be improved by better measurement. And it's virtually certain that your life has already been affected—negatively—by the lack of measurement in someone *else's* decisions.

I've made a career out of measuring the sorts of things many thought were immeasurable. I first started to notice the need for better measurement in 1988, shortly after I started working for Coopers & Lybrand as a brand-new MBA in their management consulting practice. I was surprised at how often a client would dismiss a critical quantity—something that would affect a major new investment or policy decision—as completely beyond measurement. Statistics and quantitative methods courses were still fresh in my mind and in some cases when someone called something "immeasurable," I would remember a specific example where it was actually measured. I began to suspect any claim of immeasurability as possibly premature and I would do research to confirm or refute the claim. Time after time, I kept finding that the allegedly immeasurable thing was already measured by an academic or perhaps professionals in another industry.

At the same time, I was observing that books about quantitative methods didn't focus on making the case that everything is measurable. They also did not focus on making the material accessible to the people who really needed it. They start with the assumption that the reader already believes something to be measurable, and it is just a matter of executing the appropriate algorithm. And these books tended to assume that the objective of the reader was a level of rigor that would suffice for publication in a scientific journal—not merely a decrease in uncertainty about some critical decision with a method a non-statistician could understand.

In 1995, after years of these observations, I decided that a market existed for better measurements for managers. I pulled together methods from several fields to create a solution. The wide variety of measurement-related projects I had since 1995 allowed me to fine-tune this method. Not only was every alleged immeasurable turning out not to be so, the most intractable "intangibles" were often being measured by surprisingly simple methods. It was time to challenge the persistent belief that important quantities were beyond measurement.

In the course of writing this book, I felt as if I was exposing a big secret and that once the secret was out, perhaps a lot of things will be different. I even imagined it would be a small "scientific revolution" of sorts for managers—a distant cousin of the methods of "scientific management" introduced a century ago by Frederick Taylor. This material should be even more relevant than Taylor's methods turned out to be for twenty-first century managers. Whereas scientific management originally focused on optimizing labor processes we now need to optimize measurements for management decisions. Formal methods for measuring those things management usually ignores has barely reached the level of alchemy. We need to move from alchemy to the equivalent of chemistry and physics.

The publisher and I considered several titles. All the titles considered started with "How to Measure Anything" but it wasn't always followed by "Finding the Value of Intangibles in Business." I give a seminar called "How to Measure Anything, But Only What You Need To." Since the methods in this book include computing the economic value of measurement (so that we know where to spend out measurement efforts), it seemed particularly appropriate. We also considered "How to Measure Anything: Valuing Intangibles in Business, Government and Technology" since there are so many technology and government examples in this book alongside the general business examples. But the title "How to Measure Anything: Finding the Value of Intangibles in Business" seemed to grab the right audience and convey the point of the book without necessarily excluding much of what the book is about.

The book is organized into four sections. The chapters and sections should be read in order because the first three sections rely on instructions from the earlier sections. Section I makes the case that everything is measurable and offers some examples that should inspire readers to attempt measurements even when it seems impossible. It contains the basic philosophy of the entire book and, if you don't read anything else, read this section. In particular, the specific definition of measurement discussed in this section is critical to correctly understand the rest of the book.

Section II begins to get into more specific substance about how to measure things—specifically uncertainty, risk—and the value of information. These are not only measurements in their own right but, in the approach I'm proposing, prerequisites to all measurements. The reader will learn how to measure their own subjective uncertainty with "calibrated probabilities assessments" and how to use that information to compute risk and the value of additional measurements. It is critical to understand these concepts before moving on to the next section.

Section III deals with how to reduce uncertainty by various methods of observation including random sampling and controlled experiments. It provides some short-cuts for quick approximations when possible. It also discusses methods to improve measurements by treating each observation as updating and marginally reducing a previous state of uncertainty. It reviews some material that readers may have seen in first-semester statistics courses, but it is written specifically to build on the methods discussed in the previous section. Some of the more elaborate discussions on regression modeling and controlled experiments could be skimmed over or studied in detail, depending on the needs of the reader.

Section IV is an eclectic collection of interesting measurement solutions and case examples. It discusses methods for measuring such things as preferences, values, flexibility, or quality. It covers some new or obscure measurement instruments including calibrated human judges or even the Internet. It summarizes and pulls together the approaches covered in the rest of the book with detailed discussions of two case studies and other examples.

In Chapter 1, I suggested a challenge for readers and I will reinforce that challenge by mentioning it here. Write down one or more measurement challenges you have in home life or work and read this book with the specific objective of finding a way to measure them. If those measurement influence a decision of any significance, then the cost of the book and the time to study it will be paid back many fold.

Acknowledgments

So many contributed to the content of this book through their suggestions, reviews and as sources of information about interesting measurement solutions. In no particular order I would like to thank the following:

Freeman Dyson	Pat Plunkett	Jack Stenner
Peter Tippett	Art Koines	Robyn Dawes
Barry Nussbaum	Terry Kunneman	Jay Edward Russo
Skip Bailey	Luis Torres	Reed Augliere
James Randi	Mark Day	Linda Rosa
Chuck McKay	Ray Epich	Mike McShea
Ray Gilbert	Dominic Schilt	Robin Hansen
Henry Schaffer	Jeff Bryan	Mary Lundz
Leo Champion	Peter Schay	Andrew Oswald
Tom Bakewell	Betty Koleson	George Eberstadt
Bill Beaver	Arkalgud Ramaprasad	David Grether
Juliana Hale	Harry Epstein	Todd Wilson
James Hammitt	Rick Melberth	Emile Servan-Schreiber
Rob Donat	Sam Savage	

Special thanks to Dominic Schilt at Riverpoint Group LLC who saw the opportunities with this approach in 1995 and gave so much support since then.

Measurement: The Solution Exists

## CHAPTER 1

The Intangibles and the Challenge

When you can measure what you are speaking about, and express it in numbers, you know something about it; but when you cannot express it in numbers, your knowledge is of a meager and unsatisfactory kind; it may be the beginning of knowledge, but you have scarcely in your thoughts advanced to the state of science.

—LORD KELVIN

Anything can be measured. If a thing can be observed in any way at all, it lends itself to some type of measurement method. No matter how "fuzzy" the measurement is, it's still a measurement if it told you more than you knew before. And those very things most likely to be seen as immeasurable are, virtually always, solved by relatively simple measurement methods.

As the title of this book indicates, we will discuss how to find the value of those things often called "intangibles" in business. There are two common understandings of the word intangible. First, it is routinely applied to things that, while they are literally not tangible (i.e., touchable, solid objects), can still be measured. Things like time, budget, patent ownership, and so on are good examples of things that you cannot touch but yet are measured. In fact, there is a well-established industry around valuing intangibles such as copyright and trademark ownership. But the word "intangible" has also come to mean utterly immeasurable in any way at all, directly or indirectly. It is in this context that I argue intangibles do not exist.

You've heard of "intangibles" in your own organization—things that presumably defy measurement of any type. The presumption of immeasurability is, in fact, so strong that no attempt is even made to make any observations that might tell you something—anything—about the alleged immeasurable that you might be surprised to learn. You may have run into one or more of these real-life examples:

- The "flexibility" to create new products
- The risk of failure of an information technology (IT) project
- The public health impact of a new government environmental policy
- The productivity of research
- The value of information
- The chance of one political party winning the White House
- Quality
- Public image

Each of these examples can very well be relevant to some major decision an organization must make. It could even be the single most important impact of an expensive new initiative in either business or government policy. Yet in most organizations, because the specific "intangible" was assumed to be immeasurable, the decision was not nearly as informed as it could have been.

One place I've seen this many times is in the "steering committees" that review proposed projects and decide which to accept or reject. Often the proposed projects are related to IT in some way. In some cases, the committees were categorically rejecting any investment where the benefits were primarily "soft" ones. Important factors with names like "improved word-of-mouth advertising," "reduced strategic risk," or "premium brand positioning" were being ignored in the evaluation process because they were considered immeasurable. It's not as if the project was being rejected simply because the person proposing it hadn't measured the benefit (a valid objection to a proposal); rather it was believed that the benefit couldn't possibly be measured—ever. Consequently, some of the most important strategic proposals were being overlooked in favor of minor cost-savings ideas simply because everyone knew how to measure those things and didn't know how to measure others.

The fact of the matter is that a few organizations have succeeded in analyzing and measuring all of the listed items, using methods that are probably less complicated than you would think. The purpose of this book is to show organizations two things:

1. Intangibles that appear to be completely intractable can be measured.

2. This measurement can be done in a way that is economically justified.

With a title like *How to Measure Anything*, anything less than a multivolume text would be sure to leave out something. My objective does not include every area of physical science or economics, especially where measurements are well developed. Those disciplines have measurement methods for a variety of interesting problems and are already much less inclined even to apply the label "intangible" to something they are curious about. The focus here is on measurements that are relevant—even critical—to major organizational decisions and yet don't seem to lend themselves to an obvious and practical measurement solution.

This book addresses some common misconceptions about intangibles, describes a "universal approach" to show how to go about measuring an "intangible," and backs it up with some interesting methods for particular problems. Throughout, I attempted to include some "inspirational" examples on how people have tackled some of the most "immeasurable" things I could find.

Without compromising substance, this book will also make some of the more seemingly esoteric statistics around measurement as simple as it can be. Whenever possible, math is converted into simpler charts, tables, and procedures. Some of the methods are so much simpler than what is taught in the typical "intro to stats" course that we should be able to overcome many phobias about the use of quantitative measurement methods. The reader does not need any advanced training in any mathematical methods at all. Readers just need some aptitude for clearly defining problems.

Readers are encouraged to use this book's Web site at www.howto measureanything.com. There, you will find a library of downloadable spreadsheets for many of the more detailed calculations shown in this book. There will also be additional learning aids, examples, and a discussion board for questions about the book or measurement challenges in general. It also provides a way for me to discuss new technologies or techniques that were not available when this book was printed.

I have one recommendation for a useful exercise to try. As you read through the chapters, write down those things you believe are immeasurable or, at least, you are not sure how to measure. After reading this book, my goal is that you are able to identify methods for measuring each and every one of them.

## CHAPTER 2

An Intuitive Measurement Habit: Eratosthenes, Enrico, & Emily

S etting out to develop the skills for any kind of measurement seems pretty ambitious, and a journey like that needs a light at the end of the tunnel. What we need are some best-in-class examples to follow for measurement—individuals who saw measurement solutions intuitively and often solved measurement problems with surprisingly simple methods. Fortunately, we have many people—at the same time inspired and inspirational—to show us what such a skill would look like. It's revealing, however, to find out that so many of the best examples seem to be from outside of business. In fact, this book will borrow heavily from outside of business to reveal measurement methods that can be applied to business.

Here are just a few people who, while they weren't working on measurement within business, can teach businesspeople quite a lot about what an intuitive feel for quantitative investigation should look like.

- In ancient Greece, a man estimated the circumference of Earth by looking at the different lengths of shadows in different cities at noon and by applying some simple geometry.

- A Nobel Prize–winning physicist taught his students how to estimate by estimating the number of piano tuners in Chicago.

- A nine-year-old girl set up an experiment that debunked the growing medical practice of "therapeutic touch" and, two years later, became the youngest person ever to be published in the *Journal of the American Medical Association*.

You may have heard of these individuals, or at least one or two of them. Even if you vaguely remember something about them, it is worth reviewing each in the context of the others. None of these people ever met each other personally (none lived at the same time), but each showed an ability to size up a measurement problem and identify quick and simple observations that have revealing results. They were able to estimate unknowns quickly by using simple observations. It is important to contrast their approach with what you might typically see in a business setting. The characters in these examples are or were real people named Eratosthenes, Enrico, & Emily.

How an Ancient Greek Measured the Size of Earth

Our first mentor of measurement did something that was probably thought by many in his day to be impossible. An ancient Greek named Eratosthenes (ca. 276–194 BC) made the first recorded measurement of the circumference of Earth. If he sounds familiar, it might be because he is mentioned in many high school trigonometry and geometry textbooks.

Eratosthenes didn't use accurate survey equipment, and he certainly didn't have lasers and satellites. He didn't even embark on a risky and probably lifelong attempt at circumnavigating Earth. Instead, while in the Library of Alexandria, he read that a certain deep well in Syene, a city in southern Egypt, would have its bottom entirely lit by the noon sun one day a year. This meant the sun must be directly overhead at that point in time. But he also observed that at the same time, vertical objects in Alexandria, almost straight north of Syene, cast a shadow. This meant Alexandria received sunlight at a slightly different angle at the same time. Eratosthenes recognized that he could use this information to assess the curvature of Earth.

He observed that the shadows in Alexandria at noon at that time of year made an angle that was equal to an arc of one-fiftieth of a circle. Therefore, if the distance between Syene and Alexandria was one-fiftieth of an arc, the circumference of Earth must be 50 times that distance. Modern attempts to replicate Eratosthenes's calculations vary by exactly how much the angles were, conversions from ancient units of measure, and the exact distances between the ancient cities, but typical results put his answer within 3% of the actual value.[1] Eratosthenes's calculation was a huge improvement over previous knowledge, and his error was less than the error modern scientists had just a few decades ago for the size and age of the universe. Even 1,700 years later, Columbus was apparently unaware of or ignored Eratosthenes's result; his estimate was fully 25% short (this is one of the reasons Columbus thought he might be in India, not another large, intervening landmass). In fact, a more accurate measurement than Eratosthenes's would not be available for another 300 years after Columbus. By then, two Frenchmen, armed with the finest survey equipment available in late-eighteenth-century France, numerous staff, and a significant grant, were finally able to do better than Eratosthenes.[2]

Here is the lesson for business: Eratosthenes made what might seem an impossible measurement by making a clever calculation on some simple observations. When I ask participants in my measurement and risk analysis seminars how they would make this estimate, without modern tools, they usually identify one of the "hard ways" to do it (e.g., circumnavigation). But Eratosthenes, in fact, *may not have even left the vicinity of the library* to make this calculation. One set of observations that would have answered this question would have been very difficult to make, but his measurement was based on other, simpler, observations. He wrung more information out of the few facts he could confirm instead of assuming the hard way was the only way.

ESTIMATING: BE LIKE FERMI

Another example from outside business that might inspire measurements within business is Enrico Fermi (1901–1954), a physicist who won the Nobel Prize in physics in 1938. He had a well-developed knack for intuitive, even casual-sounding measurements. One renowned example of his measurement skills was demonstrated at the first detonation of the atom bomb, the Trinity Test site, on July 16, 1945, where he was one of the atomic scientists observing the blast from base camp. While final adjustments were being made to instruments used to measure the yield of the blast, Fermi was making confetti out of a page of notebook paper. As the wind from the initial blast wave began to blow through the camp, he slowly dribbled the confetti into the air, observing how far back it was scattered by the blast (taking the farthest scattered pieces as being the peak of the pressure wave). Fermi concluded that the yield must be greater than 10 kilotons. This would have been news, since other initial observers of the blast did not know that lower limit. After much analysis of the instrument readings, the final yield estimate was determined to be 18.6 kilotons. Like Eratosthenes, Fermi was aware of a rule relating one simple observation—the scattering of confetti in the wind —to a quantity he wanted to measure.

The value of quick estimates was something Fermi was familiar with throughout his career. He was famous for teaching his students skills at approximation of fanciful-sounding quantities that, at first glance, they might presume they knew nothing about. The best-known example of such a "Fermi question" was Fermi asking his students to estimate the number of piano tuners in Chicago. His students—science and engineering majors— would begin by saying that they could not possibly know anything about such a quantity. Of course, some solutions would be to simply do a count of every piano tuner perhaps by looking up advertisements, checking with a licensing agency of some sort, and so on. But Fermi was trying to teach his students how to solve problems where the ability to confirm the results would not be so easy. He wanted them to figure out that they knew *something* about the quantity in question.

He would start by asking them to estimate other things about pianos and piano tuners that, while still uncertain, might seem easier to estimate. These included the current population of Chicago (a little over 3 million in the 1930s to 1950s), the average number of people per household (2 or 3), the share of households with regularly tuned pianos (not more than 1 in 10 but not less than 1 in 30), the required frequency of tuning (perhaps 1 a year, on average), how many pianos a tuner could tune in a day (4 or 5, including travel time), and how many days a year the turner works (say, 250 or so). The result would be computed:

Tuners in Chicago = Population/people per household

$\qquad$ × percentage of households with tuned pianos

$\qquad$ × tunings per year/(tunings per tuner per day

$\qquad$ × workdays per year)

Depending on which specific values you chose, you would probably get answers in the range of 20 to 200, with something around 50 being fairly common. When this number was compared to the actual number (which Fermi might get from the phone directory or a guild list), it was always closer to the true value than the students would have guessed. This may seem like a very wide range, but consider the improvement this was from the "How could we possibly even guess?" attitude his students often started with.

This approach also gave the estimator a basis for seeing where uncertainty came from. Was the big uncertainty about the share of households that had tuned pianos, how often a piano needed to be tuned, how many pianos can a tuner tune in a day, or something else? The biggest source of uncertainty would point toward a measurement that would reduce the uncertainty the most.

A Fermi question is not yet quite a measurement. It is not based on new observations. It is really more of an assessment of what you already know about a problem in such a way that it can get you in the ballpark. The lesson for business is to avoid the quagmire that uncertainty is impenetrable and beyond analysis. Instead of being overwhelmed by the apparent uncertainty in such a problem, start to ask what things about it you do know. As we will see later, assessing what you currently know about a quantity is a very important step for measurement of those things that do not seem as if you can measure them at all.

FERMI QUESTIONS FOR A NEW BUSINESS

Chuck McKay, with Wizard of Ads, encourages companies to use Fermi questions to estimate the market size for a product in a given area. Last year an insurance agent asked Chuck to evaluate an opportunity to open a new office in Wichita Falls, Texas, for an insurance carrier that currently had no local presence there. Is there room for another carrier in this market? To test the feasibility of this business proposition, McKay answered a few Fermi questions with some Internet searches. Like Fermi, McKay started with the big population questions and proceeded from there.

According to City-Data.com, there were 62,172 cars in Wichita Falls. According to the Insurance Information Institute, the average automobile insurance annual premium in the state of Texas was $837.40. McKay assumed that almost all cars have insurance, since it is mandatory, so the gross insurance revenue in town was $52,062,833 each year. The agent knew the average commission rate was 12%, so the total commission pool was $6,247,540 per year. According to Switchboard.com, there were 38 insurance agencies in town, a number that is very close to what was reported in Yellowbook.com. When the commission pool is divided by those 38 agencies, the average agency commissions are $164,409 per year.

This market was probably getting tight since City-Data.com also showed the population of Wichita Falls fell from 104,197 in 2000 to 99,846 in 2005. Furthermore, a few of the bigger firms probably wrote the majority of the business, so the revenue would be even less than that—and all this before taking out office overhead.

McKay's conclusion: A new insurance agency with a new brand in town didn't have a good chance of being very profitable, and the agent should pass on the opportunity.

EXPERIMENTS: NOT JUST FOR ADULTS

Another person who seemed to have a knack for measuring her world was Emily Rosa. Although Emily published one of her measurements in the *Journal of the American Medical Association* (*JAMA*), she did not have a PhD or even a high school diploma. At the time she conducted the measurement, Emily was a 9-year-old working on an idea for her fourth-grade science fair project. She was just 11 years old when her research was published, making her the youngest person ever to have research published in the prestigious medical journal and perhaps the youngest in any major, peer-reviewed scientific journal.

In 1996 Emily saw her mother, Linda, watching a videotape on a growing industry called "therapeutic touch," a controversial method of treating ailments by manipulating the patients' "energy fields." While the patient lay still, a therapist would move his or her hands just inches away from the patient's body to detect and remove "undesirable energies," which presumably caused various illnesses. Emily suggested to her mother that she might be able to conduct an experiment on such a claim. Linda, who was a nurse and a long-standing member of the National Council Against Health Fraud (NCAHF), gave Emily some advice on the method.

Emily initially recruited 15 therapists for her science fair experiment. The test involved Emily and the therapist sitting on opposite sides of a table. A cardboard screen separated them, blocking each from the view of the other. The screen had holes cut out at the bottom through which the therapist would place her hands, palms up, and out of sight. Emily would flip a coin and, based on the result, place her hand four to five inches over the therapist's left or right hand. The therapists, unable to see Emily, would have to determine whether the girl was holding her hand over their left or right hand by feeling for the girl's energy field. Emily reported her results at the science fair and got a blue ribbon—as everyone else did.

Linda mentioned Emily's experiment to Dr. Stephen Barrett, whom she knew from the NCAHF. Barrett, intrigued by both the simplicity of the method and the initial findings, then mentioned it to the producers of the TV show *Scientific American Frontiers* shown on the Public Broadcasting System. In 1997 the producers shot an episode on Emily's method, and Emily recruited 13 more therapists for the show, for a total of 28.

The 28 therapists made a total of 280 individual attempts to feel Emily's energy field. They correctly identified the position of Emily's hand just 44% of the time. Left to chance alone, they should get about 50% right with a 95% confidence interval of +/−16%. (If you flipped 280 coins, there is a 95% chance that between 34% and 66% would be heads.) So the therapists may have been a bit unlucky (since they ended up in the bottom half of the range), but their results are not out of bounds of what could be explained by chance alone. In other words, people "uncertified" in therapeutic touch—you or I—could have just guessed and done as well as or better than the therapists.

With these results, Linda and Emily thought the work might be worthy of publication. In April 1998 Emily, then 11 years old, had her experiment published in the *JAMA*. That earned her a place in the *Guinness Book of World Records* as the youngest person ever to have research published in a major scientific journal and a $1,000 award from the James Randi Educational Foundation.

James Randi, retired magician and renowned skeptic, set up a foundation for investigating paranormal claims scientifically. Randi created the $1 million "Randi Prize" for anyone who can scientifically prove extrasensory perception (ESP), clairvoyance, dowsing, and the like. Randi dislikes labeling his efforts as "debunking" paranormal claims since he just assesses the claim with scientific objectivity. But since hundreds of applicants have been unable to claim the prize by passing simple scientific tests of their paranormal claims, debunking has been the net effect. Even before Emily's experiment was published, Randi was also interested in therapeutic touch and was trying to test it. But, unlike Emily, he managed to recruit only one therapist who would agree to an objective test—and that person failed.

After these results were published, therapeutic touch proponents stated a variety of objections to the experimental method, claiming it proved nothing. Some stated that the distance of the energy field was really one to three inches, not the four or five inches Emily used in her experiment.[3] Others stated that the energy field was fluid, not static, and Emily's unmoving hand was an unfair test. (This despite the fact that patients usually lie still during their "treatment.")[4] None of this surprises Randi. "People always have excuses afterward," he says. "But prior to the experiment every one of the therapists were asked if they agreed with the conditions of the experiment. Not only did they agree, but they felt confident they would do well." Of course, the best refutation of Emily's results would simply be to set up a controlled, valid experiment that conclusively proves therapeutic touch *does* work. No such refutation has yet been offered.

Randi has run into retroactive excuses to explain failures to demonstrate paranormal skills so often that he has added another small demonstration to his tests. Prior to the taking the test, Randi has subjects sign an affidavit stating that they agreed to the conditions of the test, that they would later offer no objections to the test, and that, in fact, they expected to do well under the stated conditions. At that point Randi hands them a sealed envelope. After the test, when they attempt to reject the outcome as poor experimental design, he asks them to open the envelope. The letter in the envelope simply states "You have agreed that the conditions were optimum and that you would offer no excuses after the test. You have now offered those excuses." Randi observes, "They find this extremely annoying."

The lesson here for business is manyfold. First, even touchy-feely-sounding things like "employee empowerment," "creativity," or "strategic alignment" must have observable consequences if they matter at all. I'm not saying that such things are "paranormal," but the same rules apply.

Second, Emily's experiment demonstrated the effectiveness of simple methods routinely used in scientific inquiry, such as a controlled experiment, sampling (even a small sample), randomization, and using a type of "blind" to avoid bias from the test subject or researcher. These simple elements can be combined to allow us to observe and measure a variety of phenomena.

Also, Emily showed that useful levels of experimentation can be understood by even a child on a small budget. (Linda Rosa said she spent

$10 on the experiment.) It's also interesting to note that Emily could have constructed a much more elaborate clinical trial of the effects of this method using test groups and control groups to test how much therapeutic touch improves health. But she didn't have to do that because she simply asked a more basic question. If the therapists can do what they claimed, then they must, Emily reasoned, *at least be able to feel the energy field*. If they can't do that (and it is the basic assumption of the claimed benefits), then everything about therapeutic touch is in doubt. She could have found a way to spend much more if she had, say, the budget of one of the smaller clinical studies in medical research. But she determined all she needed with more than adequate accuracy. By comparison, how many of your performance metrics methods could get published in a scientific journal?

Emily's example shows us how simple methods can produce a useful result. I have at times heard that "more advanced" measurements like controlled experiments should be avoided because upper management won't understand them. This seems to assume that all upper management really does succumb to the Dilbert Principle[5] (the rule that states that only the least competent get promoted). In my experience, upper management will understand it just fine, if you explain it well.

Emily, explain it to them, please.

EXAMPLE: MITRE INFORMATION INFRASTRUCTURE

An interesting business example of how a business might measure an "intangible" by first testing if it exists at all is the case of the Mitre Information Infrastructure (MII). This system was developed in the late 1990s by Mitre Corporation, a not-for-profit that provides federal agencies with consulting on system engineering and information technology. MII was a corporate knowledge base that spanned insular departments to improve collaboration.

In 2000 *CIO Magazine* wrote a case study about MII. The magazine's format for this sort of thing is to have a staff writer do all the heavy lifting for the case study itself and then to ask an outside expert to write an accompanying opinion column the called "Critical Analysis." The magazine often asked me to write the opinion column when the case was anything about value, measurement, risk, and so on, so I was asked to do so for the MII case.

The Critical Analysis column is meant to offer some balance in the case study since companies talking about some new initiative are likely to paint a pretty rosy picture. The article quotes Al Grasso, the chief information officer (CIO) at the time: "Our most important gain can't be as easily measured—the quality and innovation in our solutions that become realizable when you have all this information at your fingertips." However, in the opinion column, I suggested one fairly easy measure of "quality and innovation":

> "If MII really improves the quality of deliverables, then it should affect customer perceptions and ultimately revenue.[6] Simply ask a random sample of customers to rank the quality of some pre-MII and post-MII deliverables (make sure they don't know which is which) and if improved quality has recently caused them to purchase more services from Mitre."[7]

Like Emily, I proposed that Mitre not ask quite the same question the CIO might have started with, but a simpler, related question. If quality and innovation really did get better, shouldn't someone at least be able to tell that there *is any difference*? If the relevant judges (i.e., the customers) can't tell, in a blind test, that post-MII research is "higher quality" or "more innovative" than pre-MII research, then MII shouldn't have any bearing on customer satisfaction or, for that matter, revenue. If, however, they can tell the difference, then you can worry about next question: whether the revenue improved enough to be worth the investment of over $7 million by 2000. Like everything else, if Mitre's quality and innovation benefits could not be detected, then they don't matter. I'm told by current and former Mitre employees that my column created a lot of debate. However, they were not aware of any such attempt actually to measure quality and innovation. Remember, the CIO said this would be the *most important gain* of MII, and it went unmeasured.

Notes on What to Learn from Eratosthenes, Enrico, & Emily

Taken together, Eratosthenes, Enrico, & Emily show us something very different from what we are typically exposed to in business. Executives often say "We can't even begin to guess at something like that." They dwell ad infinitum on the overwhelming uncertainties. Instead of making any attempt at measurement, they prefer to be stunned into inactivity by the apparent difficulty in dealing with these uncertainties. Fermi might say, "Yes, there are a lot of things you don't know, but what *do* you know?"

Other managers might object: "There is no way to measure that thing without spending millions of dollars." As a result, they opt not to engage in a smaller study—even though the costs might be very reasonable—because such a study would have more error than a larger one. Yet perhaps even this uncertainty reduction might be worth millions, depending on the size and frequency of the decision it is meant to support. Eratosthenes and Emily might point out that useful observations can tell you something you didn't know before—even on a budget—if you approach the topic with just a little more creativity and less defeatism.

Eratosthenes, Enrico, & Emily inspire us in different ways. Eratosthenes had no way of computing the error on his estimate, since statistical methods for computing error would not be around for two more millennia. However, if he would have had a way to compute error, the errors in measuring distances between cities and exact angles of shadows might have easily accounted for his relatively small error. The concept of measurement as "error reduction" is a central theme of this book.

Likewise, our inspiration can be attributed only in part to Enrico Fermi. Since he won a Nobel Prize, it's safe to assume that Fermi was an especially proficient experimental and theoretical physicist. But the example of his "Fermi questions" showed, even for non–Nobel Prize winners, how we can estimate things that, at first, seem too difficult even to attempt to estimate. Although his insight on advanced experimental methods of all sorts would be enlightening, I find that the reason intangibles seem intangible is almost never for lack of the most sophisticated measurement methods. Usually things that seem immeasurable in business reveal themselves to much simpler methods of observation, once we learn to see through the illusion of immeasurability. In this context, Fermi's value to us is in how we determine our current state of knowledge about a thing as a precursor to further measurement.

Unlike Fermi's example, Emily's example is not so much about initial estimation since her experiment made no prior assumptions about how probable the therapeutic touch claims were. Nor is it about using a clever calculation instead of infeasible observations, like Eratosthenes. Her calculation was merely based on standard sampling methods and did not itself require a leap of insight like Eratosthenes's simple geometry calculation. But Emily does demonstrate that useful observations are not necessarily complex, expensive, or even, as is sometimes claimed, beyond the comprehension of upper management even for ephemeral concepts like touch therapy or strategic alignment.

And as useful as these lessons are, we will build even further on the lessons Eratosthenes, Enrico, & Emily. We will learn ways to assess your current uncertainty about a quantity that improve on Fermi's methods, some sampling methods that are in some ways even simpler than what Emily used, and simple methods that would have allowed even Eratosthenes to improve on his estimate.

ENDNOTES

1. M. Lial and C. Miller, *Trigonometry*, 3rd ed. (Chicago: Scott, Foresman 1988).
2. Two Frenchmen, Pierre-Franois-André Méchain and Jean-Baptiste-Joseph, calculated Earth's circumference over a seven-year period during the French Revolution on a commission to define a standard for the meter. (The meter was originally defined to be one 10-millionth of the distance from the equator to the pole.)
3. Letter to the Editor, *New York Times*, April 7, 1998.
4. "Therapeutic Touch: Fact or Fiction?" *Nurse Week*, June 7, 1998.
5. Scott Adams, *The Dilbert Principle*. (New York: Harper Business, 1996).
6. Although a not-for-profit, Mitre still has to keep operations running by generating revenue through consulting billed to federal agencies.
7. Doug Hubbard, Critical Analysis column accompanying "An Audit Trail," *CIO Magazine*, May 1, 2000.

## CHAPTER 3

The Illusion of Intangibles: Why Immeasurables Aren't

There are three reasons why people think that something can't be measured. Each of these three reasons is actually based on misconceptions about different aspects of measurement: concept, object, and method.

1. *Concept of measurement.* The definition of measurement itself is widely misunderstood. If one understands what it actually means, a lot more things become measurable.

2. *Object of measurement.* The thing being measured is not well defined. Sloppy and ambiguous language gets in the way of measurement.

3. *Methods of measurement.* Many procedures of empirical observation are not well known. If people were familiar with some of these basic methods, it would become apparent that many things thought to be immeasurable are not only measurable but may already have been measured.

A good way to remember these three common misconceptions is by using a mnemonic like "howtomeasureanything.com," where the *c*, *o*, and *m* in ".com" stand for concept, object, and method. Once we learn that these three objections are misunderstandings of one sort or another, it becomes apparent that everything really is measurable.

In addition to these reasons why something can't be measured, there are also three common reasons why something "shouldn't" be measured. The reasons often given for why something "shouldn't" be measured are:

- The economic objection to measurement (i.e., any measurement would be too expensive)
- The general objection to the usefulness and meaningfulness of statistics (i.e., "You can prove anything with statistics")
- The ethical objection (i.e., we shouldn't measure it because it would be immoral to measure it)

These three objections don't really argue that a measurement is impossible, just that it is not cost effective, is useless, or is morally objectionable. I will show that only the economic objection has any potential merit, but even that one is overused.

THE CONCEPT OF MEASUREMENT

As far as the propositions of mathematics refer to reality, they are not certain; and as far as they are certain, they do not refer to reality.

—ALBERT EINSTEIN

Although this may seem a paradox, all exact science is based on the idea of approximation. If a man tells you he knows a thing exactly, then you can be safe in inferring that you are speaking to an inexact man.

—BERTRAND RUSSELL, BRITISH MATHEMATICIAN AND PHILOSOPHER

For those who believe something to be immeasurable, the concept of measurement, or rather the *mis*conception of it, is probably the most important obstacle to overcome. If we incorrectly think that measurement means meeting some nearly unachievable criteria, then few things will seem measurable. I routinely ask those who attend my seminars or conference lectures what they think "measurement" means. (It's interesting to see how much thought this provokes among people who are actually in charge of some measurement initiative in their organization.) I usually get answers like "to quantify something," "to compute an exact value," "to reduce to a single number," or "to choose a representative amount," and so on. Implicit or explicit in all of these answers is that measurement is certainty—an exact quantity with no room for error. If that was really what the term means, then, indeed, very few things would be measurable.

But when scientists, actuaries, or statisticians perform a measurement, they seem to be using a different de facto definition. In their special fields, each of these professions has learned the need for a precise use of certain words sometimes very different from how the general public uses a word. Consequently, members of these professions usually are much less confused about the meaning of the word "measurement." The key to this precision is that their specialized terminology goes beyond a one-sentence definition and are part of a larger theoretical framework. In physics, gravity is not just some dictionary definition, but a component of specific equations that relate gravity to such concepts as mass, distance, and its effect on space and time. Likewise, if we want to understand measurement with that same level of precision, we have to know something about the theoretical framework behind it . . . or we really don't understand it at all.

A DEFINITION OF MEASUREMENT

Measurement: A set of observations that reduce uncertainty where the result is expressed as a quantity

For all practical purposes, the scientific crowd treats measurement as a set of *observations that reduce uncertainty where the result is expressed as a quantity.* A mere reduction, not necessarily elimination, of uncertainty will suffice for a measurement. Even if they don't articulate this definition exactly, the methods they use make it clear that this is what they really mean. The fact that some amount of error is unavoidable but can still be an improvement on prior knowledge is central to how experiments, surveys, and other scientific measurements are performed.

The practical differences between this definition and the most popular definitions of measurement are enormous. Not only does a true measurement not need to be infinitely precise to be considered a measurement, but the lack of reported error—implying the number is exact—can be an indication that empirical methods, such as sampling and experiments, were not used (i.e., it's not really a measurement at all). Real scientific methods report numbers in ranges, such as "the average yield of corn farms using this new seed increased between 10% and 18% [95% confidence interval])." Exact numbers reported without error might be calculated "according to accepted procedure," but, unless they represent a 100% complete count (e.g., the change in my pocket), they are not necessarily based on empirical observation (e.g., Enron's asset valuations).

This conception of measurement might be new to many readers, but there are strong mathematical foundations—as well as practical reasons—for looking at measurement this way. Measurement is, at least, a type of information and, as a matter of fact, there is a rigorous theoretical construct for information. A field called information theory was developed in the 1940s by Claude Shannon. Shannon was an American electrical engineer, mathematician, and all-around savant who dabbled in robotics and computer chess programs.

In 1948 he published a paper titled "A Mathematical Theory of Communication," which laid the foundation for information theory and measurement in general. Current generations don't entirely appreciate this, but his contribution can't be overstated. Information theory has since become the basis of all modern signal processing theory. It is the foundation for the engineering of every electronic communications system, including every microprocessor ever built.

Shannon proposed a mathematical definition of information as the amount of uncertainty reduction in a signal, which he discussed in terms of the "entropy" removed by a signal. To Shannon, the receiver of information could be described as having some prior state of uncertainty. That is, the receiver already knew something, and the new information merely removed some, not necessarily all, of the receiver's uncertainty. The receiver's prior state of knowledge or uncertainty can be used to compute such things as the limits to how much information can be transmitted in a signal, the minimal amount of signal to correct for noise, and the maximum data compression possible.

This "uncertainty reduction" point of view is what is critical to business. Major decisions made under a state of uncertainty—such as whether to approve large information technology (IT) projects or new product development—can be made better, even if just slightly, by reducing uncertainty. Such uncertainty reduction can be worth millions.

So a measurement doesn't have to eliminate uncertainty after all. A mere *reduction* in uncertainty counts as a measurement and possibly can be worth much more than the cost of the measurement. But there is another key concept of measurement that would surprise most people: A measurement doesn't have to be about a quantity in the way that we normally think of it. Note where the definition I offer for measurement says "where the result is expressed as a quantity." The uncertainty, at least, has to be quantified, but the subject of observation might not be a quantity itself—it could be entirely qualitative, such as a membership in a set. For example, we could "measure" whether a patent will be awarded or whether a merger will happen while still satisfying our precise definition of measurement. But our uncertainty about those observations must be expressed quantitatively (e.g., there is an 85% chance we will win the patent dispute; we are 93% certain our public image will improve after the merger, etc.).

The view that measurement applies to questions with a yes/no answer or other qualitative distinctions is consistent with another accepted school of thought on measurement. In 1946 the psychologist Stanley Smith Stevens wrote an article called "On the Theory of Scales and Measurement." In it he describes different scales of measurement, including "nominal" and "ordinal." Nominal measurements are simply "set membership" statements, such as whether a fetus is male or female, or whether you have a particular medical condition. In nominal scales, there is no implicit order or sense of relative size. A thing is simply in one of the possible sets.

Ordinal scales, however, allow us to say one value is "more" than another, but not by how much. Examples of this are the four-star rating system for movies or Mohs hardness scale for minerals. A "4" on either of these scales is "more" than a "2" but not necessarily twice as much. But for homogeneous units such as dollars, kilometers, liters, volts, and the like, we can add these units in a way that makes sense. Whereas seeing four one-star movies is not necessarily as good as seeing one four-star movie, a four-ton rock weighs exactly as much as four one-ton rocks. A unit also allows us to compute ratios that make sense (e.g., four kilometers is really twice as far as two km).

Nominal and ordinal scales might challenge our preconceptions about what "scale" really means, but they are still useful observations about things. To a geologist, it is useful to know that one rock is harder than another, without necessarily having to know exactly how much harder—which is all that the Mohs hardness scale really does.

Stevens and Shannon each challenge different aspects of the popular definition of measurement. Stevens was more concerned about a taxonomy of different types of measurement but was silent on the all-important concept of uncertainty reduction. Shannon, working in a different field altogether, was probably unaware of and unconcerned with how Stevens, a psychologist, mapped out the field of measurements just two years earlier. However, I don't think a practical definition of measurement that accounts for all the sorts of things a business might need to measure is possible without both concepts of measurement.

The field of measurement theory attempts to deal with both of these issues, and more. In measurement theory, a measurement is a type of "mapping" between the thing being measured and numbers. The theory gets very esoteric, but if we focus on the contributions of Shannon and Stevens, there are many lessons for managers. The commonplace notion that presumes measurements are exact quantities ignores the usefulness of simply reducing uncertainty, if eliminating uncertainty is not possible or economical. In business, decision makers make decisions under uncertainty. When that uncertainty is about big, risky decisions, then uncertainty reduction has a lot of value—and that is why we will use that definition of measurement.

THE OBJECT OF MEASUREMENT

A problem well stated is a problem half solved.

—CHARLES KETTERING (1876–1958), AMERICAN INVENTOR,
HOLDER OF 300 PATENTS, INCLUDING ELECTRICAL IGNITION FOR
AUTOMOBILES

There is no greater impediment to the advancement of knowledge than the ambiguity of words.

—THOMAS REID (1710–1769), SCOTTISH PHILOSOPHER

Even when this more useful concept of measurement is adopted, some things seem immeasurable because we simply don't know what we mean when we first pose the question. We don't really know what it is we want to measure: the object of measurement. If someone asks how to measure "strategic alignment" or "flexibility" or "customer satisfaction," I simply ask: "What do you mean, exactly?" It is interesting how often people further refine their use of the term in a way that almost answers the measurement question by itself. At my seminars, I often ask the audience to challenge me with difficult or seemingly impossible measurements. In one case, a participant offered "mentorship" as something difficult to measure. I said, "That sounds like something one would like to measure. I might say that more mentorship is better than less mentorship. I can see people investing in ways to improve it, so I can understand the why someone might want to measure it. So, what do *you* mean by 'mentorship'?" The person almost immediately responded, "I don't think I know," to which I said, "Well, then maybe that's why it seems hard to measure to you. You have to figure out what it is first."

If I simply ask people what they mean and how it matters to them, they often answer the measurement question themselves. This is usually my first level of analysis when I conduct what I've called clarification workshops. It's simply a matter of clients stating a particular, but ambiguous, item they want to measure. I follow up by asking "What do you mean by <fill in the blank>?"

In 2000, when the Department of Veterans Affairs asked me to help them define performance metrics for IT security, I asked: "What do you mean 'IT security'?" and over the course of two or three more workshops, they defined it for me. They eventually revealed that what they meant by "IT security" were things like a reduction in unauthorized intrusions and virus attacks. They proceeded to describe that these things impact the organization through fraud losses, lost productivity, or even potential legal liabilities (which they may have narrowly averted when they recovered a stolen notebook computer in 2006 that contained the Social Security numbers of 26.5 million veterans).

All of the identified impacts were, in almost every case, obviously measurable. "Security" was a vague concept until they decomposed it into what they actually expected to observe. Still, clients often need further direction when defining these original concepts in a way that lends them to measurement. For the tougher jobs, I resort to using a "clarification chain" or, if that doesn't work, perhaps a type of thought experiment.

The clarification chain is just a short series of connections that should bring us from thinking of something as an intangible to thinking of it as a tangible. First, we recognize that if X is something that we care about, then X, by definition, must be detectable in some way. How could we care about things like "quality," "risk," "security," or "public image" if these things were totally undetectable, in any way, directly or indirectly? If we have reason to care about some unknown quantity, it is because we think it corresponds to desirable or undesirable results in some way. Second, if this thing is detectable, then it must be detectable in some amount. If you can observe a thing at all, you can observe more of it or less of it. Once we accept that much, the final step is perhaps the easiest. If we can observe it in some amount, then it must be measurable.

For example, once we figure out that we care about "public image" because it impacts specific things like advertising by customer referral which affects sales, then we have begun to identify how to measure it. Customer referrals are not only detectable, but detectable in some amount; this means they are measurable. I may not specifically take people through every part of the clarification chain, but if we can keep these three components in mind, the method is fairly successful.

CLARIFICATION CHAIN

1. If it matters at all, it is detectable/observable.
2. If it is detectable, it can be detected as an amount (or range of possible amounts).
3. If it can be detected as a range of possible amounts, it can be measured.

If the clarification chain doesn't work, I might try a thought experiment. Imagine you are an alien scientist who can clone pairs not just of sheep or even people, but entire organizations. Let's say you were studying a particular fast food chain and you were studying the effect of a particular intangible, say "employee empowerment." You create a pair of the same organization calling one the "test" group and one the "control" group. You give the test group a little bit more "employee empowerment" while holding the amount in the control group constant. What do you actually observe—in any way, directly or indirectly—that would change for the first organization? Would you expect decisions to be made at a lower level in the organization? Would this mean those decisions are better or faster? Does it mean that employees require less supervision? Does that mean you can have a "flatter" organization with less management overhead? If you can identify even a single observation that would be different between the two cloned organizations, then you are well on the way to identifying how you would measure it.

Identifying the object of measurement really is the beginning of almost any scientific inquiry, including the truly revolutionary ones. Business managers need to realize that some things seem intangible only because the managers just haven't defined what they are talking about. Figure out what you mean and you are halfway to measuring it.

THE METHODS OF MEASUREMENT

Some things may seem immeasurable only because the person considering the measurement might not be aware of basic measurement methods — such as various sampling procedures or types of controlled experiments—that can be used to solve the problem. A common objection to measurement is that the problem is unique and has never been measured before, and there simply is no method that would ever reveal its value. It is encouraging to know that several proven measurement methods can be used for a variety of issues to help measure something you may have at first considered immeasurable. Here are a few examples.

- *Measuring with very small random samples* (e.g., can you learn something from a small sample of potential customers, employees, and so on, especially when there is currently a great deal of uncertainty?)
- *Measuring the population of things that you will never see all of* (e.g., the number of a certain type of fish in the ocean, the number of plant species in the rain forests, the number of production errors in a new product or of unauthorized access attempts in your system *that go undetected*, etc.)

- *Measuring when many other, even unknown, variables are involved* (e.g., is the new "quality program" the reason for the increase in sales, or was it the economy, competitor mistakes, a new pricing policy, etc.?)
- *Measuring the risk of rare events* (e.g., the chance of a launch failure of a rocket that has never flown before, or another September 11 attack, or another levee failure in New Orleans)
- *Measuring the value of art, free time, or reducing risk to your life by assessing how much people actually pay for these things*

Most of these approaches to measurements are just variations on basic methods involving different types of sampling and experimental controls and, sometimes, choosing to focus on different types of questions. Basic methods of observation like these are mostly absent from certain decision-making processes in business, perhaps because such scientific procedures are considered to be some elaborate, overly formalized process. Such methods are not usually considered to be something you might do, if necessary, on a moment's notice with little cost or preparation. And yet they can be.

Here is a very simple example of a quick measurement anyone can do with an easily computed statistical uncertainty. Suppose you want to consider more telecommuting for your business. One relevant factor when considering this type of initiative is how much time the average employee spends commuting every day. You could engage in a formal office-wide census of this question, but it would be time consuming and expensive and will probably give you more precision than you need. Suppose, instead, you just randomly pick five people. There are some other issues we'll get into later about what constitutes "random," but, for now, let's just say you cover your eyes and pick names from the employee directory. Call these people and, if they answer, ask them how long their commute typically is. When you get answers from five people, stop. Let's suppose the values you get are 30, 60, 45, 80, and 60 minutes. Take the highest and lowest values in the sample of five: 30 and 80. There is a 93% chance that the median of the entire population of employees is between those two numbers. I call this "the Rule of Five." The Rule of Five is simple, it works, and it can be proven to be statistically valid for a wide range of problems. With a sample this small, the range might be very wide, but if it was significantly narrower than your previous range, then it counts as a measurement.

RULE OF FIVE

There is a 93% chance that the median of a population is between the smallest and largest values in any random sample of five from that population.

It might seem impossible to be 93% certain about anything based on a random sample of just five, but it's true. To understand why it is true, it is important to note that the Rule of Five estimates the median of a population. The median is the point where half the population is above it and half is below it. If we randomly picked five values that were all above the median or all below it, then the median would be outside our range. But what is the chance of that, really?

The chance of randomly picking a value above the median is, by definition, 50%— the same as a coin flip resulting in "heads." The chance of randomly selecting five values that happen to be all above the median is like flipping a coin and getting heads five times in a row. The chance of getting heads five times in a row in a random coin flip is 1 in 32, or 3.125%; the same is true with getting five tails in a row. The chance of *not* getting all heads or all tails is then 100%: 3.125% × 2, or 93.75%. Therefore, the chance of at least one out of a sample of five being above the median *and* at least one being below is 93.75% (round it down to 93% or even 90% if you want to be conservative). Some readers might remember a statistics class that discussed sampling methods for very small samples. Those methods were a little more complicated than the Rule of Five, but, for reasons I'll discuss in more detail later, the answer is really not much better.

We can improve on a rule of thumb like this by using simple methods to account for certain types of bias. Perhaps recent, but temporary, construction increased everyone's "average commute time" estimate. Or perhaps people with the longest commutes are more likely to call in sick or otherwise not be available for your sample. Still, even with acknowledged shortcomings, the Rule of Five is something that the person who wants to develop an intuition for measurement keeps handy.

Later I'll consider various methods that are proven to reduce uncertainty further. Some involve (slightly) more elaborate sampling or experimental methods. Some involve methods that are statistically proven simply to remove more error from experts' subjective judgments. There are all sorts of issues to consider if we wish to make even more precise estimates, but, remember, as long as an observation told us something we didn't know before, it was a measurement.

In the meantime, it's useful to consider why the objection "A method doesn't exist to measure this thing" is really not valid. In business, if the data for a particular question cannot already be found in existing accounting reports or databases, the object of the question is too quickly labeled as intangible. Even if measurements are thought to be possible, often the methods to do so are considered the domain of specialists or not practical for businesspeople to engage in themselves. Fortunately, this does not have to be the case. Just about anyone can develop an intuitive approach to measurement.

An important lesson comes from the origin of the word "experiment." "Experiment" comes from the Latin *ex-*, meaning "of/from," and *periri*, meaning "try/attempt." It means, in other words, to get something by trying. The statistician David Moore, the 1998 president of the American Statistical Association, goes so far as to say: "If you don't know what to measure, measure anyway. You'll learn what to measure."[1] We might call Moore's approach the Nike method: the "Just do it" school of thought. This sounds like a "Measure first, ask questions later" philosophy of measurement, and I can think of a few shortcomings to this approach if taken to extremes. But it has some significant advantages over much of the current measurement-stalemate thinking of some managers.

Many decision makers avoid even trying to make an observation by thinking of a variety of obstacles to measurements. If you want to measure how much time people spend in a particular activity by using a survey, they might say: "Yes, but people won't remember exactly how much time they spend." Or if you were getting customer preferences by a survey, they might say: "There is so much variance among our customers that you would need a huge sample." If you were attempting to show whether a particular initiative increased sales, they respond: "But lots of factors affect sales. You'll never know how much that initiative affected it." Objections like this are already presuming what the results of observations will be. The fact is, these people have no idea whether such issues will make measurement futile. They simply assume it.

Such critics are working with a set of assumptions about the difficulty of measurement. They might even claim to have a background in measurement that provides some authority (i.e., they took two semesters of statistics

20 years ago). I won't say those assumptions actually turn out to be true or untrue in every particular case. I will say they are unproductive if they are simply assumptions. Let's propose another set of assumptions that—by being assumptions—may not always be true in every single case but, in practice, turn out to be much more effective.

FOUR USEFUL MEASUREMENT ASSUMPTIONS

1. Your problem is not as unique as you think.
2. You have more data than you think.
3. You need less data than you think.
4. There is a useful measurement that is much simpler than you think.

Assumption 1

It's been done before. No matter how difficult or "unique" your measurement problem seems to you, assume it has been done before by someone else, perhaps in another field. If this assumption turns out not to be true, then take comfort in knowing that you might have a shot at a Nobel Prize for the discovery. Seriously, I've noticed that there is a tendency among professionals in every field to perceive their field as unique in terms of the burden of uncertainty. The conversation generally goes something like this: "Unlike other industries, in our industry every problem is unique and unpredictable," or "My industry just has too many factors to allow for quantification," and so on. I've done work in lots of different fields, and most of them make these same claims. So far, each one of them has turned out to have fairly standard measurement problems not unlike those in other fields.

Assumption 2

You have far more data than you think. Assume the information you need to answer the question is somewhere within your reach and if you just took the time to think about it, you might find it. Few executives are even remotely aware of all the data that are routinely tracked and recorded in their organization. The things you care about measuring are also things that tend to leave tracks, if you are resourceful enough to find them.

Assumption 3

You need far less data than you think. There are a lot of problems where the Rule of Five really does reduce uncertainty. I've met statisticians who didn't believe in the rule until they worked out the math for themselves. But, as Eratosthenes shows us, there are clever ways to squeeze interesting findings from minute amounts of data.

Assumption 4

There is a useful measurement that is much simpler than you think. Assume the first approach you think of is the "hard way" to measure. Assume that, with a little more ingenuity, you can identify an easier way. The Cleveland Orchestra, for example, wanted to measure whether its performances were improving. Many business analysts might propose some sort of randomized patron survey repeated over time. Perhaps they might think of questions that rate a particular performance (if the patron remembers) from "poor" to "excellent," and maybe they would evaluate them on several parameters and combine all these parameters into a "satisfaction index." The Cleveland Orchestra was just a bit more resourceful with the data available: It started counting the number of standing ovations. While there is no obvious difference among performances that differ by a couple of standing ovations, if we see a significant increase over several performances with a new conductor, then we can draw some useful conclusions about that new conductor. It was a measurement in every sense, a lot less effort than a survey, and—some would say—more meaningful. (I can't disagree.)

So, don't assume that the only way to reduce your uncertainty is using an impractically sophisticated method. Are you trying to get published in a peer-reviewed journal, or are you just trying to reduce your uncertainty about a real-life business decision? Think of measurement as iterative. Start measuring it. You can always adjust the method based on initial findings.

Above all else, the intuitive experimenter, as the origin of the word "experiment" denotes, *makes an attempt*. It's a habit. Unless you can precisely predict the outcome of an attempted observation—of any kind —then that observation tells you something you didn't know. Make a few more observations, and you know even more.

There might be the rare case where only for lack of the most sophisticated measurement methods, something seems immeasurable. But for those things labeled "intangible," more advanced, sophisticated methods are almost never what is lacking. Things that are thought to be intangible tend to be *so* uncertain that even the most basic measurement methods are likely to reduce some uncertainty.

ECONOMIC OBJECTIONS TO MEASUREMENT

The concept, object, and method objections, we learned, are all simply illusions. But there are also objections to measurement based not on the belief that a thing can't be measured but that it *shouldn't* be measured.

Perhaps the only valid basis to say that a measurement shouldn't be made is that the cost of the measurement exceeds its benefits. This certainly happens in the real world. In 1995 I developed a method I called Applied Information Economics, a method for assessing uncertainty, risks, and intangibles in any type of big, risky decision you can imagine. A key step in the process (in fact, the reason for the name) is the calculation of the economic value of information. I'll say more about this later, but a proven formula from the field of decision theory allows us to compute a monetary value for a given amount of uncertainty reduction. I put this formula in an Excel macro and, for years, I've been computing the economic value of measurements on every variable in dozens of various large business decisions. I found some fascinating patterns through this calculation but, for now, I'll mention just one: Most of the variables in a business case had an information value of zero. In each business case, something like one to four variables were both uncertain enough and had enough bearing on the outcome of the decision to merit deliberate measurement efforts.

ONLY A FEW THINGS MATTER

In business cases, only a few key variables merit deliberate measurement efforts. The rest of the variables have an "information value" at or near zero.

However, while there are certainly variables that do not justify measurement, a persistent misconception is that unless a measurement meets an arbitrary standard (e.g., adequate for publication in an academic journal or meets generally accepted accounting standards), it has no value. This is a slight oversimplification, but what really makes a measurement of high value is a lot of uncertainty combined with a high cost of being wrong. Whether it meets some other standard is irrelevant. If you are betting a lot of money on the outcome of a variable that has a lot of uncertainty, then even a marginal reduction in your uncertainty has a computable monetary value. For example, suppose you think developing an expensive new product feature will increase sales in one particular demographic by up to 12%, but it could be a lot less. Furthermore, you believe the initiative is not cost-justified unless sales are improved by at least 9%. If you make the investment and the increase in sales turns out to be less than 9%, then your effort will not reap a positive return. If the increase in sales is very low, or even possibly negative, then the new feature will be a disaster. Measuring this would have a very high value.

When someone says a variable is "too expensive" or "too difficult" to measure, we have to ask "Compared to what?" If the information value of the measurement is literally or virtually zero, of course, no measurement is justified. But if the measurement has any significant value, we must ask: "Is there any measurement method at all that can reduce uncertainty enough to justify the cost of the measurement?" Once we recognize the value of even partial uncertainty reduction, the answer is usually "Yes."

THE BROADER OBJECTION TO THE USEFULNESS OF "STATISTICS"

After all, facts are facts, and although we may quote one to another with a chuckle the words of the Wise Statesman, "Lies—damned lies—and statistics," still there are some easy figures the simplest must understand, and the astutest cannot wriggle out of.

—LEONARD COURTNEY, FIRST BARON COURTNEY, ROYAL STATISTICAL SOCIETY PRESIDENT (1897–1899)

Another objection is based on the idea that, even though a measurement is possible, it would be meaningless because statistics and probability itself is meaningless. ("Lies, Damned Lies, and Statistics," as it were.[2]) Even among educated professionals, there are often profound misconceptions about simple statistics. Some are so stunning that it's hard to know where to begin to address them. Here are a few examples I've run into:

"Everything is equally likely, because we don't know what will happen."

—*Mentioned by someone who attended one of my seminars*

"I don't have any tolerance for risk at all because I never take risks."

—*The words of a midlevel manager at an insurance company client of mine*

"How can I know the range if I don't even know the mean?"

—*Said by a client of Sam Savage, PhD, colleague and promoter of statistical analysis methods*

"How can we know the probability of a coin landing on heads is 50% if we don't know what is going to happen?"

—*A graduate student (no kidding) who attended a lecture I gave at the London School of Economics*

"You can prove anything with statistics."

—*A very widely-used phrase about statistics*

Let's address this last one first. I will offer a $10,000 prize, right now, to anyone who can use statistics to prove the statement "You can prove anything with statistics." By "prove" I mean in the sense that it can be published in any major math or science journal. The test for this will be that it *is* published in any major math or science journal (such a monumental discovery certainly will be). By "anything" I mean, literally, anything, including every statement in math or science that has already been conclusively disproved. I will use the term "statistics," however, as broadly as possible. The recipient of this award can resort to any accepted field of mathematics and science that even partially addresses probability theory, sampling methods, decision theory, and so on.

The point is that when people say "You can prove anything with statistics," they probably don't really mean "statistics," they just mean broadly the use of numbers (especially, for some reason, percentages). And they really don't mean "anything" or "prove." What they really mean is that "numbers can be used to confuse people, especially the gullible ones lacking basic skills with numbers." With this, I completely agree.

The other statements I list tend to be misunderstandings about more fundamental concepts behind probabilities, risk, and measurements in general. Clearly, the reason we use probabilities is specifically because we can't be certain of outcomes. Obviously, we all take some risks just driving to work, and we all, therefore, have some level of tolerance for risk.

I sometimes find that the people making these irrational claims don't even quite mean what they say, and their own choices will betray their stated beliefs. If you ask someone to enter a betting pool to guess the outcome of the number of heads in 12 coin tosses, even the person who claims odds can't be assigned will prefer the numbers around or near 6 heads. The person who claims to accept no risk at all will still fly to Moscow using Aeroflot (an airline with a safety record much worse than any U.S. carrier) to pick up a $1 million prize. The basic misunderstandings around statistics and probabilities come in a bewildering array that can't be completely anticipated. Some publications, such as the *Journal of Statistics Education*, are almost entirely dedicated to identifying basic misconceptions, even among business executives, and ways to overcome them. Suffice it to say, the reader who finishes this book will probably have fewer misconceptions about statistics.

ETHICAL OBJECTIONS TO MEASUREMENT

Let's discuss one final reason why someone might argue that a measurement shouldn't be made. This objection comes in the form of some sort of *ethical* objection to measurement. The potential accountability and perceived finality of numbers combine with a previously learned distrust of "statistics" to create resistance to measurement. Measurements can even sometimes be perceived as "dehumanizing" an issue. There is often a sense of righteous indignation when someone attempts to measure touchy topics, such as the value of an endangered species or even a human life. Yet it is done and done routinely for good reason.

The Environmental Protection Agency (EPA) and other government agencies have to allocate limited resources to protect our environment, our health, and even our lives. One of the many IT investments I helped the EPA assess was a Geographic Information System (GIS) for better tracking of methyl mercury—a substance suspected of actually lowering the IQ of children who are exposed to high concentrations.

To assess whether this system is justified, we must ask an important, albeit uncomfortable, question: Is the potentially avoided IQ loss worth the investment of more than $3 million over a five-year period? Someone might choose to be morally indignant at the very idea of even asking such a question, much less answering it. You might think that any IQ point for any number of children is worth the investment.

But wait. The EPA also had to consider investments in other systems that track effects of new pollutants that sometimes result in premature death. The EPA has limited resources, and there are a large number of initiatives it could invest in that might improve public health, save endangered species, and improve the overall environment. It has to compare initiatives by asking "How many children and how many IQ points?" as well as "How many premature deaths?"

Sometimes we even have to ask "How premature is the death?" Should the death of a very old person be considered equal to that of a younger person, when limited resources force us to make choices? At one point, the EPA considered using what it called a "senior death discount." A death of a person over 70 was valued about 38% less than a person under 70. Some people were indignant at this and, in 2003, the controversy caused then EPA administrator Christine Todd Whitman to announce that this discount was used for "guidance," not policy making and that it was discontinued.[3] Of course, even saying they are the same is itself a measurement of how we express our values quantitatively. But if they are the same, I wonder how far we can take that equivalency. Should a 99-year-old with several health problems be worth the same effort to save as a 5-year-old? Whatever your answer is, it is a measurement of the relative value you hold for each.

If we insist on being ignorant to the relative values of various public welfare programs (which is the necessary result of a refusal to measure their value), then we will almost certainly allocate limited resources in a way that solves less valuable problems for more money. This is because there is a large combination of possible investments to track such things and the best answer, in such cases, is never obvious without some understanding of magnitudes.

In other cases, it seems the very existence of any error at all (which, we know, is almost always the case in empirical measurements) makes an attempted measure morally outrageous. Stephen J. Gould, author of *The Mismeasure of Man*, has vehemently argued against the usefulness, or even morality, of measurements of the intellect like IQ or "g" (the general factor or intelligence that is supposed to underlie IQ scores). He said: "'g' is nothing more than an artifact of the mathematical procedure used to calculate it."[4] Although IQ scores and g surely have various errors and biases, they are, of course, not just mathematical procedures, but are based on observations (scores on tests). And since we now understand that measurement does not mean "total lack of error," the objection that intelligence can't be measured because tests have error is toothless.

Furthermore, other researchers point out that the view that measures of intelligence are not measures of any real phenomenon is inconsistent with the fact that these different "mathematical procedures" are highly correlated with each other[5] and even correlated with social phenomena like criminal behavior or income.[6] How can IQ be a purely arbitrary figure if it correlates with observed reality? I won't attempt to resolve that dispute here, but I am curious about how Gould would address certain issues like the environmental effects of a toxic substance that affects mental development. Since one of the most ghastly effects of methyl mercury on children, for example, are potential IQ points lost, is Gould saying no such effect can be real, or is he saying that even if it were real, we dare not measure it because of errors among the subjects? Either way, we would have to end up ignoring the potential health costs of this toxic substance and we might be forced— lacking information to the contrary—to reserve funds for another program. Too bad for the kids.

The fact is that the preference for ignorance over even marginal reductions in ignorance is never the moral high ground. If decisions are made under a self-imposed state of higher uncertainty, policy makers (or even businesses like, say, airplane manufacturers) are betting on our lives with a higher chance of erroneous allocation of limited resources. In measurement, as in many other human endeavors, ignorance is not only wasteful but can be dangerous.

Ignorance is never better than knowledge.

—ENRICO FERMI, WINNER OF THE 1938 NOBEL PRIZE FOR PHYSICS

Toward a Universal Approach to Measurement

We've heard of some people with interesting and intuitive approaches to measurement. We've also learned how to address the basic objections to measurement, including some "measurement maxims" and a few interesting measurement examples. We find that the reasons why something is considered immeasurable are each actually mere misconceptions. In different ways, all of these lessons combine to paint some of the edges of a general framework for measurement. We'll need to add a few more concepts to make it complete. This framework also happens to be the basis of the Applied Information Economics method I developed.

Even with all the different types of measurements there are to make, we can still construct a set of steps that apply to virtually any type of measurement. We can construct a universal approach. Every component of this approach is well known to some particular field of research or industry, but no one routinely puts them together into a coherent method. In this universal approach, six questions need to be asked:

1. What are you trying to measure? What is the real meaning of the alleged "intangible"?

2. Why do you care—what's the decision and where is the "threshold"?

3. How much do you know now—what ranges or probabilities represent your uncertainty about this?

4. What is the value of the information? What are the consequences of being wrong and the chance of being wrong, and what, if any, measurement effort would be justified?

5. Within a cost justified by the information value, which observations would confirm or eliminate different possibilities? For each possible scenario, what is the simplest thing we should see if that scenario were true?

6. How do you conduct the measurement that accounts for various types of avoidable errors (again, where the cost is less than the value of the information)?

I will add more detail to each step in this approach in later chapters, but I've discussed each of them in part already.

The benefits of seeing the world through "calibrated" eyes that see everything in a quantitative light have been a historical force propelling both science and economic productivity. Humans possess a basic instinct to measure, yet this instinct is suppressed in an environment that emphasizes committees and consensus over making simple observations. It simply won't *occur* to many managers that an "intangible" can be measured with simple, cleverly designed observations.

We have all been taught several misconceptions about measurement and what it means from our earliest exposure to the concept. We may have been exposed to basic concepts of measurement in, say, a chemistry lab in high school, but it's unlikely we learned much besides the idea that measurements are exact and apply only to the obviously and directly observable quantities. College statistics, however, probably helps to confuse as many people as it informs. When we go on to the workplace, professionals at all levels in all fields are inundated with problems that don't have the neatly measurable factors we saw in high school and college problems. We learn, instead, that some things are simply beyond measurement. However, as we saw, "intangibles" are a myth. The measurement dilemma can be solved. The "how much?" question frames any issue in a valuable way, and even the most controversial issues of measurement can be addressed when the consequences of not measuring are understood.

ENDNOTES

1. Cobb, George W. (1993). Reconsidering Statistics Education: A National Science Foundation Conference. Journal of Statistics Education, 1, 63–83.
2. This statement is often incorrectly attributed to Mark Twain, although he surely helped to popularize it. Twain got it from either one of two nineteenth-century British politicians, Benjamin Disraeli or Henry Labouchere.
3. Katharine Q. Seelye and John Tierney, " 'Senior Death Discount' Assailed: Critics Decry Making Regulations Based on Devaluing Elderly Lives," *New York Times,* May 8, 2003.
4. Stephen Jay Gould, *The Mismeasure of Man,* (New York: W. W. Norton & Company, 1981).
5. Reflections on Stephen Jay Gould's *The Mismeasure of Man* (1981): John B. Carroll, "A Retrospective Review," *Intelligence* 21 (1995): 121–134.
6. K. Tambs, J. M. Sundet, P. Magnus, and K. Berg, "Genetic and Environmental Contributions to the Covariance between Occupational Status, Educational Attainment, and IQ: A Study of Twins," *Behavior Genetics* 19, no. 2 (March 1989): 209–222.

Before You Measure

## CHAPTER 4

Clarifying the Measurement Problem

Confronted with apparently difficult measurements, it helps to put the proposed measurement in context. Before we measure we should ask five questions:

1. What is the decision this is supposed to support?
2. What really is the thing being measured?
3. Why does this thing matter to the decision being asked?
4. What do you know about it now?
5. What is the value to measuring it further?

In the Applied Information Economics method I developed and have used since 1995, I've been asking these questions systematically with everything we need to measure. The AIE approach has been applied in a total of over 50 major decision and measurement problems in a variety of organizations.[1] Stopping to ask these questions often completely changes not just *how* organizations should measure something but *what* they should measure.

The first three questions define what this thing is within the framework of what decisions depend on this measurement. If a measurement matters at all, it is because it must have some conceivable effect on decisions and behavior. If we can't identify what decisions could be affected by a proposed measurement and how that measurement could change them, then the measurement simply has no value.

For example, if you wanted to measure "product quality," it becomes relevant to and what could be affected by it and to ask the more general question of what "product quality" means. Are you using the information to decide on whether to change an ongoing manufacturing process? If so, how bad does quality have to be before you make changes to the process? Are you measuring product quality to compute management bonuses in a quality program? If so, what's the formula? All this, of course, depends on you knowing exactly what you mean by "quality" in the first place.

When I was with Coopers & Lybrand in the late 80's, we were on a consulting engagement with a small regional bank that was wondering how to streamline its reporting processes. The bank had been using a microfilm-based system to store the 60+ reports it got from branches every week, most of which were elective, not required for regulatory purposes. These reports were generated because someone in management thought they needed to know the information. These days, a good Oracle programmer might argue that it would be fairly easy to create and manage these queries; at the time, however, keeping up with these requests for reports was beginning to be a major burden. When I asked bank managers what decisions these reports supported, they could identify only a few cases where the elective reports had, or *ever could*, change a decision. Perhaps not surprisingly, the same reports that could not be tied to real management decisions were rarely even read. Even though someone initially had requested each of these reports, the original need was apparently forgotten. Once the managers realized that many reports simply had no bearing on decisions, they understood that those reports must, therefore, have no value.

Years later, a similar question was posed by staff of the Office of the Secretary of Defense (OSD). They wondered what the value was of a large number of weekly and monthly reports. When I asked if they could identify a single decision that each report could conceivably affect, they found quite a few that had no effect on any decision. Likewise, the information value of those reports was zero.

You also must ask the two other questions before you design a particular measurement method: How much do you know about this now and what is it worth to measure? Obviously, you have to know what it is worth to measure because you would probably come up with a very different measurement for quality if measuring it is worth $10 million per year than if it is worth $10,000 per year. And we can't compute the value until we know how much we know now and how the measurement affects specific decisions.

In the chapters that follow, we will discuss some examples regarding how to answer these questions. While exploring these "premeasurement" issues, we will show how the answers to some of these questions about uncertainty, risk, and the value of information are useful measurements in their own right.

Getting the Language Right: What "Uncertainty" and "Risk" Really Mean

As discussed, in order to measure something, it helps to figure out exactly what we are talking about and why we care about it. Information technology (IT) security is a good example of a problem that any modern business can relate to and needs a lot of clarification before it can be measured. To measure IT security, we would to ask such questions as "What do we mean by 'security'?" and "What decisions depend on my measurement of security?"

To most people, an increase in security should ultimately mean more than just, for example, who has attended security training or how many desktop computers have new security software installed. If security is better, then some risks should decrease. If that is the case, then we also need to know what we mean by "risk." Actually, that's the reason I'm starting with an IT security example. Clarifying this problem requires that we jointly clarify "uncertainty" and "risk." Not only are they measurable, they are key to understanding measurement in general.

Even though "risk" and "uncertainty" frequently are dismissed as immeasurable, a thriving industry depends on measuring both and does so routinely. One of the industries I've consulted with the most is insurance. I remember once conducting a business-case analysis for a director of IT in a Chicago-based insurance company. He said, "Doug, the problem with IT is that it is risky, and there's no way to measure risk." I replied, "But you work for an insurance company. You have an entire floor in this building for actuaries. What do you think they do all day?" His expression was one of epiphany. He had suddenly realized the incongruity of declaring risk to be immeasurable while working for an a company that measures risks of insured events on a daily basis.

The meaning of "uncertainty" and "risk" and the distinction between them seems ambiguous even for some experts in the field. Consider this quotation from Frank Knight, a University of Chicago economist in the early 1920s:

> *Uncertainty must be taken in a sense radically distinct from the familiar notion of Risk, from which it has never been properly separated. . . . The essential fact is that "risk" means in some cases a quantity susceptible of measurement, while at other times it is something distinctly not of this character; and there are far-reaching and crucial differences in the bearings of the phenomena depending on which of the two is really present and operating.*[2]

This is precisely why it is important to understand what decisions we need to support when defining our terms. Knight is speaking of the inconsistent and ambiguous use of "risk" and "uncertainty" by some unidentified groups of people. However, that doesn't mean *we* need to be ambiguous or inconsistent. In fact, these terms are described fairly regularly in the decision sciences in a way that is unambiguous and consistent. Regardless of how some might use the terms, we can choose to define them in a way that is relevant to the decisions we have to make.

DEFINITIONS FOR UNCERTAINTY, RISK, AND THEIR MEASUREMENTS

Uncertainty: The lack of complete certainty, that is, the existence of more than one possibility. The "true" outcome/state/result/value is not known.

Measurement of Uncertainty: A set of probabilities assigned to a set of possibilities. For example: "There is a 60% chance this market will more than double in five years, a 30% change it will grow at a slower rate, and a 10% chance the market will shrink in the same period."

Risk: A state of uncertainty where some of the possibilities involve a loss, catastrophe, or other undesirable outcome.

Measurement of Risk: A set of possibilities each with quantified probabilities and quantified losses. For example: "We believe there is a 40% chance the proposed oil well will be dry with a loss of $12 million in exploratory drilling costs."

We will get to how we assign these probabilities a little later, but at least we have defined what we mean—which is always a prerequisite to measurement. We chose these definitions because they are the most relevant to how we measure the example we are using here: security and the value of security. But, as we will see, these definitions also are the most useful when discussing *any* other type of measurement problem we have.

Whether others will continue to use ambiguous terms and have endless philosophical debates is of less concern to a decision maker faced with an immediate dilemma. The word "force," for example, was used in the English language for centuries before Sir Isaac Newton defined it mathematically. Today it is sometimes used interchangeably with terms like "energy" or "power"—but not by physicists and engineers. When aircraft designers use the term, they know precisely what they mean in a quantitative sense (and those of us who fly frequently appreciate their effort at clarity).

Now that we have defined "uncertainty" and "risk," we have a better tool box for defining terms like "security" (or "safety," "reliability," and "quality," but more on that later). When we say that security has improved, we generally mean that particular risks have decreased. If I apply the definition of risk given earlier, a reduction in risk must mean that the probability and/or severity (loss) of a certain list of events decrease. That is the approach I briefly mentioned earlier to help measure one very large IT security investment— the $100 million overhaul of IT security for the Department of Veterans Affairs.

EXAMPLES OF CLARIFICATION: LESSONS FOR BUSINESS FROM, OF ALL PLACES, GOVERNMENT

Many government employees imagine the commercial world as an almost mythical place of incentive-driven efficiency and motivation where fear of going out of business keeps everyone on their toes. I often hear government workers lament that they are not more like business. To those in the business world, however, the government (federal, state, or other) is a synonym for bureaucratic inefficiency and unmotivated workers counting the days to retirement. I've done a lot of consulting in both worlds, and I would say that neither generalization is entirely right or entirely wrong. Many people on either side would be surprised to learn that I think there are many things the commercial world can learn from (at least some) government agencies. The fact is that large businesses with vast internal structures still have workers so far removed from the economic realities of business that their jobs are as bureaucratic as any job in government. And I'm here to bear witness to the fact that the U.S. federal government, while certainly the largest bureaucracy in history, has many motivated and passionately dedicated workers. In that light, I will use a few examples from my government clients as great examples for business to follow.

Here is a little more background on the IT security measurement project for Veterans Affairs, which I briefly mentioned in the last chapter. In 2000, an organization called Federal CIO Council wanted to conduct some sort of test to compare different performance measurement methods. As the name implies, the Federal CIO Council is an organization consisting of the chief information officers of federal agencies and many of their direct reports. The council has its own budget and it sometimes sponsors research that can benefit all federal CIOs. After reviewing several approaches, the CIO Council decided it should test Applied Information Economics.

The CIO Council decided it would test AIE on the massive, newly proposed IT security portfolio at the Department of Veterans Affairs (VA). My task was to identify performance metrics for each of the security-related systems being proposed and to evaluate the portfolio, under the close supervision of the council. Whenever I had a workshop or presentation of findings, several council observers from a variety of agencies were often in attendance. At the end of each of the projects, they compiled their notes and wrote a detailed comparison of AIE to another popular method currently used in other agencies.

The first question I asked the VA is similar to the first question I ask on most measurement problems: "What do you mean 'IT security'?" In other words, what does improved IT security look like? What would we see or detect that was different if security was better or worse? Furthermore, what do we mean by the "value" of security?

IT security might not seem like the most ephemeral or vague concept we need to measure, but project participants soon found that they didn't *quite* know what they meant by that term.

It was clear, for example, that reduced frequency and impact of "pandemic" virus attacks is an improvement in security, but what is "pandemic" or, for that matter, "impact"? Also, it might be clear that an unauthorized access to a system by a hacker is an example of a breach of IT security, but is a theft of a laptop? How about a data center being hit by a fire, flood, or tornado? At the first meeting, participants found that while they all thought IT security could be better, they didn't have a common understanding of exactly what IT security was.

It wasn't that different parties had already developed detailed mental pictures of IT security and that they had a different picture in mind from someone else. Up to that point, *nobody* had thought about those details in the definition of IT security. Once group members were confronted with specific, concrete examples of IT security, they came to agreement on a very unambiguous and comprehensive model of what it is.

They resolved that improved IT security means a reduction in the frequency and severity of a specific list of undesirable events. In the case of the VA, they decided these events should specifically include virus attacks, unauthorized access (logical and physical), and certain types of other disasters (e.g., losing a data center to a fire or hurricane). Each of these types of events entails certain types of cost. Exhibit 4.1 presents the proposed systems, the events they meant to avert, and the costs of those events.

EXHIBIT 4.1   IT SECURITY FOR THE DEPARTMENT OF VETERANS AFFAIRS

Security Systems	Events Averted or Reduced	Costs Averted
Public Key Infrastructure (key encryption/ decryption, etc.)	Pandemic virus attacks	Productivity losses
Biometric/single sign-on (fingerprint readers, security card readers, etc.)	Unauthorized system access: external (hackers) or internal (employees)	Fraud losses
Intrusion-detection systems	Unauthorized physical access to facilities or property	Legal liability/ improper disclosure
A security-compliance certification program for new systems	Other disasters; fire, flood, tornado, etc.	Interference with mission (for the VA this mission is the care of veterans)
New antivirus software		
A security incident reporting system		
Additional security training		

Each of the proposed systems reduced the frequency or impact of specific events. Each of those events would have resulted in a specific combination of costs. A virus attack, for example, tends to have an impact on productivity, while unauthorized access might result in productivity loss, fraud, and perhaps even legal liability resulting from improper disclosure of private medical data and the like.

With these definitions, we have a much more specific understanding of "improved IT security" really means and, therefore, *how to measure it*. When I ask the question "What are you observing when you observe improved IT security?" VA management can now answer specifically. The VA participants realized that when they observe "better security," they are observing a reduction in the frequency and impact of these detailed events. They achieved the first milestone to measurement.

You might take issue with some aspects of the definition. You may (justifiably) argue that a fire is not, strictly speaking, an IT security risk. Yet the VA participants determined that, within their organization, they did mean to include the risk of fire. Still aside from some minor differences about what to include on the periphery, I think what we developed is really the basic model for any IT security measurements.

The VA's previous approach to measuring security was very different. It was actually using measures like the number of people who completed certain security training courses and the number of desktops that had certain systems installed. In other words, the VA wasn't measuring *results* at all. All previous measurement effort focused on things that were "easier" to measure. Prior to my work with the CIO Council, some people considered the ultimate impact of security immeasurable, so no attempt was made to achieve even marginally less uncertainty.

With the parameters we developed, we were set to measure some very specific things. We built a spreadsheet model that included all of these effects. This was really just another example of asking a few "Fermi" questions. For virus attacks, we asked the following:

- How often does the average pandemic (agency-wide) virus attack occur?
- When such an attack occurs, how many people are affected?
- For the affected population, how much did their productivity decrease relative to normal levels?

- What is the duration of the downtime?
- What is the cost of labor lost during the productivity loss?

If we knew the answer to each of these questions, we could compute the cost of agency-wide virus attacks as:

Average Annual Cost of Virus Attacks = number of attacks × average number of people affected × average productivity loss × average duration of downtime × annual cost of labor ÷ 2080 hours per year[3]

Of course, this calculation is only considering the cost of the equivalent labor that would have been available if the virus attack had not occurred. It does not tell us how the virus attack affected the care of veterans or other losses. Nevertheless, even if this calculation excludes some losses, at least it gives us a conservative lower bound of losses. Exhibit 4.2 shows the answers for each of these questions.

These ranges reflect the uncertainty of security experts who have had previous experience with virus attacks at the VA. With these ranges, the experts are saying that there is a 90% chance that the true values will fall between the upper and lower bounds given. I trained these experts so that they were very good at assessing uncertainty quantitatively. In effect, they were "calibrated" like any scientific instrument to be able to do this.

EXHIBIT 4.2   DEPARTMENT OF VETERANS AFFAIRS ESTIMATES FOR THE EFFECTS OF VIRUS ATTACKS

Uncertain Variable	The value is 90% likely to fall between or be equal to these points:	
Agency-wide virus attacks per year (for the next 5 years)	2	4
Average number of people affected	25,000	65,000
Percentage productivity loss	15%	60%
Average duration of productivity loss	4 hours	12 hours
Loaded annual cost per person (most affected staff would be in the lower pay scales)	$ 50,000	$ 100,000

These ranges may seem merely subjective, but the subjective estimates of some persons are demonstrably better than those of others. We were able to treat these ranges as valid because we knew the experts had demonstrated, in a series of tests, that when they said they were 90% certain, they would be right 90% of the time.

So far, you have seen how to take an ambiguous term like "security" and break it down into some relevant, observable components. By defining what security means, the VA made a big step toward measuring it. By this point, the VA had not yet made any observations to reduce their uncertainty. All they did was quantify their uncertainty by using probabilities and ranges.

It turns out that the ability of a person to assess odds can be calibrated—just like any scientific instrument is calibrated to ensure it gives proper readings. Calibrated probability assessments are the key to measuring your current state of uncertainty about anything. Learning how to quantify your current uncertainty about any unknown quantity is an important step in determining how to measure something in a way that is relevant to your needs. Developing this skill is the focus of the next chapter.

ENDNOTES

1. Between August 1995 and August 2006, there were 30 contracts with a total of 15 distinct companies or government agencies where some contracts covered the analysis of several major decisions.
2. Frank Knight, *Risk, Uncertainty and Profit* (New York: Houghton Mifflin Company, 1921), p 19–20.
3. 2080 hours per year is an Office of Management and Budget and Government Accountability Office standard for converting loaded annual salaries to equivalent hourly rates.

## CHAPTER 5

Calibrated Estimates: How Much Do You Know *Now*?

TESTING YOUR ABILITY TO ASSESS ODDS

How many hours per week do employees spend addressing customer complaints? How much would sales increase with a new advertising campaign? Even if you don't know the exact values to questions like these, you still know something. You know that some values would be impossible or at least highly unlikely. Knowing what you know now about something actually has an important and often surprising impact on how you should measure it or even whether you should measure it. What we need is a way to express how much we know now, however little that may be. On top of that, we need a way to know if we are any good at expressing uncertainty.

One method to express our uncertainty about a number is to think of it as a range of probable values. In statistics, a range that has a particular chance of containing the correct answer is called a confidence interval (CI). A 90% CI is a range that has a 90% chance of containing the correct answer. For example, you can't know for certain exactly how many of your current prospects will turn into customers in the next quarter, but you think that probably no less than 3 prospects and probably no more than 7 prospects will sign contracts. If you are 90% sure the actual number will fall between 3 and 7, then we can say you have a 90% CI of 3 to 7. You may have computed these values with all sorts of sophisticated statistical inference methods, but you might just have picked them out based on your experience. Either way, the values should be a reflection of your uncertainty about this quantity.

You can also use probabilities to describe your uncertainty about specific future events, such as whether a given prospect will sign a contract in the next month. You can say that there is a 70% chance that this will occur, but is that "right"? One way we can determine if a person is good at quantifying uncertainty is to look at all the prospects the person assessed and ask, "Of all the prospects she was 70% certain about closing, did about 70% actually close? Where she said she was 80% confident in closing a deal, did about 80% of them close?" And so on. This is how we know how good we are at subjective probabilities. We compare our expected outcomes to actual outcomes.

TWO EXTREMES OF SUBJECTIVE CONFIDENCE

Overconfidence: When an individual routinely overstates knowledge and is correct less often than he or she expects. For example, when asked to make estimates with a 90% confidence interval, many fewer than 90% of the true answers fall within the estimated ranges.

Underconfidence: When an individual routinely understates knowledge and is correct much more often than he or she expects. For example, when asked to make estimates with a 90% confidence interval, many more than 90% of the true answers fall within the estimated ranges.

Unfortunately, very few people are naturally calibrated estimators. Most of us tend to be biased either toward over- or underconfidence about our estimates. Putting odds on uncertain events or ranges on uncertain quantities is not a skill that arises automatically from experience and intuition.

Fortunately, several academic studies have proved that better estimates are attainable when estimators have been trained to remove their personal estimating biases.[1] Calibrated probability assessments were an area of research in decision psychology in the 1970s and 1980s and to a somewhat lesser degree today. Decision psychology concerns itself with how people actually make decisions, however irrational, in contrast to many of the "management science" or "quantitative analysis" methods taught in business schools, which focus on how to work out "optimal" decisions in specific, well-defined problems.

Researchers discovered that oddsmakers and bookies were generally better at assessing the odds of events than, say, executives. They also made some disturbing discoveries about how bad physicians are at putting odds on unknowns like "The chance there is a malignant tumor" or "The chance this chest pain is a heart attack." They reasoned that this variance among different professions shows that putting odds on uncertain things must be a learned skill.

Researchers learned how experts can measure whether they are systematically "underconfident," "overconfident," or have other biases about their estimates. Once this self-assessment has been conducted, they can learn several techniques for improving estimates and measuring the improvement. In short, researchers discovered that *assessing uncertainty is a general skill that can be taught with a measurable improvement.* That is, when calibrated sales managers say they are 75% confident that a new competitor will not get your major customer, there really is a 75% chance you will retain the customer.

Let's benchmark how good you are at quantifying your own uncertainty by taking a short quiz. Exhibit 5.1 contains 10 90% CI questions and 10 binary (i.e. True/False) questions. These are general knowledge questions that, unless you are a *Jeopardy* grand champion, you probably will not know with certainty. But they are all questions you probably have some idea about. These are similar to the exercises I give attendees in my workshops and seminars. The only difference is that the tests I give have more questions of each type, and I present several tests with feedback after each test. This calibration training generally takes about half a day.

But even with this small sample we will be able to detect some important aspects of your skills. More important, the exercise should get you to think about the fact that your current state of uncertainty is itself something you can quantify.

Calibration Exercise

Instructions: Exhibit 5.1 contains 10 of each of these two types of questions.

90% Confidence Interval (CI). For each of the 90% CI questions, provide both an upper bound and a lower bound. Remember that the range should be wide enough that you believe there is a 90% chance that the answer will be between your bounds.

EXHIBIT 5.1   **SAMPLE CALIBRATION TEST**

#	Question	90% Confidence Interval	
		Lower Bound	**Upper Bound**
1	In 1938 a British steam locomotive set a new speed record by going how fast (mph)?		
2	In what year did Sir Isaac Newton publish the Universal Laws of Gravitation?		
3	How many inches long is a typical business card?		
4	The Internet (then called 'Arpanet') was established as a military communications system in what year?		
5	In what year was William Shakespeare born?		
6	What is the air distance between New York and Los Angeles (miles)?		
7	What percentage of a square could be covered by a circle of the same width?		
8	How old was Charlie Chaplin when he died?		
9	How many days does it actually take the Moon to orbit Earth?		
10	The TV show *Gilligan's Island* first aired on what date?		

	Statement	Answer (True/False)	Confidence that you are correct (Circle one)
1	The ancient Romans were conquered by the ancient Greeks.		50% 60% 70% 80% 90% 100%
2	There is no species of three-humped camels.		50% 60% 70% 80% 90% 100%
3	A gallon of oil weighs less than a gallon of water.		50% 60% 70% 80% 90% 100%
4	Mars is always farther away from Earth than Venus.		50% 60% 70% 80% 90% 100%
5	The Boston Red Sox won the first World Series.		50% 60% 70% 80%90% 100%
6	Napoleon was born on the island of Corsica.		50% 60% 70% 80% 90% 100%
7	"M" is one of the three most commonly used letters.		50% 60% 70% 80% 90% 100%
8	In 2002 the price of the average new desktop computer purchased was under $1,500.		50% 60% 70% 80% 90% 100%
9	Lyndon B. Johnson was a governor before becoming vice president.		50% 60% 70% 80% 90% 100%
10	A kilogram is more than a pound.		50% 60% 70% 80% 90% 100%

Binary Questions. Answer whether each of the statements "true" or "false," then circle the probability that reflects how confident you are in your answer. For example, if you are absolutely certain in your answer, you should say you have a 100% chance of getting the answer right. If you have no idea whatsoever, then your chance should be the same as a coin flip (50%). Otherwise (probably usually), it is one of the values between 50% and 100%.

Of course, you could just look up the answers to any of these questions, but we are using this as an exercise to see how well you estimate things you can't just look up (e.g., next month's sales or the actual productivity improvement from a new IT system).

Important Hint: The questions vary in difficulty. Some will seem easy while others may seem too difficult to answer. But no matter how difficult the question seems, you still know something about it. Focus on what you *do* know. For the range questions, you know of some bounds beyond which the answer would seem absurd (e.g., you probably know Newton wasn't alive in ancient Greece or in the twentieth century). Similarly, for the binary questions, even though you aren't certain, you have some opinion, at least, about which answer is more likely.

After you've finished, but before you look up the answers, try a small experiment to test if the ranges you gave really reflect your 90% CI. Consider one of the 90% CI questions, let's say the one about when Newton published the Universal Laws of Gravitation. Suppose I offered you a chance to win $1,000 in one of the two following ways:

1. You will win $1,000 if the true year of publication of Newton's book turns out to be between the numbers you gave for the upper and lower bound. If not, you win nothing.

2. You spin a dial divided into two unequal "pie slices," one comprising 90% of the dial and the other just 10%. If the dial lands on the large slice, you win $1,000. If it lands on the small slice, you win nothing. (i.e., there is a 90% chance you win $1,000).

Which do you prefer? The dial has a stated chance of 90% that you win $1,000, a 10% chance you win nothing. If you are like most people (about 80%), you prefer to spin the dial. But why would that be? The only

EXHIBIT 5.2   **Spin to Win!**

explanation is that you think the dial has a higher chance of a payoff. The conclusion we have to draw is that the 90% CI you first estimated is really not your 90% CI. It might be your 50%, 65%, or 80% CI, but it can't be your 90% CI. This is called being overconfident, statistically speaking. You express your uncertainty in a way that indicates you have less uncertainty than you really have.

An equally undesirable outcome is to prefer option A, where you win $1,000 if the correct answer is within your range. This means that you think there is *more* than a 90% chance your range contains the answer, even though you are representing yourself as being merely 90% confident in the range.

The only desirable answer you can give is if you set your range just right so that you would be indifferent between options A and B. This means that at least you believe you have a 90% chance—not more and not less—that the answer is within your range. For an overconfident person (i.e., most of us), this means increasing the width of the range until options A and B are considered equivalent.

You can apply the same test, of course, to the binary questions. Let's say you were 80% confident about your answer to the question about Napoleon's birthplace. Again, you give yourself a choice between betting on your answer being correct or spinning the dial. In this case, however, the dial pays off 80% of the time. If you prefer to spin the dial, you are probably less than 80% confident in your answer. Now let's suppose we change the payoff odds on the dial to 70%. If you then consider spinning the dial just as good a bet (no better or worse) as betting on your answer, then you should say that you are really about 70% confident that your answer to the question is correct.

In my calibration training classes, I've been calling this the "equivalent bet test." As the name implies, it tests to see whether you are really 90%

confident in a range by comparing it to a bet that you should consider equivalent. Research indicates that even just pretending to bet money significantly improves a person's ability to assess odds.[2] In fact, *actually* betting money turns out to be only slightly better than pretending to bet (more on this in the Chapter 13 discussion about prediction markets).

Methods like the equivalent bet test help estimators give more realistic assessments of their uncertainty. People who are very good at assessing their uncertainty (i.e., they are right 80% of the time they say they are 80% confident, etc.) are called calibrated. There are a few other simple methods for improving your calibration, but first, let's see how you did on the test. The answers are in Appendix A.

To see how calibrated you are, we need to compare your expected results to your actual results. Since the range questions you answered were asking for a 90% CI, you are, in effect, saying that you expect 9 out of 10 of the true answers to be within your ranges. However, if you are like most people, you got less than that within your stated bounds. Granted, these are very small samples, so they can't measure your calibration precisely, but they're good approximate measures. Even with this small sample, if you got less than 7 answers within your bounds, then you are probably overconfident. If you got less than 5 within your bounds (as most people do), then you are very overconfident.

For the 90% CI questions in the test, you "expected" to get 9 within your ranges while the actual result was probably something less than that. Now you need to compute the "expected" value for your binary questions. For each of the answers, you said you were 50%, 60%, 70%, 80%, 90%, or 100% confident. Convert each of the percentages you circled to a decimal (i.e., 0.5, 0.6...1.0) and add them up. Let's say your confidence in your answers was 1, .5, .9, .6, .7, .8, .8, 1, .9, and .7, making your total 7.9. Your "expected" number correct was 7.9. Again, 10 is a small sample, but if your actual number correct was 2.5 or more lower than the expected correct number, you are probably overconfident.

FURTHER IMPROVEMENTS ON CALIBRATION

The academic research so far indicates that training has a significant effect on calibration. We already mentioned the equivalent bet test, which allows us to pretend we are tying personal consequences to the outcomes. Research (and my experience) also proves that another key method in calibrating a person's ability to assess uncertainty is repetition and feedback. To test this, we ask participants a series of trivia questions similar to the quiz you just took. They give me their answers, then I show them the true values, and they test again.

However, it doesn't appear that any single method completely corrects for the natural overconfidence most people have. To remedy this, I combined several methods and found that most people could be nearly perfectly calibrated.

Also, I routinely asked people to identify pros and cons for the validity of each of their estimates. A pro is a reason why the estimate is reasonable; a con is a reason why it might be overconfident. For example, your estimate of sales for a new product may be in line with sales for other start-up products with similar advertising expenditures. But when you think about your uncertainty regarding catastrophic failures or runaway successes in other companies as well as your uncertainty about the overall growth in the market, you may reassess the initial range. Academic researchers found that this method by itself significantly improves calibration.[3]

Finally, I also asked experts who were providing range estimates to look at each bound on the range as a separate "binary" question. A 90% CI interval means there is a 5% chance the true value could be greater than the upper bound and a 5% chance it could be less than the lower bound. This means that estimators must be 95% sure that the true value is less than the upper bound. If they are not that certain, they should increase the upper bound until they are certain. A similar test is applied to the lower bound. Performing this test seems to avoid the problem of "anchoring" by estimators. Anchoring is the effect of narrowing a range toward a certain number once you have that number in your mind. Some estimators say that when they provide ranges, they think of a single number and then add or subtract an "error" to generate their range. This might seem reasonable, but it actually tends to cause estimators to produce overconfident ranges (i.e., ranges that are too narrow). Looking at each bound alone as a separate binary question of "Are you 95% sure it is over/under this amount?" cures our tendency to anchor.

After a few calibration tests and practice with methods like listing pros and cons, using the equivalent bet, and anti-anchoring, estimators learn to

EXHIBIT 5.3	METHODS TO IMPROVE YOUR PROBABILITY CALIBRATION

1. *Repetition and feedback.* Take several tests in succession, assessing how well you did after each one and attempting to improve your performance in the next one.
2. *Equivalent bets.* For each estimate, set up the equivalent bet to test if that range or probability really reflects your uncertainty.
3. *Consider two pros and two cons.* Think of at least two reasons why you should be confident in your assessment and two reasons you could be wrong.
4. *Avoid anchoring.* Think of range questions as two separate binary questions of the form "Are you 95% certain that the true value is over/under (pick one) the lower/upper (pick one) bound?"

fine-tune their "probability senses." Most people get nearly perfectly calibrated after just a half day of training. Most importantly, even though subjects may have been training on general trivia, the calibration skill transfers to any area of estimation.

I've provided two additional calibration tests of each type—ranges and binary—in the Appendix. Try applying the methods summarized in Exhibit 5.3 to improve your calibration.

CONCEPTUAL OBSTACLES TO CALIBRATION

The methods just mentioned don't help if someone has irrational ideas about calibration or probabilities in general. While I find that most people in decision-making positions seem to have or are able to learn useful ideas about probabilities, some have surprising misconceptions about these issues. Here are some comments I've received while taking groups of people through calibration training or eliciting calibrated estimates after training:

- My 90% confidence can't have a 90% chance of being right because a subjective 90% confidence will never have the same chance as an objective 90%.
- This is my 90% confidence interval but I have absolutely no idea if that is right.
- We couldn't possibly estimate this. We have no idea.
- If we don't know the exact answer, we can never know the odds.

The first statement was made by a chemical engineer and it is indicative of the problem he was initially having with calibration. As long as he sees his subjective probability as inferior to objective probability, then he won't get calibrated. However, after a few calibration exercises, he did find that he could subjectively apply odds that were correct as often as the odds implied; in other words, his 90% confidence intervals contained the correct answers 90% of the time.

The rest of the objections are fairly similar. They are all based in part on the idea that not knowing exact quantities is the same as knowing nothing of any value. The woman who said she had "absolutely no idea" if her 90% confidence interval was right was talking about her answer to one specific question on the calibration exam. The trivia question was "What is the wingspan of a 747, in feet?" Her answer was 100 to 120 feet. Here is an approximate re-creation of the discussion:

> **Me:** Are you 90% sure that the value is between 100 and 120 feet?
>
> **Calibration Student:** I have no idea. It was a pure guess.
>
> **Me:** But when you give me a range of 100 to 120 feet, that indicates you at least believe you have a pretty good idea. That's a very narrow range for someone who says they have no idea.
>
> **Calibration Student:** Okay. But I'm not very confident in my range.
>
> **Me:** That just means your real 90% confidence interval is probably much wider. Do you think the wingspan could be, say, 20 feet?
>
> **Calibration Student:** No, it couldn't be that short.
>
> **Me:** Great. Could it be less than 50 feet?
>
> **Calibration Student:** Not very likely. That would be my lower bound.
>
> **Me:** We're making progress. Could the wingspan be greater than 500 feet?
>
> **Calibration Student:** [pause]. . .No, it couldn't be that long.
>
> **Me:** Okay, could it be more than a football field, 300 feet?
>
> **Calibration Student:** [seeing where I was going]. . .Okay, I think my upper bound would be 250 feet."
>
> **Me:** So then you are 90% certain that the wingspan of a 747 is between 50 feet and 250 feet?
>
> **Calibration Student:** Yes.
>
> **Me:** So your real 90% confidence interval is 50 to 250 feet, not 100 to 120 feet.

During our discussion, the woman progressed from what I would call an unrealistically narrow range to a range she really felt 90% confident contained the correct answer. She no longer said she had "no idea" that the range contained the answer because the new range represented what she actually knew.

This example is one reason I don't like to use the word "assumption" in my analysis. An assumption is a statement we treat as true for the sake of argument, regardless of whether it is true. Assumptions are necessary if you have to use deterministic accounting methods with exact points as values. You could never know an exact point with certainty so any such value must be an assumption. But if you are allowed to model your uncertainty with ranges and probabilities, you never have to state something you don't know for a fact. If you are uncertain, your ranges and assigned probabilities should reflect that. If you have "no idea" that a narrow range is correct, you simply widen it until it reflects what you do know.

It is easy to get lost in how much you don't know about a problem and forget that there are still some things you *do* know. There is literally nothing we will likely ever need to measure where our only bounds are negative infinity to positive infinity.

The next example is a little different from the last dialog, where the woman gave an unrealistically narrow range. The next conversation comes from the security example we were working on with the VA. The expert initially gave no range at all and simply insisted that it could never be estimated. He went from a saying he knew "nothing" about a variable, only to later concede that he actually is very certain about some bounds.

> **Me:** If your systems are being brought down by a computer virus, how long does the downtime last, on average? As always, all I need is a 90% confidence interval.
>
> **Security Expert:** We would have no way of knowing that. Sometimes we were down for a short period, sometimes a long one. We don't really track it in detail because the priority is always getting the system back up, not documenting the event.
>
> **Me:** Of course you can't know it exactly. That's why we only put a range on it, not an exact number. But what would be the longest downtime you ever had?
>
> **Security Expert:** I don't know, it varied so much. . .

Me: Were you ever down for more than two entire work days?

Security Expert: No, never two whole days.

Me: Ever more than a day?

Security Expert: I'm not sure. . .probably.

Me: We are looking for your 90% confidence interval of the average downtime. If you consider all the downtimes you've had due to a virus, could the average of all of them have been more than a day?

Security Expert: I see what you mean. I would say the average is probably less than a day.

Me: So your upper bound for the average would be. . .?

Security Expert: Okay, I think its highly unlikely that the average downtime could be greater than 10 hours.

Me: Great. Now let's consider the lower bound. How small could it be?

Security Expert: Some events are corrected in a couple of hours. Some take longer.

Me: Okay, but do you really think the average of all downtimes could be 2 hours?

Security Expert: No, I don't think the average could be that low. I think the average is at least 6 hours.

Me: Good. So is your 90% confidence interval for the average duration of downtime due to a virus attack 6 hours to 10 hours?

Security Expert: I took your calibration tests. Let me think. I think there would be a 90% chance if the range was, say, 4 to 12 hours.

This is a typical conversation for a number of highly uncertain quantities. Initially the experts resist giving any range at all, perhaps because they have been taught that in business, the lack of an exact number is the same as knowing nothing or perhaps because they will be "held accountable for a number." But *the lack of having an exact number is not the same as knowing nothing.* The security expert knew that an average virus attack duration of 24 working hours (three workdays), for example, would have been absurd. Likewise, it was equally absurd that it could be only an hour. But in both cases this is knowing something, and it quantifies the expert's uncertainty. A range of 6 to 10 hours is much less uncertainty than a range of 2 to 20 hours. Either way, the amount of uncertainty itself is of interest to us.

I call the method I used in the previous two dialogs the "absurdity test," and I apply it whenever I get the "there is no way I could know that" response or the "Here's my range, but it's a guess" response. No matter how little experts think they know about a quantity, it always turns out that there are still values they know are absurd. The point at which a value ceases to be absurd and starts to become unlikely but somewhat plausible is the edge of their uncertainty about the quantity. As a final test, I give them an equivalent bet to see if the resulting range is really a 90% confidence interval.

THE EFFECTS OF CALIBRATION

Since I started practicing this type of consulting in 1995, I've been tracking how well people do on the trivia tests and even how well calibrated people do in estimating real-life uncertainties, after those events have come to pass.

My calibration methods and tests have evolved a lot since 1995 but have been fairly consistent since 2001. Since then, I have taken a total of 142 people through the calibration training. For all those people, I've tracked their expected and actual results on several calibration tests, given one after the other during a half-day workshop. Since I was familiar with the research in this area, I expected significant, but imperfect, improvements toward calibration. What I was less certain of was the variance I might see in the performance from one individual to the next. The academic research usually shows aggregated results for all the participants in the research, so we can only see an average for a group. When I aggregate the performance of those in my workshops, I get a result very similar to the prior research. But because I could break down my data by specific subjects, I saw another interesting phenomenon.

Exhibit 5.4 shows the aggregated results of the range questions for all 142 participants for each of the tests given in the workshop. Those who showed significant evidence of good calibration early were excused from subsequent tests. (This turned out to be a strong motivator for performance.) The bar at the bottom of the chart shows what percentage of workshop participants ended their testing on that test number (i.e., were excused from further tests). For each test, the vertical line shows performance of the middle 90% of students and the black diamond shows the group mean. The target, of course, is to be at the thick horizontal line that indicates that 90% of the answers fell within respondents' stated 90% confidence intervals.

	Test 1	Test 2	Test 3	Test 4	Test 5	
	0	0	7	38	55	% finished on this test

142 total participants – 90% performance range and Mean for Each Test

EXHIBIT 5.4   **Aggregated Results of 90% CI Tests in Calibration Training**

The results seem to indicate significant improvement in the first three tests, but then a leveling-off short of ideal calibration. Even taking into account the fact that only the poor performers took the fourth and fifth tests, it looks like even three to four hours of intense training falls just short of the mark.

But when I broke down my data by student, I saw that most students perform superbly by the end of the training and it is a few poor performers who bring down the average. Statistically, we have to allow for some deviation from the target even for a perfectly calibrated person. Allowing only for this statistical error in the testing, fully 70% of participants are ideally calibrated after training. They are neither underconfident nor over-confident. Their 90% CI have about a 90% chance of containing the correct answer. Another 20% show significant improvement but don't quite reach ideal calibration. And 10% show no significant improvement at all from the first test they take. So why is it that about 1 in 10 people are apparently unable to improve at all in calibration training? Whatever the reason, it turns out not to be that relevant. Every single person we ever relied on for actual estimates was in the first two groups and almost all were in the first ideally calibrated group. Those who seemed to resist any attempt at calibration were, even before the testing, never considered to be the relevant expert or decision maker for a particular problem. It may be that they were less motivated, knowing their opinion would not have much bearing. Or it could be that those who lacked aptitude for such problems just don't tend to advance to the level of the people we need for the estimates. Either way, it's academic.

We see that training works very well for most people. But does proven performance in training reflect an ability to assess the odds of real-life uncertainties? The answer here is an unequivocal yes. I've had many opportunities to track how well calibrated people do in real-life situations, but one particular controlled experiment stands out. In 1997, I was asked to train the analysts of the IT advisory firm Giga Information Group (since acquired by Forrester Research, Inc.) in assigning odds to uncertain future events. Giga was an IT research firm that sold its research to other companies on a subscription basis. Giga had adopted the method of assigning odds to events they were predicting for clients, and it wanted to be sure it was performing well.

I trained 16 Giga analysts using the methods I described earlier. At the end of the training, I gave them 20 specific IT industry predictions they would answer as true or false and to which they would assign a confidence. The test was given in January 1997, and all the questions were stated as events occurring or not occurring by June 1, 1997 (e.g., "True or False: Intel will release its 300 MHz Pentium by June 1," etc.). As a control, I also gave the same list of predictions to 16 of their CIO-level clients at various organizations. After June 1 we could determine what actually occurred. I presented the results at Giga World 1997, their major symposium for the year. Exhibit 5.5 shows the results.

The horizontal axis is the chance the participants gave to their prediction on a particular issue being correct. The vertical axis shows how many of those predictions turned out to be correct. An ideally calibrated person should be plotted right along the thick dotted line. This means the person was right 70% of the time he or she was 70% confident in the predictions, 80% right when he or she was 80% confident, and so on. You see that the analysts' results (where the points are indicated by small squares) were very close to the ideal confidence, easily within allowable error. The results appear to deviate the most from "perfect calibration" at the low end of the scale, but this part is still within acceptable limits of error. (The acceptable error range is wider on the left of the chart and narrows to zero at the right.) Of all the times participants said they were 50% confident, they turned out to be right about 65% of the time. This means they might have known more than they let on and—only on this end of the scale—were a little underconfident. It's close; these results might be due to chance. There is 1% chance that 44 or more out of 68 would be right just by flipping a coin.

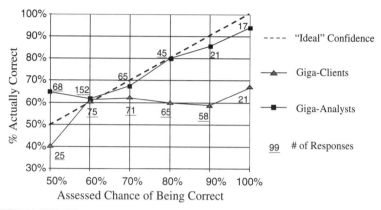

EXHIBIT 5.5 Calibration Experiment Results for 20 IT Industry Predictions in 1997

The deviation is a bit more significant—at least statistically if not visually—at the other end of the scale. Chance alone only would have allowed for slightly less deviation from expected, so they are a little overconfident on that end of the scale. But, overall, they are very well calibrated.

In comparison, the clients's results (indicated by the small triangles) who did not receive any calibration training were very overconfident. The numbers next to their calibration results show that 58 times a particular client said he or she was 90% confident in a particular prediction. Of those times, the clients got less than 60% of those predictions correct. The clients who even said they were 100% confident in a prediction in 21 specific responses got only 67% of those correct.

Equally interesting is the fact that the Giga analysts didn't actually get more answers correct. (The questions were general IT industry, not focusing on analyst specialties.) They were simply more conservative—but not overly conservative—about when they would put high confidence on a prediction. Prior to the training, however, the calibration of the analysts on general trivia questions was just as bad as the clients were on predictions of actual events. The results are clear: The difference in accuracy is due entirely to calibration training, and the calibration training works for real-world predictions.

Even though a few individuals have had some initial difficulties with calibration, most are entirely willing to accept calibration and see it as a key skill in estimation. Pat Plunkett is the program manager for Information

Technology Performance Measurement at the Department of Housing and Urban Development (HUD) and a thought leader in the U.S. government for the use of performance metrics. He has seen people from various agencies get calibrated since 2000. In 2000, Plunkett was still with the GSA and was the driver behind the CIO Council experiment that brought these methods into the VA. Plunkett sees calibration as a profound shift in thinking about uncertainty. He says: "Calibration was an eye-opening experience. Many people, including myself, discovered how optimistic we tend to be when it comes to estimating. Once calibrated, you are a changed person. You have a keen sense of your level of uncertainty."

Perhaps the only U.S. government employee who has seen more people get calibrated than Plunkett is Art Koines, a senior policy advisor at the Environmental Protection Agency, where dozens of people have been calibrated. Like Plunkett, he was also surprised at the level of acceptance. "People sat through the process and saw the value of it. The big surprise for me was that they were so willing to provide calibrated estimates when I expected them to resist giving any answer at all for such uncertain things."

The calibration skill was a big help to the VA team in the IT security case. The VA team needed to show how much it knew now and how much it didn't know now in order to quantify their uncertainty about security. The initial set of estimates (all ranges and probabilities) represent the current level of uncertainty about the quantities involved. This level provided the basis for the next steps: using odds in a decision model and computing information values.

You now understand how to quantify your current uncertainty by learning how to provide calibrated probabilities. Knowing how to provide calibrated probabilities is critical to the next steps in measurement. Chapters 6 and 7 will teach you how to use calibrated probabilities to compute risk and the value of information.

■ ENDNOTES

1. B. Fischhoff, L. D. Phillips, and S. Lichtenstein, "Calibration of Probabilities: The State of the Art to 1980," *Judgement under Uncertainty: Heuristics and Biases*, ed. D. Kahneman and A. Tversky, (New York: Cambridge University Press, 1982).
2. ibid
3. ibid

## CHAPTER 6

Measuring Risk: Introduction to the Monte Carlo Simulation

It is better to be approximately right than to be precisely wrong.

—WARREN BUFFETT

We've defined the difference between uncertainty and risk. Initially, measuring uncertainty is just a matter of putting our calibrated ranges or probabilities on unknown variables. Subsequent measurements, whatever they may be about, also measure uncertainty, with each measurement reducing uncertainty further.

Risk is simply a state of uncertainty where a possible outcome involves a loss of some kind. Generally, the implication is that the loss is something dramatic, not minor. With calibration methods, we see how to quantify our initial state of uncertainty with ranges and probabilities. The same is true when applying calibration methods to measuring risk.

What many organizations do to "measure" risk is not very enlightening. The methods for assessing risk which I'm about to describe would be familiar to an actuary, statistician, or financial analyst. But some of the most popular methods for measuring risk look nothing like what an actuary might see. Many organizations simply say a risk is "high," "medium," or "low." Or perhaps they rate it on a scale of 1 to 5. When I find situations like this, I sometimes ask how much "medium" risk really is. Is a 5% chance of losing more than $5 million a low, medium, or high risk? Nobody knows. Is a medium-risk investment with a 15% return on investment better or worse than a high-risk investment with a 50% return? Again, nobody knows.

To illustrate why these sorts of classifications are not as useful as they could be, I ask attendees in seminars to consider the next time they have to write a check (or pay over the Web) for their next auto or homeowner's insurance premium. Where you would usually see the "amount" field on the check, instead of writing a dollar amount, write the word "medium" and see what happens. You are telling your insurer you want a "medium" amount of risk mitigation. Would that make sense to the insurer in any meaningful way? It probably doesn't to you, either.

Using ranges to represent your uncertainty instead of unrealistically precise point values clearly has advantages. When you allow yourself to use ranges and probabilities, you don't really have to assume anything you don't know for a fact. But precise values have the advantage of being simple to add, subtract, multiply, and divide in a spreadsheet. So how do we add, subtract, multiply, and divide in a spreadsheet when we have no exact values, only ranges? Fortunately, a fairly simple trick can be done on any PC–Monte Carlo simulations, which were developed to do exactly that.

One of our measurement mentors, Enrico Fermi, was an early user of what was later called a Monte Carlo simulation. A Monte Carlo simulation uses a computer to generate a large number of scenarios based on probabilities for inputs. For each scenario, a specific value would be randomly generated for each of the unknown variables. Then these specific values would go into a formula to compute an output for that single scenario. This process usually goes on for thousands of scenarios.

Fermi, used Monte Carlo simulations to work out the behavior of large numbers of neutrons. In 1930, he knew that he was working on a problem that could not be solved with conventional integral calculus. But he could work out the odds of specific results in specific conditions. He realized that he could, in effect, randomly sample several of these situations and work out how large numbers of neutrons would behave in a system. In the 1940s and 1950s several mathematicians continued to work on similar problems in nuclear physics and started using computers to generate the random scenarios—most famously Stanislaw Ulam, John von Neumann, and Nicholas Metropolis. This time they were working on the atomic bomb in the Manhattan Project and, later, the hydrogen bomb at Los Alamos. At the suggestion of Metropolis, Ulam named this computer-based method of generating random scenarios after Monte Carlo, a famous gambling hotspot, in honor of Ulam's uncle, a gambler.[1]

What Fermi begat, and what was later reared by Ulam, von Neumann, and Metropolis, is today widely used in business, government, and research. A simple application of this method is working out the return on an investment when you don't know exactly what the costs and benefits will be. I once met with the chief information officer (CIO) of an investment firm in Chicago to talk about how the company can measure the value of information technology (IT). She said that they had a "pretty good handle on how to measure risk" but "I can't begin to imagine how to measure benefits."

On closer look, this is a very curious combination of positions. She explained that most of the benefits the company attempts to achieve in IT investments are improvements in basis points (1 basis point = 0.01% yield on an investment)—the return the company gets on the investments it manages for clients. The firm hopes that the right IT investments can facilitate a competitive advantage in collecting and analyzing information that affects investment decisions. But when I asked her how the company does it now, she said staffers "just pick a number." In other words, as long as enough people are willing to agree on (or at least not too many object to) a particular number for increased basis points, that's what the business case is based on. While it's possible this number is based on some experience, it was also clear that she was more uncertain about this benefit than any other. But if this is true, how is the company measuring risk? Clearly, it's a strong possibility that the firm's largest risk, if it was measured, would be the firm's uncertainty about this benefit. She was not using ranges to express her uncertainty about the basis point improvement, so she had no way to incorporate this uncertainty into her risk calculation. Even though she felt confident the firm was doing a good job on risk analysis, it's unlikely that it was doing much risk analysis at all.

In fact, *all* risk in an investment ultimately can be expressed by one method: the ranges of uncertainty on the costs and benefits. If you know precisely the amount and timing of every cost and benefit (as is implied by traditional business cases based on fixed point values), then you literally have no risk. There is no chance that any benefit would be lower or cost would be higher than you expect. But all we really know about these things is the range, not exact points. And because we only have broad ranges, there is a chance we will have a negative return. That is the basis for computing risk, and that is what the Monte Carlo simulation is for.

AN EXAMPLE OF THE MONTE CARLO METHOD AND RISK

This is an extremely basic example of a Monte Carlo simulation for people who have never worked with them before but have some familiarity with the Excel spreadsheet. If you have worked with a Monte Carlo tool before, you probably can skip these next few pages.

Let's say you are considering leasing a new machine for one step in a manufacturing process. The annual lease is $400,000 and you have to sign a multiyear contract. So if you aren't breaking even, you are stuck with it for a while. You are considering signing the contract because you think the more advanced device will save some labor and raw materials and because you think the maintenance cost will be lower than the existing process.

Your calibrated estimators gave these ranges for savings in maintenance, labor, and raw materials. They also estimated the annual production levels for this process.

- Maintenance savings (MS): $10 to $20 per unit
- Labor savings (LS):   -$2 to $8 per unit
- Raw materials savings (RMS): $3 to $9 per unit
- Production level (PL):   15,000 to 35,000 units per year
- Annual lease (breakeven): $400,000

Now you compute your annual savings very simply as:

$$\text{Annual Savings} = (\text{MS} + \text{LS} + \text{RMS}) \times \text{PL}$$

Admittedly, this is an unrealistically simple example. The production levels could be different every year, perhaps some costs would improve further as experience with the new machine improved, and so on. But we've deliberately opted for simplicity over realism in this example.

If we just took the midpoint of each of these ranges, we get

$$\text{Annual Savings} = (\$15 + \$3 + \$6) \times 25{,}000 = \$600{,}000$$

It looks like we do better than the required breakeven, but there are uncertainties. So how do we measure the risk of this investment? First, let's define risk for this context. Remember, to have a risk, we have to have uncertain future results with some of them being a quantified loss. One way of looking at risk would be the chance that we don't break even—that is, we don't save enough to make up for the $400,000 lease. The farther we undershoot the lease, the more we lost. The $600,000 is the middle of a range. How do we compute what that range really is and, thereby, compute the chance that we don't break even?

Since these aren't exact numbers, usually we can't just do a single calculation to determine whether we met the required savings or not. Some methods allow us to compute the range of the result given the ranges of inputs under some limited conditions, but in most real-life problems, those conditions don't exist. As soon as we begin adding and multiplying different types of distributions, the problem usually becomes what a mathematician would call "unsolvable" or "having no solution" with calculus. This is exactly the problem the physicists working on fission ran into. So, instead, we use a brute-force approach made possible with computers. We randomly pick a bunch of exact values—thousands—according to the ranges we prescribed and compute a large number of exact values.

The Monte Carlo simulation is an excellent method for solving this problem. We would have to randomly generate values within the stated ranges, put them into the annual savings formula, and compute a result. Some of the results will be higher than the $600,000 midpoint we computed and some will be lower. Some will even be lower than the $400,000 required to break even.

You can run a Monte Carlo simulation easily with Excel on a PC, but we need a bit more information than just the 90% confidence interval (CI) itself. We also need the *shape* of the distribution. Some shapes are more appropriate for certain values than other shapes. The one generally used with the 90% CI is the well-known "normal" distribution. The normal distribution is the familiar-looking bell curve where the probable outcomes are bunched near

What a "Normal Distribution" looks like:

Characteristics:

- Values near the middle are more likely than values farther away.
- The distribution is symmetrical, not lopsided—the mean is exactly halfway between the upper and lower bounds of a 90% CI.
- The ends trail off indefinitely to ever more unlikely values, but there is no "hard stop"; a value far outside of a 90% CI is possible but not likely.

How to make a random distribution with this shape in Excel:

=norminv(rand(),A, B)

A=mean = (90% CI upper bound + 90% CI lower bound)/2 and

B="standard deviation" =(90% CI upper bound – 90% CI lower bound)/3.29

EXHIBIT 6.1   The Normal Distribution

the middle but trail off to ever less likely values in both directions. (See Exhibit 6.1.)

With the normal distribution, I will briefly mention a related concept called the standard deviation. People don't seem to have an intuitive understanding of standard deviation, and because it can be replaced by a calculation based on the 90% CI (which people do understand intuitively), I won't focus on it here. Exhibit 6.1 shows that there are 3.29 standard deviations in one 90% CI, so we just need to make the conversion.

For our problem, we can just make a random number generator in a spreadsheet for each of our ranges. Following the instructions in Exhibit 6.1, we can generate random numbers for Maintenance savings with the Excel formula:

$$= \text{norminv}(\text{rand}(),15,(20 - 10)/3.29)$$

Likewise, we follow the instructions in Exhibit 6.1 for the rest of the ranges. Some people might prefer using the Random Number Generator in the Excel Analysis Toolpack, and you should feel free to experiment with it. I'm showing this formula in Exhibit 6.2 for a bit more of a hands-on approach.

Scenario#	Maintenance Savings	Labor Savings	Materials Savings	Units Produced	Total Savings	Breakeven Met?
1	$ 9.27	$ 4.30	$ 7.79	23,955	$511,716	Yes
2	$ 15.92	$ 2.64	$ 9.02	26,263	$724,127	Yes
3	$ 17.70	$ 4.63	$ 8.10	20,142	$612,739	Yes
4	$ 15.08	$ 6.75	$ 5.19	20,644	$557,860	Yes
5	$ 19.42	$ 9.28	$ 9.68	25,795	$990,167	Yes
6	$ 11.86	$ 3.17	$ 5.89	17,121	$358,166	**No**
7	$ 15.21	$ 0.46	$ 4.14	29,283	$580,167	Yes
⬇	⬇	⬇	⬇	⬇	⬇	⬇
9,999	$ 14.68	$ (0.22)	$ 5.32	33,175	$655,879	Yes
10,000	$ 7.49	$ (0.01)	$ 8.97	24,237	$398,658	**No**

EXHIBIT 6.2   Simple Monte Carlo Layout in Excel

We arrange the variables in columns as shown in Exhibit 6.2. The last two columns are just the calculations based on all the previous columns. The Total Savings column is the formula for annual savings (shown earlier) based on the numbers in each particular row. For example, scenario 1 in Exhibit 6.2 shows its Total Savings as ($9.27 + $4.30 + $7.79) × 23,955 = $511,716. You don't really need the "Breakeven Met?" column; I'm just showing it for reference. Now let's copy it down and make 10,000 rows.

We can use a couple of other simple tools in Excel to get a sense of how this turns out. The "=countif()" function allows you to count the number values that meet a certain condition—in this case, those that are less than $400,000. Or, for a more complete picture, you can use the histogram tool in the Analysis Toolpack. That will count the number of scenarios in each of several "buckets," or incremental groups. Then you can make a chart to display the output, as shown in Exhibit 6.3. This chart shows how many of the 10,000 scenarios came up in each $100,000 increment. For example, just over 1,000 scenarios had values between $300,000 and $400,000.

You will find that about 14% of the results were less than the $400,000 breakeven. This means there is a 14% chance of losing money. That is a

EXHIBIT 6.3   Histogram

meaningful measure of risk. But risk doesn't have to mean just the chance of a negative return on investment. In the same way we can measure the "size" of a thing by its height, weight, girth, and so on, there are a lot of useful measures of risk. Further examination shows that there is a 3.5% chance that the factory will lose more than $100,000 per year, instead of saving money. However, generating no revenue at all is virtually impossible. This is what we mean by "risk analysis." We have to be able to compute the odds of various levels of losses. If you are truly measuring risk, this is what you can do. For a spreadsheet example of this Monte Carlo problem, see the supplementary Web site at www.howtomeasureanything.com.

A shortcut can apply in some situations. If we had all normal distributions and we simply wanted to add or subtract ranges—such as a simple list of costs and benefits—we might not have to run a Monte Carlo simulation. If we just wanted to add up the three types of savings in our example, we can actually use a simple calculation. Use these six steps to produce a range:

1. Subtract the midpoint from the upper bound for each of the three cost savings ranges: or $20 − $15 = $5 for maintenance savings; we also get $5 for labor savings and $3 for materials savings.

2. Square each of the values from the last step: $5 squared is $25, and so on.

3. Add up the results: $25 + $25 + $9 = $59

4. Take the square root of the total: $59^.5 = $7.68

5. Total up the means: $15 + $3 + $6 = $24

6. Add and subtract the result from step 4 from the sum of the means to get the upper and lower bounds of the total, or $24 + $7.68 = $31.68 for the upper bound, $24 − $7.68 = $16.32 for the lower bound.

So the 90% CI for the sum of all three 90% CI for maintenance, labor, and materials is $16.32 to $31.68. In summary, the range interval of the total is equal to the square root of the sum of the squares of the range intervals.

You might see someone attempting to do something similar by adding up all the "optimistic" values for an upper bound and "pessimistic" values for the lower bound. This would result in a range of $11 to $37 for these three CI. This slightly exaggerates the 90% CI. When this calculation is done with a business case of dozens of variables, the exaggeration of the range becomes too significant to ignore. It is like thinking that rolling a bucket of dice will produces all 1's or all 6's. Most of the time, we get a combination of all the values, some high, some low. This is a common error and no doubt has resulted in a large number of misinformed decisions. Yet the simple method I just showed works perfectly well when you have a set of 90% CIs you would like to add up.

But we don't just want to add these up, we want to multiply them by the production level, which is also a range. The simple range addition method doesn't work with anything other than subtraction or addition.

A Monte Carlo simulation is also required if these were not all normal distributions. Although a wide variety of shapes of distributions for all sorts of problems are beyond the scope of this book, it is worth mentioning two others besides the normal distribution: a uniform distribution and the binary distribution. (See Exhibits 6.4 and 6.5.) Each of these will come up later when we discuss the value of information.

Tools and Other Resources for Monte Carlo Simulations

Fortunately, you really don't have to build Monte Carlo simulations from scratch these days. Many tools can be very helpful and improve the productivity of an analyst trained in the basics. They range from simple sets of Excel macros—what I use—combined with a practical consulting approach to very sophisticated packages.

What a "Uniform Distribution looks like:

100% Confidence Interval

Characteristics:

- All values between the bounds are equally likely.
- The distribution is symmetrical, not lopsided—the mean is exactly halfway between the upper and lower bounds.
- The bounds are "hard stops" and are, in effect, a "100% CI"—nothing above the upper bound nor below the lower bound is possible.

How to make a random distribution with this shape in Excel:

=rand()*(UB-LB)+LB

UB=Upper bound

LB=Lower bound

EXHIBIT 6.4   The Uniform Distribution

What a "Binary Distribution" looks like:

60%

40%

0   1

Characteristics:

- Produces only two possible values.
- There is a single probability that one value will occur (60% in the chart), and the other value occurs the rest of the time.

How to make a random distribution with this shape in Excel:

=if(rand()<P,1,0)

P=probability that a "1" will appear (a "0" appears with 1-P probability)

EXHIBIT 6.5   The Binary (a.k.a. Bernoulli) Distribution

A fellow evangelist in the use of Monte Carlo simulations in business is Sam Savage, a Stanford University professor who developed a tool he calls Insight.xls. Savage focuses on trying to sell an intuitive philosophy about using probabilistic analysis. He also has some ideas about how to institutionalize the entire process of creating Monte Carlo simulations. If different parts of the same organization are using simulations, Savage believes organizations should use a common pool of shared distributions instead of inventing their own distributions for common values. Furthermore, he believes the definition of the distribution itself can sometimes be a technical challenge that requires certain proficiency with the mathematics.

Savage has an interesting approach he calls Probability Management: "Suppose we just took [the problem of generating probability distributions] out of your hands. Now what's your excuse for not using probability distributions? Some people don't know how to generate a probability distribution—they don't know how to generate electricity either, but they still use it."

His idea is to appoint a chief probability officer, or CPO, for the firm. The CPO would be in charge of managing a common library of probability distributions for use by anyone running Monte Carlo simulations. Savage invokes concepts like the SIP, or "Stochastic Information Packet," a pregenerated set of 100,000 random numbers for a particular value. Sometimes different SIPs would be related. For example, the company's revenue might be related to national economic growth. A set of SIPs that are generated so they have these correlations are called SLURPS (Stochastic Library Units with Relationships Preserved). The CPO would manage SIPs and SLURPs so that users of probability distributions don't have to reinvent the wheel every time they need to simulate inflation or health care costs.

I would add a few other things to make Monte Carlo simulations as formally defined and accepted as accounting processes in organizations:

- *A formal certification process just for the calibrated estimators.* I've noticed that even when I've trained skilled professionals who routinely perform Monte Carlo simulations, they have rarely heard of calibrated probability assessment. As we discussed earlier, an uncalibrated estimator has a strong tendency to be overconfident. Any calculation of risk based on his or her estimates will likely be significantly understated.

- *A well-documented procedure for how models are built from the input of various calibrated estimators.* It takes some time to smooth out the wrinkles in the process. Most organizations don't need to start from scratch for every new investment they are analyzing; they can base their work on that of others or at least reuse their own prior models.

- *A single automated tool set.* Exhibit 6.6 shows a few of the many available.

THE RISK PARADOX

Building a Monte Carlo simulation is scarcely more complicated than constructing any spreadsheet-based business case. In fact, by almost any measure of complexity, the Monte Carlo simulations I built to assess the risk

EXHIBIT 6.6   A FEW MONTE CARLO TOOLS

Tool	Made by	Description
@Risk	Palisade Corporation Ithaca, NY	Excel-based; a wide variety of distributions; a fairly sophisticated tool. Broad user base and technical support.
AIE	Hubbard Decision Research Glen Ellyn, IL	Excel-based set of macros; also computes value of information and portfolio optimization; emphasizes methodology over the tool and provides consulting for practical implementation issues.
Crystal Ball	Decisioneering, Inc. Denver, CO	Another Excel-based tool; strong competitor to @Risk. Many users and technical support.
Risk Solver Engine	Frontline Systems Incline Village, NV	Unique Excel based development platform to perform "Interactive" Monte Carlo simulation at unprecedented speed. Supports SIP and SLURP formats for probability management.
SAS	SAS Corporation Raleigh NC	Goes well beyond the Monte Carlo simulation; extremely sophisticated package used by many professional statisticians.
SPSS	SPSS Inc. Chicago, IL	Also goes far beyond the Monte Carlo; tends to be more popular among academics.
XLSim	Stanford U. Professor Sam Savage, AnalyCorp	An inexpensive package designed for ease of learning and use. Savage also provides seminars and management protocols for making Monte Carlo methods practical in organizations.

of large information technology projects are in every case significantly less complex than the IT system I'm analyzing.

Are Monte Carlo simulations a little complex? Sure, by some standards. Are Monte Carlo simulations too complex to be practical in business? Not by modern business standards. Just like any other complex business problem, management can bring in people with the skills to do it.

Despite this, quantitative risk analysis based on Monte Carlo simulations has not been universally adopted. Many organizations employ fairly sophisticated risk analysis methods on particular problems; for example, actuaries in an insurance company define the particulars of an insurance product, statisticians analyze the ratings of a new TV show, and production managers are using Monte Carlo simulations to model changes in production methods. But those very same organizations do *not* routinely apply those same sophisticated risk analysis methods to much bigger decisions with more uncertainty and more potential for loss.

In 1999, I was teaching a seminar to a group of executives wanting to learn about risk analysis for IT. I began to explain a few basic concepts for Monte Carlo simulations and asked whether anyone was using such methods to assess risk. Usually respondents who claim to assess risk just apply subjective "high," "medium," or "low" assessments with no quantitative basis whatsoever. My objective is to help attendees to differentiate between this kind of fluff and the kind of analysis an actuary would recognize. One of my students said he routinely applied analysis just like this using a common Monte Carlo tool. Impressed, I said, "You are the first IT executive I've ever met who already does this." He said, "No, I'm not in IT. I do analysis of production methods for Boise Cascade" (the paper and wood company). I asked, "Which do you think is more risky, IT investments or paper production?" He agreed that IT was riskier but added that the company never applies Monte Carlo simulations methods to IT.

Risk Paradox

If an organization uses quantitative risk analysis at all, it is usually for routine operational decisions. The largest, most risky decisions get the least amount of proper risk analysis.

Over the years, in case after case, I have found that if organizations apply quantitative risk analysis at all, it is on relatively routine, operational-level decisions. The largest, most risky decisions are subject to almost no risk analysis—at least not any analysis that an actuary or statistician would be familiar with. I've named the phenomenon the "risk paradox."

Almost all of the most sophisticated risk analysis is applied to less risky operational decisions while the riskiest decisions—mergers, IT portfolios, big research and development initiatives, and the like—receive virtually none. Why is this true? Perhaps it is because there is a perception that operational decisions—approving a loan or computing an insurance premium—seem simpler to quantify, but the truly risky decisions are too elusive to quantify. This is a serious mistake. As I have shown, there is nothing "immeasurable" about the big decisions.

Now that you understand the concepts of uncertainty and risk in specific quantitative terms, we can move on to a rarely used but very powerful tool in measurement: computing the value of information.

ENDNOTE

1. Stanislaw Ulam, *Adventures of a Mathematician* (Berkeley: University of California Press) 1991.

## CHAPTER 7

Measuring the Value of Information

I f we could measure the value of information itself, we could use that to determine the value of conducting measurements. If we did compute this value, we would probably choose to measure completely different things. We would probably spend more effort and money measuring things we never measured before, and we would probably ignore some things we routinely measured in the past.

THE MCNAMARA FALLACY

"The first step is to measure whatever can be easily measured. This is OK as far as it goes. The second step is to disregard that which can't easily be measured or to give it an arbitrary quantitative value. This is artificial and misleading. The third step is to presume that what can't be measured easily isn't important. This is blindness. The fourth step is to say that what can't easily be measured really doesn't exist. This is suicide."

—Charles Handy, "The Empty Raincoat," 1995 pg. 219

There are really only three basic reasons why information ever has a value to a business:

1. Information reduces uncertainty about decisions that have economic consequences.

2. Information affects the behavior of others, which has economic consequences.

3. Information sometimes has its own market value.

The solution to the first of these three has existed since the 1950's in a field of mathematics called decision theory, an offshoot of game theory. It is also the method we focus on, mostly because it is more relevant to most common needs and because the other two are somewhat simpler. The value of information affecting human behavior is exactly equal to the value of the difference in human behavior. If measuring performance itself gets a 20% increase in productivity, then the monetary value of that productivity increase is the value of the measurement. If the value of information is its market value, then we have a market forecasting problem no different from estimating the sales for any other product. If we are collecting information on traffic at city intersections at various times of day to sell to firms that evaluate retail locations, then the value of that measurement is our expected profit from the sale of that information. But most of the reasons we measure something in business are at least partially related to how the measurement affects decisions. This is what the rest of this chapter is about.

The Chance of Being Wrong and the Cost of Being Wrong: Expected Opportunity Loss

The esoteric field of game theory provided a formula for the value of information over 50 years ago, and it can be understood both mathematically and intuitively. We can make better "bets" (i.e., decisions) when we can reduce uncertainty (i.e., make measurements) about them. Knowing the value of the measurement affects how we might measure something or even whether we need to measure it at all.

If you are uncertain about a business decision (and a calibrated person should be realistic about the level of uncertainty), then that means you have a chance of making the wrong decision. By "wrong" I mean that the consequences of some alternative would have turned out to be preferable,

THE CHANCE OF BEING WRONG AND THE COST OF BEING WRONG

and you may have selected that alternative, if only you had known. The cost of being wrong is the difference between the wrong choice you took and the best alternative available—that is, the one you would have chosen if you had perfect information. For example, if you are going to invest in a bold new ad campaign, you are hoping the investment will be justified. But you don't know for a fact that it will be successful. Historically, you know there have been ad campaigns that, while they initially appeared to have all the look of a great idea, turned out to be a market flop. Some of the more catastrophic examples have even helped competitors. On the plus side, the right campaign sometimes can directly result in a major increase in revenue. It does no good to stand still and make no investments in your business just because there is a chance of being wrong. So, based on the best information you have so far, the default decision is to go ahead with the campaign—but there may be a value to measuring it first.

To compute the value of measuring the likelihood of success of a campaign, you have to know both what your loss would be if this campaign turns out to be a bad investment and the chance it will turn out to be a bad investment. If there was no chance that the campaign would fail, then there would be no need whatsoever to reduce uncertainty about it—the decision would be risk-free and obvious.

Just to keep the example simple, let's look at a binary situation—you either fail or succeed, period. Suppose you could make $40 million profit if the ad works and lose $5 million (the cost of the campaign) if it fails. Then suppose your calibrated experts say they would put a 40% chance of failure on the campaign. With this information, you could create a table, as shown in Exhibit 7.1.

The Opportunity Loss (OL) for a particular alternative is just the cost if we chose that path and it turns out to be wrong. This Expected Opportunity Loss (EOL) for a particular strategy is the chance of being wrong times the

EXHIBIT 7.1   EXTREMELY SIMPLE OPPORTUNITY LOSS EXAMPLE

	Campaign Works	Campaign Fails
Chance of Success	60%	40%
Approve Campaign	+$40 million	−$5 million
Reject Campaign	$0	$0

cost of being wrong. For the example, you get these answers:

Opportunity Loss if Campaign Approved: $5 M
Opportunity Loss if Campaign Rejected: $40 M
Expected Opportunity Loss if Approved: $5 M × 40% = $2 M
Expected Opportunity Loss if Rejected: $40 M × 60% = $24 M

EOL exists because you are uncertain about the possibility of negative consequences of your decision. If you could reduce this uncertainty, then EOL would also be reduced. *That* is what a measurement does.

All measurements that have value result in the reduction of uncertainty of some quantity that affects some decision with economic consequences. The bigger the reduction in EOL, the higher the value of a measurement. The difference between the EOL before a measurement and the EOL after a measurement is called the Expected Value of Information (EVI).

Computing the EVI of a measurement before we make the measurement requires us to estimate how much uncertainty reduction we can expect. This sometimes is complicated, depending on the variable being measured, but there is a shortcut. The easiest measurement value to compute is the Expected Value of Perfect Information (EVPI). If you could eliminate uncertainty, EOL would be reduced to zero. So the EVPI is simply the EOL of your chosen alternative. In the example, the "default" decision (what you would do if you didn't make a further measurement) was to approve the campaign and—as explained—that EOL was $2 million. So the value of eliminating any uncertainty about whether this campaign would succeed is simply $2 million. If you could only reduce, but not eliminate uncertainty, then the EVI would be something less.

THE VALUE OF INFORMATION

Expected Value of Information(EVI) = Reduction in Expected Oportunity loss (EOL)

i.e. EVI = $EOL_{Before\ Info} - EOL_{After\ Info}$

where EOL = chance of being wrong x cost of being wrong

Expected Value of Perfect Information (EVPI) = $EOL_{Before\ Info}$
(EOL after is Ø if information is perfect)

A slightly more complicated, but much more common and realistic, method is the EOL calculation where your uncertainty is about a continuous value, not just two extremes like "succeed" and "fail." It's more common to need to compute the value of a measurement where the uncertain variable has a range of possible values. The method for computing this information value is not fundamentally different from how we computed the value of a simple binary problem. We still need to compute an EOL.

THE VALUE OF INFORMATION FOR RANGES

In the ad example, suppose instead of expressing the results as only two possible outcomes, the results are a range of possible values. A calibrated expert in marketing was 90% certain that the sales directly resulting from this ad campaign could be anywhere from 100,000 units to 1 million units. However, we have to sell at least a certain amount to make this ad campaign break even. Let's say that after taking into account the cost of the campaign and the gross margin on the product, we determine that a minimum of 200,000 units sold is required to break even. Anything less than that and the campaign is a net loss, but more so as we drop farther below this point. If we sell exactly 200,000, we neither lose nor gain. If we didn't sell any, we would have lost the cost of the ad campaign, $5 million (you might say the business would lose more than just the cost of the campaign, but let's keep it simple). Another way of looking at this is that for every unit we are short of the breakeven point, we are losing $25. In this situation, what is the value of reducing uncertainty about the effect of the campaign?

One way to compute EVPI for ranges like this is to take these five steps:

1. Slice the distribution up into hundreds or thousands of small segments.
2. Compute the opportunity loss for the midpoint of each segment.
3. Compute the probability for each segment.
4. Multiply the opportunity loss of each segment times its probability.
5. Total all the products from step 4 for all segments.

The best way to do this is to make a macro in Excel, or write some software, that chops up the distribution into 1,000 or so slices, then makes the required calculation. This ensures that we handle all sorts of important situations and exceptions. To make it a little easier, I did most of the work for you. Now all you need to do is use a couple of the following charts and perform some simple arithmetic.

As a prelude to this calculation, we need to decide which of the upper and lower bounds on the 90% confidence interval (CI) is the "best bound" (BB) and "worst bound" (WB). Clearly, sometimes a bigger number is better (e.g., revenue) and sometimes a smaller number is better (e.g., costs). In the ad campaign example, small is bad, so the WB is the 100,000 units and the BB is 1,000,000 units. From this, we are going to compute a value I'll call the Relative Threshold (RT). This quantity tells us where the threshold sits relative to the rest of the range. See Exhibit 7.2 for a visual explanation of RT.

We are going to use this value to compute EVPI in four steps:

1. Compute Relative Threshold: $RT = (\text{Threshold-WB})/(\text{BB-WB})$. For our example, the best bound is 1,000,000 units, the worst bound is 100,000 units, and the threshold is 200,000 units so $RT = (200,000 - 100,000)/(1,000,000 - 100,000) = 0.11$

2. Locate the RT in the vertical axis of Exhibit 7.3.

3. Look directly to the right of the RT value and you will see two sets of curves—one for normal distributions on the left and one for uniform distributions on the right. Because our example is a normal distribution, find the point on the curve for normal distributions that is directly to the right of our RT value. I will call this value the Expected Opportunity Loss Factor (EOLF). Here our EOLF is 15.

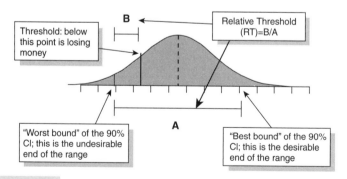

EXHIBIT 7.2   An Example of the "Relative Threshold"

*RT=(Threshold-Worst Bound)/(Best Bound-Worst Bound); See Exhibit 7.2

for more detail.

EXHIBIT 7.3   **The Expected Opportunity Loss Factor (EOLF) Chart**

4. Compute EVPI as: EVPI = EOLF/1000 × OL per unit × (BB-WB). Our example has an opportunity loss per unit of $25. This gives an EVPI = 15/1000 × 25 × (1,000,000 − 100,000) = $337,500. See Exhibit 7.3.

This calculation shows that a measurement (in this case, a forecast) about the number of units that will be sold could theoretically be worth as much as $337,500. This number is an absolute maximum and assumes a measurement that eliminates uncertainty. Although eliminating uncertainty is almost always impossible, this simple method provides an important benchmark for how much we should be willing to spend.

The procedure for a uniform distribution is the same, except, of course, we need to use the uniform distribution column of curves. In either the uniform or the normal distribution case, some important caveats should be understood. First, this simple method applies only to linear losses. That is, for each unit we undershoot the threshold by, we lose a fixed amount—$25 in our example. If we plotted the loss against the units sold, it would be a straight line. That's linear. But if the loss accelerated or decelerated in some way, the EOLF chart may not be a very close estimate. For example, if we are uncertain about a compounding interest rate, then the loss we have below whatever threshold we define would not go up like a straight line. It's also important to note that if the normal distribution has to be truncated in some way, or if any other distribution shape besides normal or uniform is required, then the chart may not be a close approximation.

> ### VALUE OF INFORMATION ANALYSIS ON SUPPLEMENTARY WEB SITE:
>
> www.howtomeasureanything.com
>   Go to the "Value of Information Analysis" link. You can download a detailed Excel-based calculator for VIA with examples from this book.

If you have an important measure with a high information value, it may be worth doing the extra math I described for breaking down the distribution into a large number of slices. But, instead of making such a spreadsheet from scratch, you can download the Value of Information Analysis spreadsheets and examples on the supplementary Web site, www.howtomeasureanything .com.

THE IMPERFECT WORLD: THE VALUE OF PARTIAL UNCERTAINTY REDUCTION

The last example, for the Expected Value of Perfect Information, shows the value of eliminating uncertainty, not just reducing it. The EVPI calculation can be useful by itself, since at least we know a cost ceiling we should never exceed to make the measurement. But often we have to live with merely reducing our uncertainty, especially when we are talking about something like sales forecasts from ad campaigns. At such times it would be helpful to know not just the maximum we might spend under ideal conditions, but what a given real-life measurement (with real-life error remaining) should be worth. In other words, we need to know the Expected Value of Information, not the Expected Value of *Perfect* Information.

The EVI is, again, best computed with a bit more elaborate modeling, but we can make some simple estimates. To do this, it's helpful to get a mental picture of what an EVI would look like if we graphed EVI versus information quantity (see Exhibit 7.4).

The EVI curve is generally convex and asymptotic. That is, the value of information tends to rise more quickly with small reductions in uncertainty but levels off as the uncertainty approaches zero. As you can see in the chart, the value of information initially rises more quickly but then levels off at EVPI (which, of course, EVI can never exceed).

It is also worth keeping in mind that the EVI for a normal distribution is usually closer to a straight line than the EVI for a binary or uniform distribution. For a normal distribution, a measurement that would have just half the uncertainty of the original range would have an EVI of about half the EVPI, a quarter of the uncertainty would be a quarter of the EVPI, and so on. The EVI curve for a normal distribution is not exactly straight, of course, since it still has to level off at the EVPI. For a binary or uniform distribution, the EVI curve is generally a little more curved than it is for a normal distribution so the EVI increases even faster with a little more measurement.

EXHIBIT 7.4   The Expected Value of Information Curve

Thus, a measurement that reduces uncertainty by half is generally worth more than half the EVPI. For the ad campaign example, the EVPI was $337,500. If you think you could reduce your uncertainty by half for a study that costs $150,000, then you are justified to do the study (but probably not justified by much). If you can do the study for $30,000, then it's a no-brainer bargain.

Another characteristic of the EVI curve to keep in mind, specifically for uniform distributions, is that uniform distributions are flat, with sharply truncated bounds; nothing outside the bounds is possible, and everything inside the bounds is equally likely. If the calibrated expert wanted to give our range a uniform distribution of 100,000 to 1,000,000 units sold, the expert is saying, in effect, that there is no chance of selling more than 1 million units or selling less than 100,000. If we can make a measurement that at least allows us to move up the lower bound to some value greater than the threshold of 200,000 units sold, we will have eliminated the possibility of a loss. In examples like this, the biggest jump in EVI is up to the point where the uncertainty reduction is just enough that it becomes possible to eliminate a chance of loss. The difference in value between a measurement that could reduce uncertainty by half and one that could reduce uncertainty by three-quarters may be very small. Once we have eliminated the chance of a loss (or determined for certain that the loss will occur), any additional measurement has much less value.

Although this method for computing an EVPI with Exhibit 7.3 for normal distributions is just an approximation, it should be within 10% or so of the true answer for a normal distribution. You can estimate the EVI by recognizing EVPI as an absolute ceiling and keeping the general shape of an EVI curve in mind. You may think that we are making approximations upon approximation, but it results in a "good enough" measurement. Estimating the EVPI for a proposed measurement already has some uncertainty of its own, so fine precision on the EVI is not that useful. Also, those variables that you should measure—those that have high information values—tend to be the highest information value by an extremely large margin. Often they are 10 or 100 times as much (or more) as the value of the next best measurements. The estimation error for an EVI usually won't come close to making a difference.

Knowing the monetary value of the information in a measurement puts a new light on what is "measurable." If someone says a measurement would be too expensive, we have to ask "compared to what?" If a measurement that would just reduce uncertainty by half costs $50,000 but the EVPI is $500,000, then the measurement certainly is not too expensive. But if the information value is zero, then any measurement is too expensive. Some measurements might have marginal information values—say, a few thousand dollars—not enough to justify some formal effort at measurement but a bit too much just to ignore. For those measurements, I try to think of approaches that can quickly reduce a little uncertainty, say making a few phone calls to a few more experts.

With the EVI curve, we also learn the value of iterative measurements. While the EVI curve shows that the value of information levels off, a curve showing the cost of information takes off like a rocket as we approach the usually unattainable state of perfect certainty. This fact tells us that we should normally think of measurement as iterative. Don't try to hit it out of the ballpark in the first attempt. Each measurement iteration can tell you something about how—and whether—to conduct the next iteration.

THE EPIPHANY EQUATION: KNOWING THE VALUE OF CONDUCTING MEASUREMENTS CHANGES EVERYTHING

In my consulting practice, I've been applying a slightly more sophisticated version of the process I described above.

By 1999, I had completed the very quantitative Applied Information Economics analysis on about 20 major information technology (IT) investments. Each of these business cases had 40 to 80 variables, such as initial development costs, adoption rate, productivity improvement, revenue growth, and so on. For each of these business cases, I ran a macro in Excel that computed the information value for each variable. I used this value to figure out where to focus measurement efforts.

When I ran the macro that computed the value of information for each of these variables, I began to see this pattern:

- The vast majority of variables had an information value of zero. That is, the current level of uncertainty about that variable was acceptable and no further measurement was justified (first mentioned in Chapter 3).

- The variables that had high information values were routinely those that the client never measured. Usually the high-value variables were completely absent from previous business cases.

- The variables that clients used to spend the most time measuring were usually those with a very low (even zero) information value (i.e., it was highly unlikely that additional measurements of the variable would have any affect on decisions).

After organizing and evaluating all the business cases and their information value calculations, I was able to confirm this pattern. I wrote an article about my findings that was published in *CIO Magazine* in 1999 titled "The IT Measurement Inversion."[1]

Subsequent data continues to confirm my original observations. But I also noticed the same phenomenon on non-IT projects, such as those relating to military logistics, the environment, venture capital, and facilities expansion. The highest value measurements almost always are a bit of a surprise to the client. Again and again, I found that clients spent a lot of time, effort, and money measuring things that just didn't have a high information value while ignoring variables that could significantly affect real decisions. Finally, I quit calling the concept the IT Measurement Inversion and renamed it the "Measurement Inversion." In quite a few different fields, the things that get measured just don't matter as much as what is ignored.

Furthermore, I often find that when clients measure something completely different—as a result of knowing the information value—they would often view the actual findings as a great revelation. In other words, if you want an epiphany, look at a high-value measurement you were previously ignoring. Exhibit 7.5 summarizes these findings.

THE MEASUREMENT INVERSION

In a business case, the economic value of measuring a variable is usually inversely proportional to how much measurement attention it usually gets.

Attributes of Business Cases
Information Value versus
Measurement Priorities of Most Organizations

Lowest Information Value

Most Measured

- Initial cost (development, procurement, etc.)

- Long-term costs (maintenance, training, etc.)

- Cost saving benefits other than labor productivity

  (energy, raw materials, capital costs, etc.)

- Labor productivity

- Revenue enhancement

- Technology adoption rate

- Project completion (chance of cancellation,

Highest Information Value

completion date, rescoping, etc.)

Least Measured

EXHIBIT 7.5   The Measurement Inversion

Because most organizations lack a method for measuring the value of conducting a measurement, they measure all the wrong things. It is not that project costs and the like should not be measured, but an inordinate amount of attention is given to them when there are much bigger uncertainties in other areas.

A stark illustration of the Measurement Inversion can be seen in a large UK-based insurance client of mine that was an avid user of a software complexity measurement method called function points. This method was popular in the 1980s and 1990s as a basis of estimating the effort for large software development efforts. This organization had done a very good job of tracking initial estimates, function point estimates, and actual effort expended for over 300 IT projects. The function point estimation required three or four full-time persons as "certified" function point counters. This was by far the most deliberate effort the company expended on measuring any aspect of proposed software development projects.

But a very interesting pattern arose when I compared the function point estimates to the initial estimates provided by project managers and the final effort calculated by the time tracking system. The costly, time-intensive function point counting did change the initial estimate but, on average, it was no closer to the actual project effort than the initial estimate. In other words, sometimes function point estimates improved the initial estimate and sometimes they gave an answer that was farther for the actual effort at the completion of the project. Not only was this the single largest measurement effort in the IT organization, it literally added *no* value since it didn't reduce uncertainty at all.

A few reasons might explain why Measurement Inversion happens. First, people measure what they know how to measure or what they believe is easy to measure. You probably know the old joke about the drunk looking for his watch in the well-lit street, even though he knows he lost it in the dark alley. He justifies this by saying the light is better out in the street. If the organization is used to using, say, surveys to measure things, then things that are best measured with other methods probably don't get measured as often. If the organization is good at measuring things based on data-mining methods, it will tend to measure only things that lend themselves to that approach.

My graduate quantitative methods professor used to tell the class "If your only tool is a hammer, then every problem is a nail." This seems to apply to quite a lot of businesses and government agencies. There is a comfort zone in the measurement methods they use. Even though methods to measure something like the impact of, for example, customer satisfaction on revenue are well developed in some firms, other firms will resist using them and instead focus on lower-value measurements they feel more familiar with.

Also, managers might tend to measure things that are more likely to produce good news. After all, why measure the benefits if you have a suspicion there might not be any? Of course, that tends to be the thinking of people asking for money or justifying their jobs, not the person who has to sign the checks.

Finally, not knowing the business value of the information from a measurement means people can't put the difficulty of a measurement in context. A measurement they feel is "too difficult" might actually be perceived as practical if they understood that the information value was many times the expected cost. A large consumer credit company once asked me for a proposal on measuring the benefits of a worldwide IT infrastructure investment that would exceed $100 million. After hearing more about the nature of the problem, I estimated that the study would cost $100,000 or so. The company responded by saying that it needed to keep costs down to $25,000 (I declined the business). The original proposal was less than one-tenth of 1% of the estimated size of a highly uncertain, risky investment. In some industries, a much less risky investment would get an even more detailed analysis than what I proposed. Conservatively, the value of the information the study would have produced would likely have been in the millions of dollars.

I call the formula for the value of information the "epiphany equation" because it seems that to have a truly profound revelation, you almost always have to look at something other than what you have been looking at. Being able to compute the value of information has caused organizations to look at completely different things—and frequently that has resulted in a surprise that changed the direction of a major decision.

SUMMARIZING UNCERTAINTY, RISK, AND INFORMATION VALUE: THE FIRST MEASUREMENTS

Understanding how to measure uncertainty is key to measuring risk. Understanding risk in a quantitative sense is key to understanding how to compute the value of information. Understanding the value of information tells us what to measure and about how much effort we should put into measuring it. Putting all of this in the context of quantifying uncertainty reduction is central to understanding what measurement is all about.

LESSONS FROM COMPUTING THE VALUE OF INFORMATION

Be Iterative—the highest value measurement is the beginning of the measurement, so do it in bits and take stock after each.

The Value of Measurement Matters—If you don't compute the value of measurements, you are probably measuring the wrong things, the wrong way.

Putting everything from this chapter together, we can come away with a few new ideas. First, we know that the early part of any measurement usually is the high-value part. Don't attempt a massive study to measure something if you have a lot of uncertainty about it now. Measure a little bit, remove some uncertainty, and evaluate what you have learned. Were you surprised? Is further measurement still necessary? Did what you learn in the beginning of the measurement give you some ideas about how to change the method? Iterative measurement gives you the most flexibility and the best bang for the buck.

Finally, if you aren't computing the value of a measurement, you are very likely measuring some things that are of little or no value and ignoring some high-value items. Furthermore, if you aren't computing the value of the measurement, you probably don't know how to measure it efficiently. You may even be spending too much or spending too little time measuring something. You might dismiss a high-value measurement as "too expensive" because you could not put the cost in context with the value.

Everything up to this point in the book is just "Phase 1" for measuring those things often thought to be impossible to measure. We have taken what might have been a very ambiguous concept and defined it in terms of how it matters to us and how we observe it. We have measured uncertainty, risk, and the value of information. Now we can get to the next step.

Interestingly, this is as far as the Department of Veterans Affairs went with the IT security metrics project. The object of the project was just to figure out what to measure; actual measurements would be carried out over the next several years. To the VA, knowing the value of measurement was useful in itself since it provided the framework for all future security metrics.

The next step for us is to go beyond just stating current uncertainty and computing the value of measuring it. Now that we know what to measure and about how much we can spend on the measurement, we can set out to design a way to measure it.

■ ENDNOTE

1. "The IT Measurement Inversion," *CIO Enterprise Magazine,* April 15, 1999.

Measurement Methods

CHAPTER 8

The Transition: From What to Measure to How to Measure

If you've applied the lessons of the previous sections to your measurement problem, you've defined the issue in terms of how you observe it, you've quantified your uncertainty about it, and you've computed the value of additional information. All of that was really what you do before you begin measuring. Now we need to figure out how to reduce our uncertainty further—in other words, measure it.

Now it's time to introduce some powerful and practical empirical methods. Given the way we have defined measurement, the oft-heard phrase "empirical measurement" is entirely redundant. "Empirical" refers to the use of observation as evidence for a conclusion (you might also hear the redundant phrase "empirical observation"). "Empirical methods" are formal, systematic approaches for making observations to avoid or at least reduce certain types of errors that observations (and observers) are like likely to have. And observation is not limited to sight, although this is a commonly assumed notion. Observation may not even be direct; it may be augmented by the use of measurement instruments. This is, in fact, almost always the case in the modern physical sciences.

Clever empirical methods of observation often appear in various academic literature, surprising experts in the field as well as the general public. Many people would be shocked to discover that statistical methods have been used to estimate the number of tanks manufactured by Germany in World War II (discussed in detail later) based on no more than the serial numbers of captured tanks. Even the age when infants gain depth perception has been measured, even though they are too young to talk.

But we are focusing on those things that are often considered to be immeasurable in business. Fortunately, the approach to addressing many of these issues does not involve the most sophisticated methods. It's worth restating that the objective for this book is to show that many of the things a manager might consider immeasurable are actually measurable. The only question is whether they are important enough to measure (e.g., had a high information value relative to the cost of measurement).

A few relatively simple methods will suffice to measure most of these issues. The real obstacles to measurement, as we are discovering, are mostly conceptual, not the lack of understanding of dozens of much more complicated methods. After all, in those areas where fairly sophisticated methods are used, there is little debate about whether the object of measurement is measurable. Such sophisticated measurement methods were developed precisely because someone understood that the object was measurable. Why write a two-volume treatise on quantitative clinical chemistry, for example, if both the author and the targeted readers didn't assume from the beginning that the topic is entirely measurable?

I will leave it to others to describe specialized quantitative methods for specific scientific disciplines. You picked up this book because you are unclear how other, "softer" topics can be treated with rigor.

In this chapter, we will ask a few questions so that we might be able to determine the appropriate category of measurement methods. Those questions are:

- *What are the parts of the thing we're uncertain about?* Decompose the uncertain thing so that it is computed from other uncertain things.

- *How has this (or its decomposed parts) been measured by others?* Chances are, you're not the first to encounter a particular measurement problem and there may even be extensive research on the topic already. Reviewing the work of others is called "secondary research."

- *How do the "observables" identified lend themselves to measurement?* You've already answered how you observe the thing. Follow through with that to identify how you observe the parts you identified in the step above. Secondary research may already answer this for you.

- *How much do we really need to measure it?* Take into account the previously computed current state of uncertainty, the threshold, and value of information. These are all clues that point toward the right measurement approach.

- *What are the sources of error?* Think about how observations might be misleading.

- *What instrument do we select?* Based on your answers to the previous questions, identify and design a measurement instrument. Once again, secondary research may provide guidance.

With these questions in mind, it is time to discuss how tools are used for measurement.

Tools of Observation: Introduction to the Instrument of Measurement

The names we use for things and how those names change throughout history reveal a lot about how our ideas about them have changed. The scientific instrument is a good example of this. Prior to the industrial revolution, especially during the European Renaissance, scientific instruments were often called "philosophical engines." They were devices for answering what were the "deep" questions of the time. Galileo used a pendulum and an inclined plane down which he would roll balls to measure the acceleration due to gravity. (The story of him dropping weights from the Leaning Tower of Pisa might be fiction.) Daniel Fahrenheit's mercury thermometer quantified what was previously considered the "quality" of temperature. These devices revealed not just a number but something fundamental about the nature of the universe the observers lived in. Each one was a keyhole through which some previously secret aspect of the world could be observed.

The users of these devices weren't even called scientists yet, but natural philosophers. These natural philosophers were not part of the kind of research labs we would recognize today; instead, they were often a sort of gentleman scholar. With a few exceptions, they had the time and the means to build expensive devices or they had wealthy private patrons—just as artists in their time might. The devices they used were often ornate, not just utilitarian, and were purchased by men of means to showcase their taste as well as intellectual curiosity. (In some cases, both the former and latter were facades.)

By the time of the industrialist inventors like Thomas Edison and Alexander Graham Bell in the later nineteenth century, research and development had become a mass production business. Prior to this time, instruments were often made to specification for an individual; by the time of Edison and Bell, devices were being produced uniformly and in large quantities. Scientific instruments started to become much more utilitarian. While the gentlemen philosophers of the natural world might have displayed their new microscopes alongside expensive art, the microscopes used by the industrialist inventors were fit for display only in laboratories that, by today's standards, would almost be considered sweatshops. Perhaps not surprisingly, it was at this time that much of the public began to perceive science and scientific observation as a bit less of a fanciful pursuit of deep knowledge and more like drudgery.

Even today, for many people, a measurement instrument generally connotes a device—perhaps a complicated-looking piece of electronic equipment—designed to quantify some obscure physical phenomenon, such as a Geiger counter measuring radiation or a scale measuring weight. Actually, the term "instrument" is used much more broadly by many people in different fields. In education assessment, for example, researchers call a survey, a test, or even an individual question an instrument. And that is a legitimate a use of the term.

The measurement instrument, like any tool, gives an advantage to the user. The simple mechanical tool gives an advantage like leverage for the human muscle by multiplying the force it can exert. Likewise, the measurement instrument enhances the human senses by detecting things we cannot detect directly. It also can aid reasoning and memory by doing quick calculations and storing the result. Even a particular experimental method arguably aids human perception and in this sense is itself a measurement instrument. If we want to know how to measure anything, it is in this broadest sense that we need to use the term.

I often find managers who believe something is immeasurable simply because all the data have not yet been compiled and available for easy access. They can imagine how to measure sales; it is already compiled and reported to them. But the idea that some measurements require a deliberate effort of observation with the aid of specific measurement instruments, such as a survey or an experiment, is not something they think of right away.

Part of the solution for this initial lack of imagination about measurement instruments may be to try to recapture the fascination Galileo and Fahrenheit had for observing the "secrets" of their environment. They didn't think of devices for measurement as complex contraptions to be used by esoteric specialists in arcane research. The devices were simple and obvious. Nor were they, like some managers today, dismissive of instruments because they had limitations and errors of their own. *Of course* they have errors. The question is "Compared to what?" Compared to the unaided human? Compared to no attempt at measurement at all? Keep the purpose of measurement in mind: uncertainty reduction, not necessarily uncertainty elimination.

Instruments generally have six advantages. They don't need to have all the advantages to qualify as an instrument. Any combination will suffice. Often even one advantage is an improvement on unaided human observation.

1. *Instruments detect what you can't detect.* A voltmeter detects voltage across a circuit, a microscope magnifies, a cloud chamber shows the trails of subatomic particles. This ability is what is most commonly thought of in relation to an instrument, but it is overemphasized.

2. *Instruments are more consistent.* Left to their own devices, humans are very inconsistent. An instrument, whether it is a scale or a customer survey, is generally more consistent.

3. *Instruments can be calibrated to account for error.* Calibration is the act of measuring something for which you already know the answer to test not the object of measurement, but the instrument itself. We might calibrate a scale by placing on it a weight we know to be exactly 1 gram. We calibrated your ability to assess odds by asking questions where the answer was already known. In this way, we know what the error is for a proper instrument.

    An instrument often includes a method for offsetting a particular error, which is often called a control. A controlled experiment, for example, compares the thing being measured to some baseline. If you want to know if a new sales force automation system improves repeat business, you need to compare it to customers and sales reps who aren't using the system. Perhaps some sales reps use it more than others or perhaps the rollout has not gone to every region or product line. Doing this allows for comparisons between those using and those not using the new system (more on this in the next chapter).

4. *Instruments deliberately don't see some things.* Instruments are useful when they ignore factors that bias human observations. For example, removing names from essay tests graded by teachers removes the possible bias a teacher might have about some students. In clinical research studies, neither doctors nor patients know who is taking a drug and who is taking a placebo. This way, patients cannot bias their experience and doctors cannot bias their diagnosis.

5. *Instruments record.* The image of the old electrocardiograph machine spinning out long ribbons of paper displaying the activity of the heart is a good example of how the instrument is a recording tool. Of course, today the record is often entirely electronic. Instruments don't rely on selective and faulty human memory. Gamblers, for example, routinely overestimate their skill because they don't really keep track of their progress. The best measure of their progress is the drop in cash in their bank accounts.

6. *Instruments take a measurement faster and cheaper than a human.* It could be possible to hire enough people to physically count inventory every hour of every day in a large grocery store. But point-of-sale scanners do it cheaper. A state trooper could compute highway speeds with a stopwatch and distance markers, but a radar gun would give the answer before the speeder got away and give it more accurately. If an instrument does nothing else, cost alone could be reason enough to use it.

According to these criteria, a shepherd who counts sheep using beads on a rope is using an instrument. The string is calibrated, it records, and without it the shepherd would probably make more errors. Sampling procedures and experimental approaches themselves are instruments and are often referred to in that way even if they do not use any mechanical or electronic devices. Some would question the value of broadening this definition. A customer survey, for example, doesn't necessarily detect anything humans can't. But it should at least be consistent as well as calibrated. And if it is a Web-based survey, it will be cheaper to conduct and easier to analyze (more about this in Chapter 13). Those who would reject the idea of a customer survey being a measurement instrument forget the whole point of measurement. How uncertain would they be *without* the instrument?

There are so many measurement methods for so many types of measurement challenges that no one book could address them all in detail. But the abundance of available methods reassures us that no matter what the measurement issue is, a well-developed solution exists. And even though it is impractical to try to fit a complete measurement encyclopedia in this book, broad basic categories of methods solve quite a few problems. Furthermore, these methods can be used in combination to create a variety of approaches to specific measurement problems.

In our resolve to measure anything, the "Four Useful Measurement Assumptions" (mentioned in Chapter 3) are worth reiterating:

1. Don't reinvent the wheel—it's been done before.

2. You have access to more data than you think—it might just involve some resourcefulness and original observations.

3. You need less data than you think, if you are clever about how to analyze it.

4. The method you need is probably simpler than you first thought.

DECOMPOSITION

Some very useful uncertainty-reducing methods are technically not actual measurements because they do not involve making new observations of the world. But they are often a very practical next step in determining how to measure something. Often they can reveal that the estimator actually knew more than he or she let on in the initial calibrated estimate. One of these is what I'm going to call decomposition. Decomposition involves figuring out how to compute something very uncertain from other things that are a lot less uncertain or at least easier to measure.

DECOMPOSE IT

Many measurements start by decomposing an uncertain variable into constituent parts to identify directly observable things that are easier to measure.

As you recall from earlier in this book, decomposition is, in fact, what Eratosthenes did. He didn't attempt to measure the circumference of Earth directly. Instead, he worked out the mathematical relationship between the angle of the sun in the sky from different latitudes, indicated by the lengths of shadows, to the circumference of Earth. The length of shadows was a very easy observation from which he could compute what he wanted to know. "Fermi questions" were also simply a method to decompose a given problem into its constituents. Instead of being exasperated by a difficult estimate, Fermi just started to break it down and answer each part. While his original question (the number of piano tuners in Chicago) seemed unknowable, it is just a function of other easier-to-estimate variables.

In fact, most measurements in the empirical sciences are done exactly like this: indirectly. For example, neither the mass of an electron nor the mass of Earth is observed directly. Other observations are made from which these values can be computed.

One example of the usefulness of decomposition is estimating the cost of a big construction project. Your first calibrated estimate might be $10 million to $20 million based on similar-size projects. However, when you break your specific project down into several components and put a range on each of those, you can end up with an aggregate range that is narrower than your original range. You didn't make any new observations. You simply made a more detailed model based on things you already knew. Furthermore, you may find that your big uncertainty is the cost of one particular item (e.g., the cost of labor in a particular specialty). This realization alone brings you that much closer to a useful measurement.

Another example of decomposition as a step in measurement is a potential productivity improvement. Let's say there is a new process or technology that is expected to improve productivity, but the best estimate is that it will improve productivity by 5% to 40% for a particular set of employees. Part of the uncertainty for estimators comes from the fact that they are trying to approximate, in their head some other variables they don't know firsthand. They don't know, for example, exactly how many people work in the area that would be affected the most.

Measuring how many people work in the area seems like an obvious and simple step in measurement. Yet, those who insist that something cannot ever be measured resist even this. In such cases, a facilitator can be a big help in getting people through this blockage.

> **Facilitator:** Previously you gave me a calibrated estimate of a 5% to 40%
> productivity improvement for your engineers with this new

engineering document management software. Because this particular variable had the highest information value for the business case of whether to invest in the new software or not, we have to reduce our uncertainty further.

Engineer: That's a problem. How can we measure a soft thing like productivity? We don't even track document management as an activity, so we have no idea how much time we spend in it now.

Facilitator: Well, clearly you think that productivity will improve because there are certain tasks they will spend less time doing, right?

Engineer: I suppose so, yes.

Facilitator: What activities do engineers spend a lot of time at now that they will spend much less time at if they used this tool? Be as specific as possible.

Engineer: Okay. I guess they would probably spend less time searching for relevant documents. But that's just one item.

Facilitator: Great, it's a start. How much time do they spend at this now per week, and how much do you think that time will be reduced? Calibrated estimates will do for now.

Engineer: I'm not sure....I suppose I would be 90% confident the average engineer spends between 1 hour to 6 hours each week just looking for documents. Equipment specs, engineering drawings, procedural manuals, and so on are all kept in different places, and most are not in electronic form.

Facilitator: Good. How much of that would go away if they could sit at their desks and do queries?

Engineer: Well, even when I use automated search tools like Google, I still spend a lot of time searching through irrelevant data, so automation could not reduce time spent in searching by 100%. But I'm sure it would go down at least by half.

Facilitator: Does this vary for the type of engineer?

Engineer: Sure. Engineers with management roles spend less time at this. They depend on subordinates more often. On the other hand, engineers who focus on particular compliance issues have to research lots of documents. Various technicians also would use this.

Facilitator: Okay. How many engineers and technicians fall into each of these categories, and how much time do they each spend in this activity. . . .

We go on in this way until we've identified a few different categories of staff, each spending a different amount of time in document searching and each with a different potential reduction in this time spent. The staff members may also vary by how much they adopt the new technology and other factors.

The previous dialog is actually a reconstruction of a specific conversation I had with engineers in a major U.S. nuclear power utility. During the meeting, we also identified other tasks, such as distribution, quality control, and the like, that might be reduced by document management systems. As before, the time spent in each of these tasks varied by the type of engineer or technician.

In short, part of the reason these engineers gave such a wide range for a productivity improvement is that they were imagining all of these variances among different types of engineers without explicitly breaking it down this way. Once they broke it down, they found that some numbers were fairly certain (e.g., the head count for each engineer type, or the fact that some types spend most or little of their time in this activity) and that the uncertainty about the original number came primarily from one or two specific items. If we found that they were more uncertain just about time spent replicating or tracking down lost documents and then only for a certain class of engineers, we would have a big clue about where to begin a measurement.

"DECOMPOSITION EFFECT"

The phenomenon that the decomposition itself often turns out to provide such a sufficient reduction in uncertainty that further observations are not required.

The 55 major risk/return analyses I've done in the last 10 years consisted of a total of over 3,300 individual variables, or an average of a little over 60 variables per model. Of those, about 120 (about 2 per model) required further measurement according to the information value calculation. Most of these, about 100, had to be decomposed further to find a more easily measured component of the uncertain variable. Other variables offered more direct and obvious methods of measurement; for example, having to determine the gas mileage of a truck on a gravel road (by just driving a truck with a fuel flow meter) or estimating the number of bugs in software (by inspecting samples of code).

But almost a third of those variables that were decomposed (about 30) required no further measurement after decomposition. In other words, about 25% of all the high-value measurements were (decomposed or not) addressed with decomposition alone. Calibrated experts already knew enough about the variable, they just needed a more detailed model that more explicitly expressed the detailed knowledge they had.

About two-thirds of those variables that were decomposed had one or more of their components measured; for example, as part of a larger productivity improvement measurement, a survey was administered to one group of people to measure time spent on a specific activity. For these variables, decomposition was one critical step in understanding how to learn more about the thing being analyzed. The entire process of decomposition itself is a gradual conceptual revelation for those who think that something is immeasurable. Like any engineer who faces the initially daunting task of how to build a suspension bridge in a way that has never been done before, decomposition addresses any measurement problem systematically, identifying its component parts. And, like the bridge engineer, this analysis of parts at each step redefines and refines the nature of the problem we face. The decomposition of an "immeasurable" variable is an important step toward measurement and sometimes a sufficient uncertainty reduction, itself.

Secondary Research: Assuming You Weren't the First to Measure It

The standard approach to measurement in business, it seems, is for some smart people to start with the assumption that, being smart, they themselves will have to invent the method for a new measurement. In reality, however, such innovation is almost never required.

No scientific research starts with the first random sample or experimental observation. Nor does it start with the design of a sampling method or experiment. It starts with "secondary" research. Secondary research is reviewing the research of others; it is distinct from "primary" research, where the researchers make the observations directly themselves. In seeming contrast to the nomenclature, secondary research always precedes primary research. All researchers assume, as a matter of course, that others came before them. This is the point of the first of the four proposed "working assumptions" for measurement (in Chapter 3): Your measurement problem is not as unique as you think. As a working assumption, you proceed as if your measurement problem has already been solved by others or at least has been further clarified. This working assumption almost always turns out to be true.

Library research, however, still does not seem to be an ingrained skill among management. But it has gotten a lot easier. Almost all my research now starts with the Internet. No matter what measurement problem I'm attempting to resolve, I start by doing homework with Google and Yahoo. Then, of course, I still usually end up in the library, but with more direction and purpose.

There are just a few "tricks" in using the Internet for secondary research. If you are looking for information that has been applied to measurement methods, you will probably find that most Internet searching is unproductive unless you are using the right search terms. It takes practice to use Internet searches effectively, but these tips should help.

- *If I'm really new to a topic, I don't start with Google.* I start with Wikipedia.org, the online collaborative encyclopedia. Wikipedia contains well over a million articles, and a surprising number cover business and technology topics that might be considered too obscure for traditional encyclopedia sets. A good article usually includes links to other sites, and controversial topics tend to have lengthy discussions attached so you can decide for yourself what information to accept.

- *Use search terms that tend to be associated with research and quantitative data.* If you need to measure "software quality" or "customer perception," don't just search on those terms alone—you will get mostly fluff. Instead, include terms like "table," "survey," "control group," "correlation," and "standard deviation," which would tend to appear in more substantive research. Also, terms like "university," "PhD," and "national study" tend to appear in more serious (less fluffy) research.

- *Think of Internet research in two levels: search engines and topic-specific repositories.* The problem with using powerful search engines like Google is that you might get thousands of hits, none of which is relevant. But try searching specifically within industry magazine Web sites or online academic journals. If I'm curious about macroeconomic or international analysis, I'll go straight to government Web sites like the Census, Department of Commerce, even the CIA (the CIA *World Fact Book* is my go-to place for a variety international statistical data). These will give fewer hits but will mostly likely generate more relevant hits.

- *Try multiple search engines.* Even the seemingly all-powerful Google seems to miss a few items I find quickly when I use other engines. I like to use clusty.com and yahoo.com to supplement searches on Google.

- *If you find marginally related research that still doesn't directly address your topic of interest, be sure to read the bibliography.* The bibliography is sometimes the best method for branching out to find more research.

THE BASIC METHODS OF OBSERVATION: IF ONE DOESN'T WORK, TRY THE NEXT

Describing in detail how you see or detect the proposed object of measurement is a useful way to begin to describe a measurement method. If you have any basis for the belief that the object even *exists*, then you are observing it in some way. If someone claims customer satisfaction will increase significantly if we can only reduce call-waiting time, then the person must have some reason for believing it. Have there been some complaints? Have there been downward trends in customer satisfaction as the company grew? Measurements are almost always performed to test the truth of some idea, and those ideas don't just come from a vacuum.

If you've identified your uncertainty, identified any relevant thresholds, and computed the value of information, then you've already identified something that is observable in principle. Consider these five questions about the nature of the observation. This is a sort of cascade of empirical methods. If the first approach doesn't work, go to the next, and so on. These aren't in any particular order, but you will probably find that for some situations, it's best to start with one then move to the others.

1. *Does it leave a trail of any kind?* Just about every imaginable phenomenon leaves some evidence that it occurred. Think like a forensic investigator. Does the thing, event, or activity that you are trying to measure lead to consequences that themselves have a trail of any kind? Example: Longer waits on customer support lines cause some customers to hang up. This has to at least cause some loss of business, but how much? Did they hang up because of some unrelated reason on their end or out of frustration from waiting? People in the first group tend to call back; people in the second group tend not to. If you can identify even some of the customers who hang up and notice that they tend to purchase less, then you have a clue. Now can you find any

correlation between customers who hung up after long waits and a decrease in sales to that customer? (See "Example for Leaving a Trail.")

2. *If the trail doesn't already exist, then can you observe it directly, or at least a sample of it?* Perhaps you haven't been tracking how many customers in a retail parking lot have out-of-state license plates, but you could look now. And even though staking out the parking lot full time is impractical, you can at least count license plates at some randomly selected times.

3. *If it doesn't appear to leave behind a detectable trail of any kind, and direct observation does not seem feasible without some additional aid, can you devise a way to begin to track it now?* If it hasn't been leaving a trail, you can "tag" it so it at least begins to leave a trail. One example is how Amazon.com provides free gift wrapping in order to help track how many of its books are purchased as gifts. At one point Amazon was not tracking the number of items sold as gifts; Amazon added the gift wrapping feature to be able to track it. Another example is how consumers are given coupons so retailers can see, among other things, what newspapers their customers read.

4. *If tracking the existing conditions does not suffice (with either existing or newly collected data), can the phenomenon be "forced" to occur under conditions that allow easier observation (i.e., an experiment)?* Example: If a retail store wants to measure whether a proposed returned-items policy will detrimentally affect customer satisfaction and sales, try it in some stores while holding others unchanged. Try to identify the difference.

SOME BASIC METHODS OF OBSERVATION

1. Follow its trail like a clever detective. Do "forensic analysis" of data you already have.

2. Use direct observation. Start looking, counting, and/or sampling if possible.

3. If it hasn't left any trail so far, add a "tracer" to it so it *starts* leaving a trail.

4. If you can't follow a trail at all, then create the conditions to observe it (an experiment).

These methods apply regardless of whether this is a measurement of something that is occurring now (current sales due to customer referral) or a forecast (the expected improvement in customer referrals due to some new product feature, improvement in customer service, etc.). If it is something that describes a current state, the current state has all the information you need to measure it. If the measurement is actually a forecast, then consider what you have observed already that gives you any reason to expect improvement change. If you can't think of anything you ever observed that causes you to have that expectation, why is your expectation justified at all?

And remember that in order to detect a trail, add a tracer/tag, or conduct an experiment, you only need to observe a few in a random sample. Also remember that different elements of your decomposition may have to be measured differently. Don't worry just yet about all of the problems that each of these approaches could entail. Just identify whichever approach seems the simplest and most feasible for now.

> ### EXAMPLE FOR LEAVING A TRAIL: THE VALUE OF FASTER PICKUP OF CUSTOMER CALLS
>
> A large European paint supplies distributor asked me how to measure the impact of network speed on sales, since the network affected how quickly inbound calls could be answered. Since the PBX phone system kept logs of calls and hang-ups while on hold, and since the network kept a history of its utilization levels (and, therefore, response time), I recommended cross-referencing the two data sets. This showed that hang-ups increased when demand on the network increased. They also looked at past situations where the network was slower because of other use, not increased use by customer service, as well as the sales history by day. Altogether, they were able to isolate the difference in sales that was due just to slower network speed.

Measure Just Enough

Chapter 7 reviewed how to compute the value of information for a particular decision. The uncertainty, thresholds, and information value you determined say a lot about what measurement method you really need. If the information value of knowing whether your customers think your product quality has improved with a new manufacturing process (e.g., the "new" beverage formulation or the "classic" beverage formulation) is a couple of thousand dollars, you can't justify a two-month pilot market or even a major blind taste test. But if the information value is in the range of millions of dollars (which is more likely if this is the product of even a medium-size company), then we should not feel daunted by a study that might cost $100,000 and lasts a few weeks. Keeping the information value in mind along with the threshold, the decision, and current uncertainty provides the purpose and context of the measurement.

The information value puts an upper limit on what you should even theoretically be willing to spend. But the best measurement expenditure is probably far below this maximum. As a ballpark estimate, I shoot for spending about 10% of the EVPI on a measurement, and sometimes even as low as 2%. (This is about the least amount you should consider.) I use this estimate for three reasons. First, the EVPI is the value of perfect information. Since all empirical methods have some error, we are only shooting for a reduction in uncertainty, not perfect information. So the value of our measurement will probably be much less than the EVPI. Second, initial measurements often change the value of continued measurement. If the first few observations are surprising, the value of continuing the measurement may drop to zero. This means there is a value in iterative measurement. And since you always have the option of continuing a measurement if you need more precision, there is usually a manageable risk in underestimating the initial measurement effort. Finally, remember that the information value curve is usually steepest at the beginning—the first 100 samples reduce uncertainty much more than the second 100.

The threshold also tells you something about how to measure a thing. If you need to measure a market to set production levels or productivity to pay bonuses, then you don't really have a "threshold." Every improvement in accuracy is worth something, although the incremental increase in value is less and less as you approach EVPI. But, suppose you need to measure the size of the market because a particular investment in your organization breaks even if your market increased by at least 12% from last year. Your measurement method should stay focused on the fact that measuring within a 1% error is not as important as simply knowing which side of that threshold you are on. If you can determine with confidence that the value is less than a 5% increase in the market, then the difference in value between a 1% error is virtually identical to a measure with a 5% error. In this case, the only error you care about is the chance that your measurement said the value was less (or more) than 12% when in fact the opposite was true.

Finally, the initial state of uncertainty tells you a lot about how to measure it. Remember, the more uncertainty you started out with, the more the initial observation will tell you. When starting from a position of extremely high uncertainty, even methods with a lot of inherent error can give you more information than you had before.

CONSIDER THE ERROR

All measurements have error. As with all problems, the solution starts with the recognition that we have the problem—which allows us to develop strategies to compensate, at least partially. Those who tend to be easily thwarted by measurement challenges, however, often assume that the existence of *any* error means that a measurement is impossible. If that were true, then virtually nothing would ever have been measured in any field of science. Fortunately, for the scientific community and for the rest of us, it's not. Enrico Fermi can rest easy.

Scientists, statisticians, economists, and most others who make empirical measurements separate measurement error into two broad types: systemic and random. Systemic errors are those that are consistent and not just random variations from one observation to the next. For example, if the sales staff routinely overestimates next quarter's revenue by an average of 50%, that is a systemic error. The fact that it isn't always exactly 50% too optimistic, but varies, is an example of random error. Random error, by definition, can't be individually predicted, but it falls into some quantifiable patterns that can be computed with the laws of probability.

Systemic error and random error are related to the measurement concepts of precision and accuracy. "Precision" refers to the reproducibility and conformity of measurements, while "accuracy" refers to how close a measurement is to its "true" value. While the terms "accuracy" and "precision" (as well as "inaccuracy" and "imprecision") are used synonymously by most people, to measurement experts they are clearly different.

A bathroom scale that is calibrated to overstate or understate weight (as some people apparently do, deliberately) could be precise but inaccurate. It is precise because if the same person stepped on the scale several times within an hour—so that the actual weight doesn't have a chance to change—the scale would give the same answer very consistently. Yet it is inaccurate because every answer is always, say, eight pounds over. Now imagine a perfectly calibrated bathroom scale in the bathroom of a moving motor home. Bumps, acceleration, and hills causes the readings on the scale to move about and give different answers even when the same person steps on it twice within one minute. Still, you would find that after a number of times on the scale, the answers average out to be very close to the person's actual weight. This is an example of fairly good accuracy but low precision. Calibrated experts are similar to the latter. They may be inconsistent in their judgments, but they are not consistently overestimating or underestimating.

QUICK GLOSSARY OF ERROR

Systemic error/systemic bias: An inherent tendency of a measurement process to favor a particular outcome; a consistent bias.

Random error: An error that is not predictable for individual observations; not consistent or dependent on known variables (although such errors follow the rules of probability in large groups).

Accuracy: A characteristic of a measurement having a low systemic error—that is, not consistently over- or underestimating a value.

Precision: A characteristic of a measurement having a low random error; highly consistent results even if they are far from the true value.

To put it another way, precision is low random error, regardless of the amount of systemic error. Accuracy is low systemic error, regardless of the amount of random error. Each of the types of error can be accounted for and reduced. If we know the bathroom scale gives an answer eight pounds higher than the true value, then we can adjust the reading accordingly. If we get highly inconsistent readings with a well-calibrated scale, then we can remove random error by taking several measurements and computing the average. Any method to reduce either of these errors is called a control.

Random sampling, if used properly, is itself a type of control. Random effects, while individually unpredictable, follow specific predictable patterns in the aggregate. For example, I can't predict a coin flip. But I can tell you that if you flipped a coin 1,000 times, there will be 500 +/− 26 heads. (We'll talk about computing the error range later.) It is often much harder to compute an error range for systemic error. Systemic errors—like those from using biased judges to assess the quality of a work product or using an instrument that constantly underestimates a quantity—don't necessarily produce random errors that can be quantified probabilistically.

If you had to choose, would you prefer the weight measurement from an uncalibrated but precise scale with an unknown error or a calibrated scale on a moving platform with highly inconsistent readings each time you weigh yourself? I find that, in business, people often choose precision with unknown systemic error over a highly imprecise measurement with random error. For example, to determine how much time sales reps spend in meetings with clients versus other administrative tasks, they might choose a complete review of all timesheets. They would generally not conduct a random sample of sales reps on different days at different times. Time sheets have error, especially those completed for the whole week at 5 p.m. on Friday in a rush to get out the door. People underestimate time spent on some tasks, overestimate time spent on others, and they are inconsistent in how they classify tasks.

If a complete review of 5,000 time sheets (say, 100 reps for 50 weekly time sheets each) tells us that sales reps spend 34% of their time in direct communication with customers, we don't know how far from the truth it might be. Still, this "exact" number seems reassuring to many managers. Now, suppose a sample of direct observations of randomly chosen sales reps at random points in time finds that sales reps were in client meetings or on client phone calls only 13 out of 100 of those instances. (We can compute this without interrupting a meeting by asking as soon as the rep is available.) As we will see in Chapter 9, in the latter case we can statistically compute a 90% CI to be 7.5% to 18.5%. Even though the random sampling approach only gives us a range, we should prefer its findings to the census audit of time sheets. The census of time sheets gives us an exact number, but we have no way to know by how much and in which direction the time sheets err.

SMALL RANDOM SAMPLES VERSUS LARGE NONRANDOM SAMPLES: THE KINSEY SEX STUDY

A famous debate about small random versus large nonrandom samples concerned the work of Alfred Kinsey in the 1940s and 1950s regarding sexual behavior. Kinsey's work was both controversial and popular at the time. Funded by the Rockefeller Foundation, he was able to conduct interviews of 18,000 men and women. But they were not exactly random samples. He tended to meet people by referral and tended to sample everyone in a specific group (a bowling league, a college fraternity, a book club, etc.). Kinsey apparently assumed that any error could be offset by a large enough sample. But that's not how most systemic error works—it doesn't "average out." John W. Tukey, a famous statistician who was retained by the same Rockefeller Foundation to review Kinsey's work, was quoted as saying: "A random selection of three people would have been better than a group of 300 chosen by Mr. Kinsey." In another version of this quote, he was said to prefer a random sample of 400 to Kinsey's 18,000. If the first quote is Tukey's, he may have exaggerated, but not by much. Tukey meant that the groups Kinsey sampled were often very close to homogeneous. Therefore, these groups may only have counted as something closer to one random sample, statistically speaking. In the second version of the quote, Tukey is almost certainly correct: A random sample of 400 will have an easily quantifiable error, and that error may actually be much less than the systemic error of 18,000 poorly chosen samples.

Why do people choose a false sense of exactitude over the quantifiable error of a random sample? When they are pressed for an answer, I find they are confusing the error of a single sample with the error of the entire study. Yes, in the sales rep sampling example, in some snapshots in time you would find a sales rep doing something that is not representative of how their time is spent, such as making travel arrangements, when he or she is hardly ever out of town. If that sales rep were sampled only once, then this would not say much of anything useful about how *that* rep spends his or her time. But if 25 of 100 sales reps, each sampled at different times, are making travel arrangements, then you can be safe in concluding that sales reps spend about

25% of their time, on average, making travel arrangements and a little math from Chapter 9 shows the 90% CI for this measurement is 18% to 32%. Since there is an obvious unreliability in one sample, people assume that random samples have some kind of cumulative error, not an error that tends to average out.

The error you can't count on averaging out—systemic error—is also called a bias. The list of types of biases seems to grow with almost every year of research in decision psychology or empirical sciences in general. But there are three big biases that you need to control for: expectancy, selection, and observer biases.

TYPES OF OBSERVATION BIASES

Expectancy bias: Seeing what we want to see. Observers and subjects sometimes, consciously or not, see what they want. We are gullible and tend to be self-deluding. Clinical trials of new drugs have to make sure that subjects don't actually know whether they have taken the real drug or a placebo. This is the previously mentioned blind test. When those who are taking the real drug are hidden from the doctors as well as the patients, this is a double-blind test. The approach I recommended for the Mitre Corporation example in Chapter 3 is an example of a blind test.

Selection bias: Even when attempting randomness in samples, we can get inadvertent nonrandomness. If we sample 500 voters for a poll and 55% say they will vote for candidate A, it is fairly likely—98.8%, to be exact—that candidate A actually has the lead in the population. There is only a 1.2% chance that a random sampling could have just by chance chosen more voters for A if A wasn't actually in the lead. But this assumes the sample was random and didn't tend to select some types of voters over others. If the sample is taken by asking passersby on a particular street corner in the financial district, then you are more likely to get a particular type of voter even if you "randomly" picked which passersby to ask.

Observer bias (or the "Heisenberg and Hawthorne" bias): Subatomic particles and humans have something in common—the act of observing them causes them both to change behavior. In 1927 the physicist Werner Heisenberg derived a formula that showed that there is a limit to how much we can know about a particle's position and velocity. When we observe particles, we have to interact with them (e.g., bounce light off them), causing their paths to change. That same year a research project was begun at the Hawthorne Plant of the Western Electric Company in Illinois. Initially led by Professor Elton Mayo from the Harvard Business School, the study set out to determine the effects of the physical environment and working conditions on worker productivity. Researchers altered lighting levels, humidity, work hours, and so on in an effort to determine under which conditions workers worked best. To their surprise, they found that worker productivity improved no matter how they changed the workplace. The workers were simply responding to the knowledge of being observed; or perhaps, researchers hypothesized, management taking interest in them caused a positive reaction. Either way, we can no longer assume observations see the "real" world if we don't take care to compensate for how observations affect what we observe. The simplest solution is to keep observations a secret from those being observed.

CHOOSE AND DESIGN THE INSTRUMENT

After decomposing the problem, placing one or more of the decomposed parts in an observation hierarchy, aiming for "just good enough" uncertainty reduction, and accounting for the main types of error, the measurement instrument should be almost completely formed in your mind. Just answering the questions up to this point should have made some measurement methods more apparent.

Let's summarize how to identify the instrument:

1. *Decompose the measurement so that it can be estimated from other measurements.* Some of these elements may be easier to measure, and sometimes the decomposition itself will have reduced uncertainty.

2. *Consider your findings from secondary research:* Look at how others measured similar issues. Even if their specific findings don't relate to your measurement problem, is there anything you can salvage from the methods they used?

3. *Place one or more of the elements from the decomposition in one or more of the methods of observation: trails left behind, direct observation, tracking with "tags," or experiments.* Think of at least three ways you detect it, and then follow its trail forensically. If you can't do that, try a direct observation. If you can't do that, tag it or make other changes to it so it *starts* leaving a trail you can follow. If you can't do that, create the event specifically to be observed (the experiment).

4. *Keep the concept "just enough" squarely in mind.* You don't need great precision if all you need is more certainty that a productivity improvement will be over the minimum threshold needed to justify a project. Keep the information value in mind; a small value means little effort is justified, and a big value means you should think big about the measurement method. Also, remember how much uncertainty you had to begin with. If you were originally very uncertain, how much of an observation do you really need to reduce the uncertainty?

5. *Think about the errors specific to that problem.* If it is a series of human judges evaluating the quality of work, beware of expectation bias and consider a blind. If you need a sample, make sure it is random. If your observations themselves can affect outcome, find a way to hide the observation from the subject.

Now, if you can't yet fully visualize the instrument, consider these tips, listed in no particular order. Some have been mentioned already, but all are worth reviewing.

- *Work through the consequences.* If the value you are seeking is surprisingly high, what should you see? If the value is surprisingly low, what should you see? In the example cited in Chapter 2, young Emily reasoned that if the therapeutic touch specialists could do what they claimed, they should at least be able to detect a human "aura." For a quality measurement problem, if quality is better, then you probably should see fewer complaints from customers. For a sales-related software application, if a new information technology system really helps salespeople sell better, then why would you see sales go down for those who use it more?

- *Imagine how others would do it.* Think the problem through like a forensic investigator, a detective, an experimental psychologist, a paleontologist, a librarian, a military intelligence officer, a journalist, or a librarian. Get out of your current occupational box and consider something other than the "standard" measurement methods of the field.

- *Be iterative.* Don't try to eliminate uncertainty in one giant study. Start making a few observations, and recalculate the information value. It might have a bearing on how you continue measurement.

- *Consider multiple approaches.* If one type of observation on one of the elements in your decomposition doesn't seem feasible, focus on another. You have many options. If the first measurement method works, great. But in some cases I've measured things three different ways, after the first two were unenlightening. Are you sure you are exploring all the methods available? If you can't measure one variable in a decomposition, can you measure another?

- *What's the really simple question that makes the rest of the measurement moot?* Again, Emily didn't try to measure how well therapeutic touch worked, just whether it worked at all. In the Mitre example discussed earlier, I suggested the company determine if clients could detect *any* change in the quality of research before they tried to measure a value of the expected improvement in quality. Some questions are so basic that it is possible that their answers could make more complicated measurements irrelevant. What is the basic question you need to ask to see if you need to measure any more?

- *Just do it.* Don't let anxiety about what could go wrong with measurement keep you from just *starting* to make some organized observations. Don't assume you won't be surprised by the first few observations and considerably reduce your uncertainty.

By now you should have a pretty good idea of what you need to observe and, generally, how to observe it in order to make your measurement. Now we can talk about some specific methods of observation in two general categories: observations analyzed with "traditional" statistics and a method called Bayesian analysis. Together, these two broad categories cover just about all empirical methods applied to physics, medicine, environmental studies, or economics. Although the traditional methods are by far the most prevalent methods, the newer Bayesian analysis has some distinct advantages.

## CHAPTER 9

Sampling Reality: How Observing Some Things Tells Us about All Things

If you want 100% certainty about the percentage of defective bricks from a kiln, you have to test all of them. Since testing the failure load of a brick requires destroying it, this would require the destruction of every brick you make. If you want to have most of the bricks left over to use or sell, you only get to test a few bricks to learn something about all the bricks.

The group you want to learn about is the population, in this case, the bricks produced. A test of every single item in a group you want to learn (e.g., testing every brick produced) is a census. Obviously, a census is impractical for bricks, since you would have no bricks left where the census is complete, but it is practical in other situations. A monthly inventory is usually a census, and the balance sheet is a census of every asset and liability. The U.S. Census tries to count every human being in the country, although in reality it falls a bit short of this.

But lots of things are more like bricks than like accounting transactions. There are a number of reasons it is impractical to test, track, weigh, or even count every item in a population. But we can still reduce uncertainty by looking at just some items from a population. Anything short of a complete census of the population is a sample. In effect, sampling is observing just some of the things in a population to learn something about all of the things in a population.

It might seem remarkable that looking at some things tells us anything about things we aren't looking at but, in fact, this is most of what science is about. Experiments only look at some phenomena in a universe full of phenomena. But when science discovers a "law," it says that the law applies to everything in that population, not just the few examples observed so far.

For example, the speed of light was determined with, literally, some samples of light. And no matter what measurement method was used, it had error. So scientists measured the speed of light more than once. Each measurement is another sample. And yet the speed of light is a universal constant that should apply to the light reflecting off this page and hitting your eyes as well as the light sampled in a lab. Even a census could just be a sample of a still larger population over time. A complete inventory is just one snapshot in time, as is a balance sheet.

This point might be disconcerting to some who would like more certainty in their world, but everything we know from "experience" is just a sample. We didn't actually experience everything; we experienced some things and we extrapolated from there. That is all we get—fleeting glimpses of a mostly unobserved world from which we draw conclusions about all the stuff we didn't see. Yet people seem to feel confident in the conclusions they draw from limited samples. The reason they feel this way is because experience tells them sampling often works. (Of course, that experience too is based on a sample.)

We may only need a very small number of samples to draw useful conclusions about the rest of the unsampled population. If we are taking a sample to test for something completely homogeneous, like the DNA in someone's blood or octane levels in gasoline, then we need only one sample from a person or batch. However, if the samples vary a lot, such as the size of fish in a lake or the time spent by employees dealing with PC problems, then we generally need more—sometimes a lot more. But perhaps not as many as many people think.

How can looking at just a few things tell us something about all things in a population? If we sample 12 people in a city to find out how often they go to the movies or whether they trust the mayor, can we learn anything about all the people we *didn't* ask? Yes, we can. And if you think about it, that's kind of amazing; but whether this small sample tells us much depends, in part, on how we took the sample. If we just ask our friends or all the men in a barbershop, there is good reason to believe that this group might not be representative of the total population, and it is hard to tell how far off our conclusions about the larger population might be. We need a method to ensure that we don't just systematically choose samples of a particular type.

The solution for this is genuinely random sampling from the entire population we are trying to examine. If we can pick samples randomly, then we still have error, but the rules of probability can tell us something about the error. We can work out the chance that we just happened to pick Democrats in a political poll of an area that, in reality, has more Republicans. As the number of people randomly sampled grows, the chance of accidentally getting a nonrepresentative group becomes smaller and smaller.

If you've seen reports of political polls or have read any research that used some sort of sample, you've seen reference to the concept of statistical significance. Statistical significance simply tells us whether we are seeing something real and not just something that just happened by chance. How big of a sample do we need to get a "statistically significant" result? Do we have to survey 1,000 customers? Do we have to spot-check welds on the chassis of 50 cars? Does a drug have to be tested with more than 100 patients in a clinical trial?

I've heard many authoritative-sounding proclamations on this topic. Someone will state that unless there is at least some specific number, the results won't be statistically significant. How did the person come up with this number? At best, the individual will make a vague reference to some rule from a statistics text, but, in all but the rarest cases, he or she won't be able to show a specific calculation.

In short, the concept of statistical significance is vastly overused by those who don't quite understand what it means. Do they mean that unless this threshold is met for the sample size, we will have *no* reduction in uncertainty? Do they mean that the uncertainty reduction we get from a smaller sample won't have an economic value of information that exceeds the cost of the measurement? My experience is that when it comes to conducting some sort of random sampling in business, a lot of "experts" come out of the woodwork to state what can and can't be done in statistics. I have found that the error rate in their foggy memory of first-semester statistics can be much, much higher than the error of a small sample.

Someone who really does know something about statistical significance is Barry Nussbaum, Chief Statistician of Statistical Support Services at the Environmental Protection Agency. I've worked with him on how to import some of my methods into statistical analysis at the EPA. He fields questions from all over the agency about how to conduct statistical analysis on different types of problems. He tells me: "When people ask for statistics support, they ask 'What's the sample size?' It is the wrong question, but it's the first one most people ask." Of course, Nussbaum needs to find out more about what they are measuring and why. I couldn't agree more.

In fact, a very small sample can probably tell you much more than you think. Especially when your uncertainty is great, even a small sample can produce a big reduction in uncertainty. If you already know a quantity is within a very narrow range—say, the percentage of customers satisfied with their service being within 80% to 85%— then you would probably need a lot of samples to improve on that (more than 1,000, actually). But this book is more about those things that are considered immeasurable, and in those cases the uncertainty is generally much greater. And it is exactly in those types of problems where even a few observations can tell us a lot.

For someone who needs to review the material from first-semester college statistics, there are a lot of accessible statistics books. This book doesn't try to cover all of those topics. We focus instead on the most basic and useful methods and including a bit on what the standard statistics text books tend to leave out or at least deemphasize. The limitations of statistics textbooks are part of the problem for managers seeking solutions for measurement challenges. The entire industry of statistical analysis seems less concerned about practical accessibility or the broader issue of how to measure the "immeasurable." Nussbaum has noticed the same general disposition among those who get published in the *Journal of the American Statistical Association* (*JASA*), "If you look at the *JASA*, even what they call 'applications' are pretty theoretical."

This chapter discusses some simple methods for drawing a lot of information from a few samples. But unlike most stats books, we focus on "intuition building" before we show any math, and the math presented is as limited as possible. When we do get into how to compute specific values, we emphasize quick estimates and simple tables and charts over memorizing equations.

Furthermore, every example in this chapter (as well as most in this book) can be downloaded as spreadsheet examples from the supplementary Web site, www.howtomeasureanything.com. Make full use of that resource.

HOW MANY CARS BURN THE WRONG FUEL?

A Government Agency Takes a "Just do it" Approach to Measurement

In the 1970s, the Environmental Protection Agency (EPA) knew it had a public policy problem. After 1975, automobiles were designed with catalytic converters to use unleaded gasoline. But leaded gasoline was cheaper and drivers were inclined to continue using leaded fuel in cars with the new catalytic converters. The now-familiar narrower nozzle restrictor at the opening to the gas tank was mandated by the EPA to keep people from adding leaded gasoline to new cars. (Leaded gasoline came out of wider nozzles that wouldn't fit in the nozzle restrictors.) A driver could still simply remove the restrictor and use leaded gasoline. Barry Nussbaum, Chief Statistician of Statistical Support Services at the EPA, said: "We knew people were putting leaded fuel in the new cars because when DMV [Department of Motor Vehicle] inspections were done, they looked at the restrictor to see if it was removed." Using leaded fuel in the new cars could cause air pollution to be worse, not better, as the unleaded gasoline program was meant to achieve. There was a moment of consternation at the EPA. How could it possibly measure how many people were using leaded gasoline in unleaded cars? In the "Just Do It" spirit of measurement, members of the EPA simply staked out gas stations. First, they randomly selected gas stations throughout the county. Then, armed with binoculars, EPA staff observed cars at the pump, recorded whether they took leaded or unleaded gasoline, and compared license plate numbers to a DMV list of vehicle types. This method got the EPA some bad exposure—a cartoonist for the *Atlanta Constitution* showed the EPA as Nazi-like characters arresting people who used the wrong gas, even though the EPA only observed and arrested no one. Still, Nussbaum said, "This got us into trouble with a few police departments." Of course, the police had to concede that anyone is free to observe others on and from a public street corner. But the important thing is that the EPA found an answer: 8% of cars that should use only unleaded gas were using leaded gas. As difficult as the problem first sounded, the EPA recognized that if it took the obvious observation and just started sampling, it could improve on the relative uncertainty.

BUILDING AN INTUITION FOR RANDOM SAMPLING: THE JELLY BEAN EXAMPLE

Here is a little experiment you can try. What is your 90% CI for the weight, in grams, of the average jelly bean? Remember, we need two numbers—a lower bound and an upper bound—just far apart enough that you are 90% confident that the average weight of a jelly bean, in grams, is between the bounds. Just like every other calibrated probability estimate, you have some idea, regardless of how uncertain you feel about it. A gram, by the way, weighs as much as 1 cubic centimeter of water. Write down your range before you go any further. As explained in Chapter 5, be sure to test it with the equivalent bet, consider some pros and cons for why the range is reasonable, and test each bound against anchoring.

I have a typical bag of jelly beans, the type you can buy anywhere candy is sold. I took such a bag and began sampling jelly beans. I put several jelly beans one at a time on a digital scale. Now consider these questions. Answer each one before you go to the next point.

1. Suppose I told you the weight of the first jelly bean I sampled was 1.4 grams. Does that change your 90% CI? If so, what is your updated 90% CI? Write down your new range before proceeding.

2. Now I give you the results of the next 4 randomly sampled jelly bean weights, for a total of 5 so far: 1.4, 1.5, 1.6, and 1.1. Does that change your 90% CI even further? If so, what is your 90% CI, now? Again, write down this new range.

3. Finally, I give you the results of the next 3 randomly sampled weights of jelly beans, for a total of 8 samples so far: 1.5, 0.9, 1.7. Again, does that change your 90% CI and, if so, what is it now? Write down this final range.

Your range usually would have gotten at least a little narrower each time you were given more data. If you had an extremely wide range as a first estimate (before you were told any sampling results), then even the first sample would have significantly narrowed your range.

I gave this test to nine calibrated estimators and I got fairly consistent results. The biggest difference among the estimators was how uncertain they were about the initial estimate. The narrowest ranges were 1 to 3 grams for the average jelly bean, and the widest was 0.5 to 50 grams, but most ranges were closer to the narrowest ranges. As the estimators were given additional information, most reduced the width of their range, especially those who started with very wide ranges. The estimator who gave a range of 1 to 3 grams did not reduce the range at all after the first sample. But the person who gave a range of 0.5 to 50 grams reduced the upper bound significantly, resulting in a range of 0.5 to 6 grams.

The true average of the population of this bag of jelly beans is close to 1.45 grams per jelly bean. Interestingly, the ranges of the estimators narrowed in on this value fairly quickly as they were given just a few additional samples.

Exercises like this help you gain a sense of intuition about samples and ranges. Asking calibrated estimators for subjective estimates without applying what some would call "proper statistics" is actually very useful and even has some interesting advantages over traditional statistics, as we will soon see. But first, let's look at how most statistics texts handle small samples.

A Little about Little Samples: A Beer Brewer's Approach

There is a way to compute the 90% CI for the jelly bean problem objectively, without any reliance on calibrated estimators, using a method developed by a beer brewer. This method is widely taught in basic statistics courses and can be used for computing errors for samples sizes as small as two. In the earliest years of the twentieth century, William Sealy Gosset, a chemist and statistician at the Guinness brewery in Dublin, had a measurement problem. Gosset needed a way to measure which types of barley produced the best beer-brewing yields. Prior to that time, a method alternatively called the z-score or normal-statistic was developed to estimate a confidence interval based on random samples—as long as there were at least 30 samples. This method produces distributions in the shape of the normal distribution discussed earlier. Unfortunately, Gosset did not have the luxury of sampling a large number of batches of beer for each type of barley. But instead of assuming he couldn't measure it, he set out to derive a new type of distribution for very small sample sizes. By 1908 he had developed a powerful new method he called the t-statistic, and he wanted to publish it.

To guard against the loss of trade secrets (a problem Guinness had previously experienced), the company forbade its employees from publishing anything about its business processes. While Gosset valued his job, he apparently wanted to publish this idea more than he needed immediate recognition. So Gosset published his t-statistic under the pseudonym "Student." Although the true author has been long known, virtually all statistics texts call this the Student's t-statistic.

The t-statistic is similar in shape to the normal distribution we discussed previously. But for very small samples, the shape of the distribution is much flatter and wider. The 90% CI computed with a student's t-statistic is much more uncertain (i.e., broader) than a normal distribution would indicate. For sample sizes larger than 30, the shape of the t-distribution is virtually the same as the normal distribution.

With either type of distribution, there is a relatively simple procedure (compared to much of the rest of statistics methods) for computing the 90% CI of the average of a population. Some might find the procedure to be unintuitive, and those familiar with the approach might find this to be a trivial rehash of information available in statistics texts. The first group might want to hold out for a much simpler solution (coming in the next chapter) while the second group might just skim over this material. Aiming for readers who consider themselves to be somewhere in the middle, I've opted to make my explanation as simple as possible. Here is how we compute a 90% CI, using the first five samples from the jelly bean example:

1. Compute the sample variance as follows: (This is a concept we'll refer to more often later).
   a. Compute the average of the samples: $(1.4 + 1.4 + 1.5 + 1.6 + 1.1)/5 = 1.4$
   b. Subtract this average from each of the samples and square the result for each sample: $(1.4 - 1.4)^2 = 0, (1.4 - 1.4)^2 = 0, (1.5 - 1.4)^2 = .01$, etc.
   c. Add all the squares and divide by one less than the number of samples: $(0 + 0 + .01 + .04 + .09)/(5 - 1) = .035$
2. Divide the sample variance by the number of samples and take the square root of the result. In a spreadsheet we could write "= SQRT(.035/5)" to get .0837.

   (This is called the standard deviation of the estimate of the mean in statistics texts.)

EXHIBIT 9.1   **SIMPLIFIED T-STATISTIC**
PICK THE NEAREST SAMPLE SIZE
(OR INTERPOLATE IF YOU PREFER
MORE PRECISION)

Sample size	t-score
2	6.31
3	2.92
4	2.35
5	2.13
6	2.02
8	1.89
12	1.80
16	1.75
28	1.70
Larger Samples	(z-score) 1.645

3. Look up the t-stat in Exhibit 9.1, the simplified t-statistic table, next to the sample size: Next to the number 5 is the t-score 2.13. Note that for very large sample sizes, the t-score gets closer to the z-score (for the normal distribution) of 1.645.

4. Multiply the t-stat by the answer from step 2: $2.13 \times .0837 = .178$. This is the sample error in grams.

5. Add the sample error to the mean to get the upper bound of a 90% CI, and subtract the same sample error from the mean to the lower bound: upper bound $= 1.4 + .178 = 1.578$, lower bound $= 1.4 - .178 = 1.222$

So we get a 90% CI of 1.222 to 1.578 after just five samples. This same procedure also gives us the answer for larger samples needed for the traditional z-score. The only difference is that the z-score we need to compute a 90% CI is always 1.645 (it doesn't change further as sample size increases).

Exhibit 9.2 shows the cumulative results of another hypothetical sampling problem using the t-statistic. It could have been the yields of brewed batches at Guinness, the time spent in line by customers, or the shoe sizes Nebraskans. Regardless of the specific type of problem, you need a 90% CI for the average of the population but, for some reason, you can only sample a few, not hundreds or thousands. The reason could be economics, time constraints, or the shyness of Nebraskans about having their feet measured.

Estimating the true average by taking of few samples

Values could be "Amount of time spent in Line by Customers" or anything else

Upper Bound of 90% CI

Running Average of Sample

True Mean of the Population

Each Sample Value

- With a few samples, there is still high uncertainty but...
- ...each new sample reduces uncertainty a lot and...
- ...the first few samples reduce uncertainty the most when initial uncertainty is high.

- As number of samples increae, the 90% CI gets much narrower but...

- ...each new sample reduces uncertainty only slightly and...

- ...beyond about 30 samples, you need to quadruple the sample size to cut error by half.

0   5   10   15   20   25   30

Number of Samples

EXHIBIT 9.2   Example of How Uncertainty Changes w/Sample Size

The lower part of the graph shows each of the samples gathered by a random method, compared to the true mean of the population shown by a straight dashed line. Some are high, some are low. For the purposes of this chart, the actual values are omitted, but you still get the point. Just above that is something that looks like a tornado on its side, made of three jagged curves. The middle of the three shows the running average of the samples (the average of the first 3 after the first 3, the first 4 after the first 4, etc.) compared, again, to the true mean of the population, shown by a straight dashed line. The outer two shows the upper and lower bound of a 90% CI, recomputed after each new sample.

Note that after just a few samples, the 90% CI is still wide, but narrows rapidly with each new sample. While the value of each randomly selected sample still bounces back and forth wildly, the running average of the samples tends to get closer to the true mean after several samples. Also note that while the 90% CI is much narrower at 30 samples, it wasn't much narrower than at

20 or even 10 samples. In fact, once you get to 30 samples, you have to quadruple the number of samples (120) if you want the error to go down by half again. If you want only one-quarter as much error as you have at 30 samples, you need 16 times as many samples (480). In short, each halving of error requires multiplying the sample size by 4.

Both the t-statistic and the normal z-statistic are types of "parametric" statistics. Parametric statistics are those that have to assume a particular underlying shape to the distribution. And while often it is safe to assume that a distribution is normal to start with, it can be far off base. Even though these parametric statistics don't rely strictly on the "subjective" estimates of calibrated experts, they still start with a fairly arbitrary assumption.

Ultimately, the subjective versus objective distinction may not mean that much, anyway, when we measure the performance of these methods. The only thing we should concern ourselves with is how well the two methods work in reality. Are the calibrated estimators better or worse at estimating based on a small sample with a parametric method? Are calibrated estimators wrong more often than parametric statistics?

In the experiment with the calibrated estimators and the jelly beans, the estimators consistently gave wider ranges than what we would get if we used the t-statistic, but not by much. This means that doing a little more math reduces error further than calibrated estimators alone. After 8 samples, the most conservative calibrated estimator had a range of 0.5 to 2.4 grams while the most confident estimator gave a range of 1 to 1.7 grams. After the same number of samples, the t-statistic would compute a 90% CI for the estimate of the mean of 1.21 to 1.57 grams, considerably narrower than even the narrowest range among the estimators. But even though the uncertainty reduction according to the estimators was conservative (not as narrow as it could have been), it was not irrational and was still a significant reduction from the prior state of uncertainty. As we will see in Chapter 10, further studies bear out these findings.

In summary, we find:

- When you have a lot of uncertainty, a few samples greatly reduce it.
- Calibrated estimators were able to reduce uncertainty even with only one sample—which is impossible with traditional parametric statistics.
- Calibrated estimators are rational yet conservative. Doing more math reduces uncertainty even further.

THE EASIEST SAMPLE STATISTICS EVER

Clearly, the estimators could greatly reduce uncertainty with just a few observations, and using a parametric method will reduce uncertainty even further. But are calibrated estimates just inferior to parametric statistics? Not always. Both the t-statistic and the normal statistic can only consider the values of the samples. They can't take into account the context of a sample, prior information the estimator had before conducting the measurement, or other information. In other words, many of the things we consider "common sense" are excluded from parametric methods since they fail to consider information that calibrated estimators intuitively include.

Suppose that instead of measuring the weight of jelly beans, we were asking sales managers how much time they spend managing under-performing sales reps. If we sampled only 5 sales managers, they might give us their answers in average hours per week. Let's say they said 6, 12, 12, 7 and 1 hours per week. The t-statistic would compute a 90% CI of 3.8 to 13. However, that equation doesn't know that the 1 comes from Bob, whom you know has more problem sales staff members than anyone else and is probably deliberately underestimating. The calibrated estimator, in contrast, easily handles that sort of additional information. Taking the latter approach might seem unreliable, since it depends on the judgment of an expert, but, on average, it is nearly as good as "objective" statistics and in some cases better.

Furthermore, on very small samples, a t-statistic can produce a confidence interval that just doesn't make sense given other known constraints. Suppose you cross-referenced some time sheets and saw that no sales manager ever meets with sales reps individually more than 12 hours a week, not all of which is dealing with underperforming sales reps. And the sales reps who are underperforming show they meet with the sales manager no more than 12 hours per week. Now the upper part of our 90% CI seems unrealistic. But that's the best the t-statistic can do.

There is another, simpler method I developed that does not rely on the opinions of calibrated estimators, since it only uses the data in the sample. But it avoids some of the problems of the t-statistic. In Chapter 3, I briefly mentioned the Rule of Five. Remember, that rule states that if you randomly sample 5 of any population, there is a 93.8% chance that the median of the population is between the largest and smallest values in the sample. But that is only one rule from a set of similar rules for highly simplified small sample statistics. Like the Rule of Five, if we can come up with a method where sample values themselves can be used to directly estimate a 90% CI, then we can quickly estimate a range without any math at all.

If we sample 8 items, the largest and smallest values would make a range much wider than a 90% CI (actually, about 99.2% CI). But it turns out that if we take the second largest and smallest values, we get back to something closer to a 90% CI—about 93%. If we sample 11, the 90% CI can be approximated with the third largest and third smallest values.

Exhibit 9.3 shows similar rules for the first 11 sample sizes that can approximate a 90% CI just by counting in from the largest and smallest values by the amount shown. For example, if you can sample 18 things, the sixth largest and sixth smallest values out of the 18 samples approximated the upper and lower bounds for a 90% CI. I picked a set of sample sizes that get can get close to a 90% CI with a clear preference for conservatively wider ranges when an exact 90% CI is not possible. The third column gives the "Actual Confidence" to show the odds that the median will be between the bounds given by the nth largest/smallest samples. Don't worry about how to use the third column. It is sufficient to know that it is as close as possible to the true 90% CI without being too narrow. (Therefore, it is a slightly conservative estimate of the 90% CI.)

EXHIBIT 9.3   THE "MATHLESS" 90% CI

Lower bound:__th smallest
Upper bound:__th largest

Sample Size	nth largest and smallest sample value	Actual Confidence
5	1st	93.8%
8	2nd	93.0%
11	3rd	93.5%
13	4th	90.8%
16	5th	92.3%
18	6th	90.4%
21	7th	92.2%
23	8th	90.7%
26	9th	92.4%
28	10th	91.3%
30	11th	90.1%

I call this the mathless 90% CI since it only requires you to count in a certain number from the largest and smallest values in the data. There is no computing sample variance, no square roots, and no t-statistics tables. I computed this table based on some nonparametric methods and checked it with some Monte Carlo simulations of small samples. The derivation was a little more complicated than we can get into here, but the result makes estimating a 90% CI from small samples very easy. Try to commit to memory the first few sample sizes: 5, 8, 11, and 13. From those you take the first, second, third, and fourth largest and smallest, respectively, to estimate a 90% CI. Now you can quickly compute a 90% CI even by casual observations of data in your environment, without having to pull out a calculator.

The reason this method works as well as it does is because, in short, the "middle" of the data doesn't matter very much when computing a 90% CI. To explain this, we need just a little more exposure to parametric methods. The parametric methods include a step where we compute something called sample variance, just as we saw with the parametric t-statistic. Remember, for each sample, we subtract the mean from the sample value and square the results. Then we add up all the squares to get the sample variance. When you perform this brief calculation, you find that almost all of the variance comes from those samples farthest from the mean. Even for large sample sizes, the middle third of a sample typically makes up just 2% of the variance; the other 98% of the variance comes from the upper and lower thirds of the sample data. When the sample size is smaller than 12, the variance is mostly just the single largest and single smallest sample—the two extreme points.

This mathless approach generates a 90% CI just slightly wider than the t-statistic, but it avoids some of the problems of the t-statistic. Recall the example where five sales managers said they spent 6, 12, 12, 11, and 1 hours per week on managing underperforming sales reps. While the t-statistic gave us an upper bound of 13, we know that other constraints make this impossible. But using the mathless method, we get a range of 1 to 12. We *know* 12 is a possible value because it is, in fact, one of the values in our sample. If we sampled 6 more sales managers to get 4, 5, 10, 7, 9, 10, we get a total of 11 samples. If we look up 11 samples in our table, we see that the 90% CI is approximated by the third largest and third smallest values. Now we have a 90% CI of 5 to 11 hours per week. In this (somewhat rare) case, the t-statistic actually gives us a slightly wider range of 4.5 to 11.3.

It is important to note that the nonparametric method I used is a 90% CI of the median, not the mean, as the t-statistic provides. The median of a population is a value where exactly half of the population is below it and half above it. The mean of a population is the total of all the values divided by the size of the population. In a skewed (i.e., lopsided) population distribution, the median and mean can be different values. However, if we assumed that the population distribution is close to symmetrical, then the mean and the median are the same. In this case, the mathless table works just as well to compute a 90% CI for a mean as a 90% CI for a median.

This assumption might be a stretch in some cases, but it's actually much less of an assumption than is made in parametric statistics. In parametric statistics, we have to assume the distribution has certain specific shapes. In the case of the mathless table, we make *no* assumption at all about the distribution of the population to estimate the median. The population can be distributed in all sorts of irregular ways, like the "camel-back" age distribution in the United States caused by the baby boomers and their children or a uniform distribution like the spin of a roulette wheel. The mathless table still works for the median in these cases. But if the distribution is also symmetrical, regardless of whether it is uniform, normal, camel-back or bow-tie shaped, then the mathless table also works for the mean.

A BIASED SAMPLE OF SAMPLING METHODS

How would your average executive measure the population of fish in a lake? I regularly ask this question of a room full of seminar attendees. Usually someone in the room produces the most extreme answer: Drain the lake. The average executive, like the average accountant or even the average midlevel IT manager thinks that "measure" is synonymous with "count." So when asked to measure the population of fish, they assume they are being asked for an exact count, not just a reduction in uncertainty. With that goal in mind, they drain the lake and, no doubt, would come up with a very organized procedure where a team picks up each dead fish, throws it in the back of a dump truck, and clicks it off on a handheld counter. Perhaps someone else counts the fish again in the truck and inspects the now-empty lake bed to "audit" the quality of the count. They could then report that there were exactly 22,573 fish in the lake; therefore, last year's restocking effort was successful. Of course, they're all dead now.

If you told marine biologists to measure the fish in the lake, they would not confuse a "count" with a "measure." Instead, the biologists might employ a method called release and recatch. First, they would catch and tag a sample of fish—let's say 1,000—and release them back into the lake. Then, after the tagged fish had a chance to disperse among the rest of the population, they catch another sample of fish. Suppose they caught 1,000 fish again, and this time 50 of those 1,000 fish were tagged. This means that about 5% of the fish in the lake are tagged. Since the marine biologists know they originally tagged 1,000 fish, they conclude that the lake contains about 20,000 fish (5% of 20,000 is 1,000).

This type of sampling follows the "binomial distribution," but, for large numbers like these, we can approximate it with the normal distribution. The error for this estimate can be computed using a slight variation on the previous error estimate methods. All we have to do is change how we compute the sample variance; the rest is the same. The sample variance in this case is computed as the share within the group we are trying to measure times the share outside of the group. In other words, we take the share of tagged fish (.05) times the share of fish not tagged (.95), resulting in .0475.

Now we follow the rest of the previously defined procedure. We divide the sample variance by the number of samples and take the square root of the total: $SQRT(.0475/1000) = .007$. To get our 90% CI of the share of tagged fish in the lake, we take the share we think are tagged (.05) plus or minus .007 times 1.645 (the 90% CI z-statistic) to get a range of 3.8% to 6.2% of the fish in the lake are tagged. We know we tagged 1,000, so this must mean there are a total of $1000/.062 = 16,256$ to $1000/.032 = 25,984$ fish in the lake.

To some people, this might seem like a wide range. But suppose our previous level of uncertainty gave us a calibrated estimate of 2,000 to 50,000. Furthermore, suppose our objective was simply to determine if the population was increasing or dying off, and we originally stocked the lake with 5,000 fish. Anything greater than 6,000 is at least increasing population and 10,000 or more would be healthy enough that no expensive intervention would be required. Given the initial range and the relevant threshold, this new level of uncertainty is definitely a significant improvement and an easy acceptable error. In fact, we could have sampled just a quarter of what we did in the initial catch and the recatch (250 fish each time), and we would still be confident the population had increased to a number greater than 6,000.

This method is a particularly powerful example of how sampling reveals something about the unseen. It has been used for estimating such things as how many people the U.S. Census missed, how many species of butterflies are still undiscovered in the Amazon, how many unauthorized intrusions have been made in an IT system, and how many prospective customers you have not yet identified. Just because you will never see all of a group doesn't mean you can't measure the size of a group.

"Release-Recatch" in its various forms is just one of many varieties of sampling. No doubt, quite a few more powerful methods are yet to be invented. Still, knowing a little about a few important sampling methods gives you enough background to figure out how to assess observations for a wide variety of problems.

Spot Sampling

Spot sampling consists of taking random "snapshots" of people, processes, or things instead of tracking them constantly throughout a period of time. For example, if you wanted to see the share of time that employees spend in a given activity, you randomly sample people through the day to see what they were doing *at that moment*. If you find that in 12 instances out of 100 random samples, people were on a conference call, then you can conclude they spend about 12% of the time on conference calls (90% CI is 8% to 18%). This example is also a binomial distribution, just like the release-recatch example. At a particular point in time they are either doing this activity or not, and you are simply asking what share of the time this takes. This example is just big enough that we can also approximate it with a normal distribution, as we did above.

But what if you could only spot sample 30 people, and 5 of them were engaged in the activity of interest? Is this nearly enough information? Again, it depends on how uncertain you were before you started sampling. This could easily be enough information to reduce your uncertainty. Exhibit 9.4 provides a way to quickly estimate the 90% CI of a population proportion when you have smaller samples. Following the instructions on the exhibit, you should get about 9% for the lower bound of a 90% CI and about 31% for the upper bound. Suppose your prior calibrated estimate was 5% to 50% and the threshold where you would make a different decision with this information was 40%. The sample would have been sufficient to support that decision.

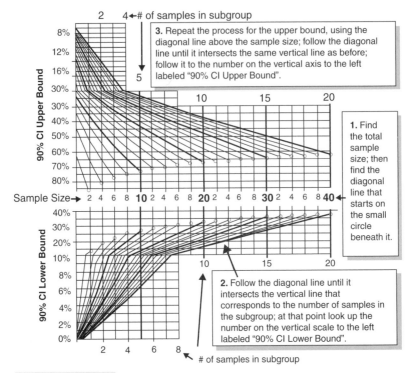

Clustered Sampling

Clustered sampling is defined as taking a random sample of groups then conducting a census or more concentrated sampling within the group. For example, if you want to see what share of households has satellite dishes or correctly separate plastics in recycling, it might be cost effective to randomly choose several city blocks, then conduct a complete census of everything in a block. (Zigzagging across town to individually selected households would be time consuming.) In such cases, we can't really consider the number of elements in the groups (in this case, households) to be the number of random samples. Within a block, households may be very similar, so we can't really treat the number of households as the size of the "random" sample. When households are highly uniform within a block, it might be necessary to treat the effective number of random samples as the number of blocks, not the number of households.

Stratified Samples

In stratified sampling, different sample methods and/or sizes are used for different groups within a population. This method may make sense when you have some groups within a population that vary widely from each other but are fairly homogeneous inside a group. If you are a fast-food restaurant and you want to sample the demographic of your customers, it might make sense to sample drive-through customers differently from walk-ins. If you run a factory and you need to measure "safety habits," you might try observing janitors and supervisors for safety procedure violations differently from welders. (Don't forget the Hawthorne effect. Try using a blind in this case.)

Serial Sampling

The serial sampling approach is generally not discussed in statistics texts. Nor would it be here if the title of this book was *How to Measure Most Things*. But this approach was a big help in intelligence gathering in World War II,[1] and it could be a very powerful sampling method for certain types of business problems. During World War II, spies for the Allies produced reports on enemy production of military equipment, including Germany's Mark V tanks. The reports about the Mark V were highly inconsistent, and Allied Intelligence rarely knew whom to believe. In 1943 statisticians working for the Allies developed a method for estimating production levels based on the serial numbers of captured tanks. Serial numbers were sequential and had a date embedded in them. However, looking at a single serial number did not tell them exactly where the series started (it might not have started at 001). Common sense tells us that the minimum tank production must be at least the difference between the highest and lowest serial numbers of captured tanks for a given month. But can we infer even more?

By treating captured tanks as a random sample of the entire population of tanks, the statisticians saw that they could compute the odds of various levels of production. Working backward, it would seem unlikely, for example, to capture by chance alone 10 tanks produced in the same month with serial numbers all within 50 increments of each other, if 1,000 tanks were produced that month. It is more likely that randomly selecting from 1,000 tanks would give us a more dispersed series of serial numbers than that. If, however, only 80 tanks were produced that month, then getting a sample of 10 tanks with that narrow range of serial numbers seems at least feasible.

EXHIBIT 9.5   **COMPARISON OF WORLD WAR II GERMAN MARK V TANK PRODUCTION ESTIMATES**

Month of Production	Intelligence Estimate	Statistical Estimate	Actual (based on captured documents after the war)
June 1940	1,000	169	122
June 1941	1,550	244	271
August 1942	1,550	327	342

Exhibit 9.5 shows how the Mark V tank production estimates from Allied Intelligence and from the statistical method compared to the actual number confirmed by postwar analysis of captured documents. Clearly, the statistical method based on the analysis of serial numbers of captured tanks is the hands-down winner in this comparison.

Furthermore, an estimate with an error still considerably less than the original intelligence estimates could probably have been done with surprisingly few captured tanks. Exhibit 9.6 shows how a random sample of serial-numbered items can be used to infer the size of the entire population. Following the directions on the exhibit, consider the example of just 8 "captured" items. (This could be a competitor's products, pages of a competitor's report retrieved from the garbage, etc.) The largest in the series is 100220 and the smallest is 100070, so step 1 gives us 150 as a result. Step 2 gives us a result of about 1.0 where the "Upper Bound" curve intersects the vertical line for our sample size of 8. In step 3 we take $(1 + 1.0) \times 150 = 300$, where the result is the upper bound. Repeating these steps for the mean and lower bound, we get a 90% CI of 156 to 300 with a mean of 195 (note the mean is not the middle of the range—the distribution is lopsided). Just 8 captured tanks could easily have been a reasonable number of captured tanks to work with.

Two caveats: If several tanks are captured from the same unit, we might not be able to treat each as a separate randomly selected tank, since tanks in the same unit might be in the same series of numbers. However, that fact is usually apparent just by looking at the numbers themselves. Also, if the serial numbers are not really sequential (so that each number in a range is assigned to one tank) and some numbers are skipped, then this method requires some modification. Again, the distribution of numbers used should be easy to detect. For example, if only even numbers or increments of 5 are used, then that should be obvious from the sample.

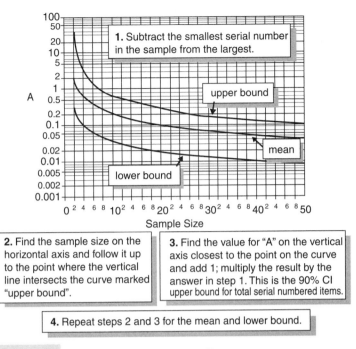

EXHIBIT 9.6   Serial Number Sampling

Where could this apply in business? "Serial numbers"—that is, a sequential series—show up in a variety of places in the modern world. In this way, competitors offer free intelligence of their production levels just by putting serial numbers on items any retail shopper can see. (To be random, however, this sample of items should include those from several stores.) Likewise, a few pages from a discarded report or numbers from discarded receipts tell something about the total number of pages in the report or receipts from that day. I'm not encouraging dumpster-diving but, then again, the dumpster has been used to measure a lot of interesting activities.

Measure to the Threshold

Remember, usually you want to measure something because it supports some decision. And these decisions tend to have thresholds where, if a value is above it, one action is required, and another is required if the value is below it. But most statistical methods aren't about asking the most relevant question: "When is X enough to warrant a different course of action?" Here I want to show you a "statistic" that directly supports the goal of not just reducing uncertainty in general but a measurement, relative to an important threshold.

Suppose you needed to measure the average amount of time spent by employees in meetings that could be conducted remotely with one of the Web meeting tools. This could save staff a lot of travel time and even avoid canceled or postponed meetings due to travel difficulties. To determine whether a meeting can be conducted remotely, you need to consider what is done in the meeting. If a meeting is among staff members who communicate regularly and for a relatively routine topic, but someone has to travel to make the meeting, you can probably conduct it remotely. You start out with your calibrated estimate that the average employee spends 3% to 15% traveling to meetings that could be conducted remotely. You determine that if this percentage is actually over 7%, then you should make a significant investment in tele-meetings. The Expected Value of Perfect Information (EVPI) calculation shows that it is worth no more than $15,000 to study this. According to our rule of thumb for measurement costs, we should try to spend about $1,500 so anything like a complete census of meetings is out of the question if you have thousands of employees.

Let's say you sampled 10 employees and, after a detailed analysis of their travel time and meetings in the last few weeks, you find that only one employee spends less time in these activities than the 7% threshold. Given this information, what is the chance that the average time spent in such activities is actually below 7%, in which case the investment would not be justified? One "commonsense" answer is 1/10, or 10%. Actually, this is another example where mere "common" sense isn't as good as a little math. The real chance is much smaller.

Exhibit 9.7 shows how to estimate the chance that the median of a population is on one particular side of a threshold, given that an equal or greater number of the samples in a small sample set came up on the other side.

Try this example to practice with the calculator.

1. Look at the top of the exhibit, where it gives sample sizes, and find the number 10. Follow the solid curve below it.

2. Look at the bottom of the exhibit, where it lists the number of samples below the threshold, and find the number 1. Follow the dashed line above it.

3. Find the intersection of the curve and the dashed line.

4. Read the percentage to the left of the chart that corresponds with the vertical position of the intersection point. You will find it reads about 0.6%.

This small sample says there is a much less than 1% chance that the average is actually below the threshold. While this statistic seems counterintuitive, the fact is that the uncertainty about which side of a threshold the median (or even the mean) of a population sits on can be reduced a lot very quickly. Suppose we would have sampled just 4 and none of the 4 was below the threshold. Referring to the exhibit again, we find that there would be just under a 4% chance that the median is actually under the threshold and consequently a 96% chance that the median is above the threshold. It may seem impossible that a sample of 4 could provide that much certainty, but some math or a Monte Carlo simulation will confirm it.

Note that the uncertainty about the threshold can fall much faster than the uncertainty about the quantity in general. It's possible that after just a few samples you still have a fairly wide range, but, if the threshold is well

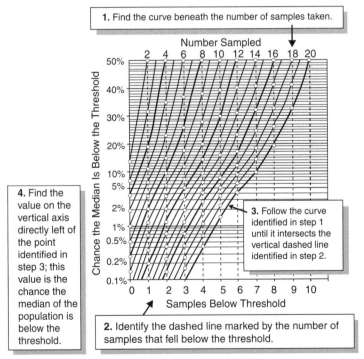

EXHIBIT 9.7   The Threshold Probability Calculator

outside the range, the uncertainty about the threshold can drop to virtually nothing.

An important limitation of this exhibit is that it assumes maximum uncertainty about the threshold. That is, it starts with the assumption that there is no prior information about whether it is more likely that the median is really on one side of the threshold than the other. This means that we start with a 50/50 chance regarding which side of the threshold the median is really on. If there was some prior knowledge that it was much more likely that the median was below the threshold, then the exhibit won't be accurate, but it will still give us a useful result. If the chance of being below the threshold is lower than the chance of being above it, then the exhibit will actually overestimate the odds that the real value is below the threshold. In our example, the range of 3% to 15% indicates that being below the threshold of 7% is less likely than being above it. The exhibit tells us that the chance of being below this threshold is 0.6%, but knowing what we do about the range, we can determine that the chance is even less than that.

If, however, our range was, say, 1% to 8%, then we start with the knowledge that the true value is probably below the threshold of 7%. In that case, the exhibit underestimates the chance that the value is below the threshold. But let's consider another benchmark to help us zero in on a value. We could look at the actual midpoint of our original range and compute the threshold probability for that. With this range, we are saying that there is a 50/50 chance that the value is less than 4.5%. Of the 10 employees sampled, let's say none was below that. Our exhibit tells us that, in this situation, the chance that the true value is actually below 4.5% is less than 0.1%. Although this doesn't tell us exactly how unlikely it is to be below the 7% threshold, it's obvious that being much below 7% is vanishingly unlikely.

So, generally, if the samples strongly confirm prior knowledge (e.g., you get just 1 out of 10 samples below the threshold when you already knew that there is a low chance the median is below the threshold), then the uncertainty drops even faster. If the samples contradict prior knowledge, it will take more samples to decrease uncertainty by the same amount. Also, remember that the exhibit gives the chance that the median—not the mean—is below or above a threshold. Of course, you can do some more math and reduce uncertainty even further. If four samples are above the threshold by a large margin, that would give a higher level of confidence than if the four samples were just barely above the threshold.

EXPERIMENT

My first online buying experience was sometime in the mid-1990s. I had several texts on empirical methods in various subject areas but was looking for a book on more of a general philosophy of scientific measurement—something I could recommend to my management customers. I read all the basics (Kuhn, Popper, etc.), but that wasn't what I was looking for. Then, I saw a book on www.amazon.com called *How to Think like a Scientist*.[2] The reviews were great and it seemed like it would be something I could recommend to a typical executive. I purchased the book and within a couple of weeks it came in the mail. It wasn't what I expected. It was a children's book—recommended for ages 8 and up. I felt pretty foolish and chalked it up as another reason not to buy things on the Web in the early phase of Internet retail. In a bookstore I would not have browsed the children's section (being childless at the time). And if I saw such a book in the discount pile, the cover[3] would have told me that it wasn't the serious "science for business" type of text I was looking for. But then I started to flip through the pages. Although each page was two-thirds cartoon and one-third text, it seemed to capture all the basic concepts and explain it as simply as possible. I saw how it gave a simple explanation of testing a hypothesis and making observations. I changed my mind about the purchase being a mistake. I realized I found this gem on the web precisely because I couldn't prejudge it as a children's book. And the most important message of this book is what was implied on the front cover: scientific method is for ages 8 and up.

The idea of performing an experiment to measure some important business quantity, unfortunately, does not come often enough to many managers. As Emily Rosa showed us, experiments can be simple affairs. As Enrico Fermi showed us, a handful of confetti used in a clever way can reveal something as incredible as the yield of an atom bomb. The idea is quite simple. As Chapter 3 on selecting measurement instruments instructed, if you need to know it, can't find where it is already measured, and can't track it in any way without overt intervention, then try to create the conditions for observation with an experiment.

The word "experiment" could be broadly used to mean any phenomena deliberately created for the purpose of observation. You "experiment" when you run a security test to see if and how quickly a threat is responded to. But, usually, a key feature of the *controlled* experiment is that you observe two things, not just one. You watch what you are testing (the test group), and you watch something to compare it to (the control group). This is ideal in a situation where it would be hard to track an existing phenomenon or where the thing being measured has not yet happened, such as the effect of a new product formulation or the implementation of a new information technology.

You could pilot the new product or the new technology by itself. But how would you know the customers preferred the new product or if productivity really increased? Your revenue might have increased for many reasons other than the new formulation, and the productivity might change for other reasons as well. In fact, if businesses could be affected by only one thing at a time, the whole idea of a control group would be unnecessary. We could change one factor, see how the business changed, and attribute that change entirely to that factor. Of course, we have to be able to measure even when complex systems are affected by many factors we can't even identify.

If we change a feature on a product and want to determine how much this affects customer satisfaction, we might need an experiment. Customer satisfaction and, consequently, repeat business might change for lots of reasons. But if we want to see if this new feature is cost-justified, then we need to measure *its* impact apart from anything else. By comparing customers who have bought products with this new feature to customers who did not, we should be better able to isolate the effects of the new feature alone.

Most of the methods you use in experiments to interpret results are the same as we already discussed—they involve one or another sort of sampling, perhaps some blinds, and so on. One important extra control, however, is to be able to compute the difference between a test group and a control group. If we are confident that the test group is really different from the control group, then we should be able to conclude that something other than just pure chance is causing these two groups to be different. Comparing these two groups is really very similar to how we previously computed the standard deviation of the estimate, but with one small change. In this case, the standard deviation we want to compute is the standard deviation of the difference between two groups. Consider this example.

Suppose a company wanted to measure the effect of customer relationship training on the quality of customer support. The customer support employees typically take incoming calls from clients who have questions or problems with a new product. It is suspected that the main effect of a positive or negative customer support experience is not so much the future sales to that customer but the positive or negative word-of-mouth advertising the company gets as a result. As always, the company started by assessing its current uncertainty about the effects of training, it identified the relevant threshold, and it computed the value of information.

After considering several possible measurement instruments, managers decided that "quality of customer support" should be measured with a postcall survey of customers. The questions, they reasoned, should not just ask whether the customers were satisfied but whether they would be more or less likely to refer the company to friends as a result of the customer support experience. Using previously gathered marketing data, the calibrated managers determined that the new customer relationship training could improve sales by 0% to 12% but that they needed to improve it by only 2% to justify the expense of the training.

They begin conducting this survey before anyone attends training, so they can get a baseline. For each employee, they sample only one customer who called in. The key question was "Based on your experience with our customer support, how likely are you to recommend us to friends: (1) more likely, (2) about as likely as before, (3) less likely?" Each response is recorded as a value of 1, 2, or 3. Knowing some previous research about the impact of customer satisfaction on sales, the marketing department has determined that an improvement of one-tenth of a point on the average score to this question results in a 2% increase in sales.

The training is expensive, so at first managers decide to send 30 randomly chosen customer support staffers to the training as a test group. Nevertheless, the cost of training this small group is still much less than the computed information value. The control group is the entire set of employees who did not receive training. After the test group receives training, managers continue the survey of customers, but again, they sample only one customer for each employee. For the original baseline, the test group, and the control group, the mean and variance are computed (as shown in the jelly bean example at the beginning of this chapter). Exhibit 9.8 shows the results.

The responses from customers seem to indicate that the training did help; could it just be chance? Perhaps the 30 randomly chosen staff members were already, on average, better than the average of the group, or perhaps those 30 people were, by chance, getting less problematic customers. For the test group and control group, we apply the following five steps.

EXHIBIT 9.8	EXAMPLE FOR A CUSTOMER SUPPORT TRAINING EXPERIMENT

	Sample Size	Mean	Variance
Test group (received training)	30	2.433	0.392
Control group (did not receive training)	85	2.094	0.682
Original baseline (before anyone received training)	115	2.087	0.659

1. Divide the sample variance of each group by the number of samples in that group. We get .392/30 = .0131 for the test group and 0.682/85 = .008 for the control group.

2. Add the results from step 1 for each group together: .031 + .008 = .021

3. Take the square root of the result from step 2. This gives us the standard deviation of the difference between the test group and control group. The result in this case would be 0.15.

4. Compute the difference between the means of the two groups being compared: 2.433 − 2.094 = .339

5. Compute the chance that the difference between the test group and control group is greater than zero—that is, that the test group really is better than the control group (and not just a fluke). Use the "normdist" formula in Excel to compute this:

$$= \text{normdist}(0, 0.339, 0.15, 1)$$

resulting in 0.01.

This shows us that there is only a 1% chance that the test group is really just as good or worse than the control; we can be 99% certain that the test group is better than the control.

We can compare the control group to the original baseline in the same way. The difference between the control group and the original baseline is just .007. Using the same method that we just used to compare the test and the control groups, we find that there is a 48% chance that the control group is less than the baseline or a 52% chance it is higher. This tells us that the difference between these groups is negligible and, for all practical purposes, they are no different.

We have determined with very high confidence that the training contributes to a real improvement in customer satisfaction. Since the difference between the test and control groups is about .4, the marketing department concludes that the improved training would account for about an 8% improvement in sales, easily justifying the cost of training the rest of the staff and ongoing training for all new staff. In retrospect, we probably could have used even fewer samples (using a student's t- distribution for samples under 30).

SEEING RELATIONSHIPS IN THE DATA: AN INTRODUCTION TO REGRESSION MODELING

One of the most common questions I get in seminars is something like "If sales increase due to some new IT system, how do I know it went up because of the IT system?" What surprises me a bit about the frequency of this question is the fact that much of the last few centuries of scientific measurement has been about isolating the effect of a single variable. I can only conclude that those individuals who asked the question do not have an understanding of some of the most basic concepts in scientific measurement. Clearly, the experiment example given earlier in this chapter shows how something that has many possible causes can be traced to a particular cause by comparing a test group to a control group. But the use of a control and test group are really just one method we have for separating out the effect of one single variable from all the noise that exists in any business. We can also consider how well one variable correlates with another.

Correlation between two sets of data is generally expressed as a number between $+1$ and -1. A correlation of 1 means the two variables move in perfect harmony: As one increases, so does the other. A correlation of -1 also indicates two closely related variables, but as one increases, the other decreases in lockstep. A correlation of 0 means they have nothing to do with each other.

To get a feel for what correlated data looks like, consider the four examples of data in Exhibit 9.9. The horizontal axis could be scores on an employment test and the vertical axis could be a measure of productivity. Or the horizontal axis could be number of TV advertisements in a month and the vertical axis could be the sales for a given month. They could be anything. But it is clear that in some of the charts, the data in the two axes are more closely related than the data are in other charts. The chart in the upper left-hand corner shows two random variables. The variables have nothing to do with each other, and there

No Correlation

0.8 Correlation

−0.6 Correlation

0.99 Correlation

EXHIBIT 9.9   **Examples of Correlated Data**

is no correlation. This is shown by the lack of a "slope" in the data points. The data appears flat because there is more variability in the horizontal data than the vertical data. If the two were equally variable, the scatter would be more circular, but there would still be no slope. The chart in the lower right-hand corner shows two data points that are very closely related.

Before you do any math, you should plot the data just to see if the correlation is visually obvious. If you were tracking estimated project costs versus actual project costs, and the plot comparing them looked like the graph in the lower right, then your cost estimation is extraordinarily accurate. If it looked like the graph in the upper left-hand corner, a person rolling dice would estimate project costs just as well.

If we use regression modeling with historical data, we may not need to conduct a controlled experiment. Perhaps, for example, it is difficult to tie an IT project to an increase in sales, but we might have lots of data about how something *else* affects sales, like faster time to market of new products. If we know that faster time to market is possible by automating certain tasks, then we can make the connection.

I once analyzed the investment in a particular software project at a major cable TV network. The network was considering the automation of several administrative tasks in the production of new TV shows. One of the hoped-for benefits was an improvement in ratings points for the show, which generally results in more advertising revenue. But how could the network forecast the effect of an IT project on ratings when, as is so often the case, so many other things affect ratings?

The entire theory behind how this production automation system could improve ratings was that it would shorten certain critical-path administrative tasks. If those tasks were done faster, then the network could begin promotion of the new show sooner. The network did have historical data on ratings and, by rooting through some old production schedules, we could determine how many weeks each of these shows was promoted before airing. (We had previously computed the value of this information and determined that this minor effort was easily justified.) Exhibit 9.10 shows a plot of what these TV shows could look like on a chart showing the weeks in promotion and the ratings points for the shows. These are not the actual data from the client, but roughly the same correlation is illustrated.

Before we do any additional analysis with these data, do you at least *see* a correlation? If so, which of the charts from Exhibit 9.9 does this most resemble? Making such a chart is always my first step in regression analysis because usually the correlation will be obvious. In Excel, it's simple to make two columns of data—in this case promotion weeks and ratings points—where each pair of numbers represents one TV show. Just select the entire set of data, click on the "chart" button in Excel, choose an "XY (Scatter)" chart, follow the rest of the prompts, and you will see a chart just like the one in Exhibit 9.10

EXHIBIT 9.10   **Promotion Period vs. Ratings Points for a Cable Network**

It *looks* correlated, so exactly how correlated is it? For that, we have to get a little more technical. Instead of explaining all the theory behind the regression modeling, I'll jump right into how to do it in Excel.

One simple method in Excel is to use the "=correl()" function to compute the correlation. Suppose the promotion weeks and ratings data were in the first 28 rows of columns A and B, respectively, in a spreadsheet. You would write =correl(A1:A28,B1:B28). With our data, we get a correlation of about 0.7. Therefore, we can be fairly certain that being able to spend more time promoting a new show does help improve ratings. Now we can focus on whether and by how much we can streamline the production process and increase the amount of time we spend promoting the shows.

Another way to do this in Excel is to use the regression wizard in the "Data Analysis Toolpack." (Navigating to it has changed a little between versions of Excel, so just look it up in Help.) The regression wizard will prompt you to select the "Y range" and the "X range." In our example, these are the ratings points and weeks in promotion, respectively. This wizard will create a table that shows several results from the regression analysis. Exhibit 9.11 is an explanation of some of those results.

This information can be used to create a formula that would be the best approximation of the relationship between ratings and promotion time. In the formula that follows, we use Promotion Weeks to compute Estimated Ratings Points. It is conventional to refer to the computed value (in this case,

---

EXHIBIT 9.11   SELECTED ITEMS FROM EXCEL'S REGRESSION TOOL "SUMMARY OUTPUT" TABLE

Variable Name	What It Means
Multiple R	The correlation of one or more variables to the "dependent" variable (eg., ratings points): 0.7 in this example.
R square	The square of the multiple R. This can be interpreted as the amount of variance in ratings points explained by promotion weeks.
Intercept	The ratings point if promotion weeks were set to zero. This is where the best fit line would intersect the vertical axis.
X variable 1	The coefficient (i.e., weight) for promotion weeks.

EXHIBIT 9.12   **The Promotion Time vs. Ratings Chart with the "Best fit" Regression Line Added**

Estimated Ratings Points) as the "dependent variable" and the value used to compute it (Promotion Weeks) as the "independent variable."

$$\text{Estimated Ratings Points} = \text{"X Variable 1"} \times \text{Promotion weeks} + \text{Intercept}$$

If we plot the line this simple formula gives us on the chart we made, it would look like Exhibit 9.12.

Exhibit 9.12 shows that, while there is a correlation, there are still other factors that cause Ratings not to be entirely dependent on promotion time. We use this information together with the controlled experiment to address the infamous "How do I know this if there are so many other factors?" question. It is clear that the ratings have some effect; it doesn't matter if you have quantified or can even *name* all the other factors that affect ratings.

The advantage of using Excel's regression tool over some of Excel's simpler functions, such as =correl(), is that the regression tool can do "multiple regression". That is, it can simultaneously compute the coefficients for several independent variables at once. If we were so inclined, we could create a model that would correlate not only promotion time but also season, category, focus group results, and several other factors to ratings. Each of these additional variables would have a coefficient shown as "X

Variable 2," "X Variable 3," and so on in the summary output table of the regression tool. Putting all these together, we would get a formula like this:

$$\text{Estimated Ratings Points} = \text{"X Variable 1"} \times \text{Promotion weeks} \\ + \text{"X Variable 2"} \times \text{Focus Group Results} \\ + \cdots + \text{Intercept}$$

Having said all this, it is important to state several caveats about regression models. First, correlation does not mean "cause." The fact that one variable is correlated to another does not necessarily mean that one variable causes the other. If church donations and liquor sales are correlated, it is not because of some collusion between clergy and the liquor industry. It is because both are affected by how well the economy is doing. Generally, you should conclude that one thing causes another only if you have some *other* good reason besides the correlation itself to suspect a cause-and-effect relationship. In the case of the ratings points and promotion weeks, we did have such reasons.

Second, keep in mind that these are simple linear regressions. It's possible to get even better correlations by using some other function of a variable (e.g., its square, inverse, the product of two variables, etc.) than by using the variable itself. Some readers may want to experiment with that. Finally, in multiple regression models, you should be careful of independent variables being correlated to each other. Ideally, independent variables should be entirely unrelated to each other.

I've only covered the basics of multiple regression modeling. It is a useful tool, but proceed with caution.

ENDNOTES

1. Goodman, "Serial Number Analysis," *Journal of the American Statistical Association* 47 (1952): pp. 622–634. Kramer, Stephen P., "How to Think like a Scientist," (New York: HarperCollins, 1987).
2. "At the time, Amazon did not show book covers online."

## CHAPTER 10

Bayes: Adding to What You Know Now

SIMPLE BAYESIAN STATISTICS

In the first semester of business statistics, students learn a few methods, based on a few "simplifying" assumptions. Often the assumptions don't end up simplifying very much of anything. Later on in statistics, students learn about some more "advanced" methods that, to me, always seemed much more intuitive than the earlier sections.

A key assumption in most introduction-to-statistics courses is that the only thing you ever knew about a population are the samples you are about to take. In fact, this is virtually never true in real-life situations.

Imagine that you are sampling several sales reps about whether an advertising campaign had anything to do with recent sales. You would like to measure the campaign's "contribution to sales." One way would be simply to poll all of your sales team. But you have more information than just what they reveal. You had some knowledge prior to the poll based on historical experience with sales and advertising. You have knowledge about current seasonal effects on sales as well as the economy and measures of consumer confidence. Should this matter? Intuitively, we know this prior knowledge should count, statistics somehow. But until students get much further into their textbook, they won't (or, perhaps, will never) get to the part where they deal with prior knowledge.

A PRIOR-KNOWLEDGE PARADOX

1. All conventional statistics assume the observer had no prior information about the subject of the observation.
2. The above assumption is almost never true in the real world.

Dealing with this prior knowledge is what is called Bayesian statistics. The inventor of this approach, Thomas Bayes, was an eighteenth-century British mathematician and Presbyterian minister whose most famous contribution to statistics would not be published until after he died. Bayesian statistics deals with the issue of how we update prior knowledge with new information. With Bayesian analysis, we start with how much we know now and then consider how that knowledge is changed by new information. The non-Bayesian statistics covered in most courses about sampling assume that your only knowledge about a group of things is the sample you just took.

In fact, a Bayesian analysis was the basis of most of the charts I provided in Chapter 9 as well as the mathless 90% CI table. For example, in the "population proportion" table, I started with the prior knowledge that, without information to the contrary, the proportion in the subgroup was uniformly distributed between 0% and 100%. Again, in the "Threshold Probability Calculator" I started with the prior knowledge that there was a 50/50 chance that the true median of the population was on either side of the threshold. In both of these cases, I took the position of maximum uncertainty.

Bayes' theorem states that the probability of a "situation" given an "observation" is equal to the probability of that situation times the probability of the observation, given the situation and all that divided by the probability of the observation, as shown in Exhibit 10.1.

Suppose we were considering whether to release a new product. Historically, new products make a profit in the first year after release only 30% of the time. A mathematician could write this as P(FYP) = 30%, meaning the probability of a first year profit is 30%. Often a product is released in a test market first before there is a commitment to full-scale production. Of those times when a product was profitable in the first year, it was also successful in the test market 80% of the time (where by "successful" we might mean that a particular sales threshold is met). A mathematician

---

EXHIBIT IO.I   **BAYES THEOREM**

P(A|B)=P(A)×P(B|A)/P(B)

Where:

P(A|B)=The "conditional" probability of A given B

P(A)=Probability of A

P(B)=Probability of B

P(B|A)=The conditional probability of B given A

---

might write this as "P(S|FYP) = 80%" meaning the "conditional" probability that a product had a successful test market (S) given (where "given" is the "|" symbol) that we knew it had a first year profit is 80%.

But we probably wouldn't be that interested in the probability that the market test *was* successful given that there was a first year profit. What we really want to know is the probability of a first year profit given that the market test was successful. That way, the market test can tell us something useful about whether to proceed with the product. This is what Bayes theorem does. In this case we set up Bayes' theorem with these inputs:

- P(FYP|S) is the probability of a first-year profit given a successful test market—in other words, the "conditional" probability of FYP given S.

- P(FYP) is the probability of a first-year profit.

- P(S) is the probability of a successful test market.

- P(S|FYP) is the probability of a successful test market given a product that would be widely accepted enough to be profitable the first year.

Let's say that test markets give a successful result 40% of the time. To compute the probability of a first-year profit given a successful test market, we set up an equation as follows using the probabilities already given:

$$P(FYP|S) = P(FYP) \times P(S|FYP)/P(S) = 30\% \times 80\%/40\% = 60\%$$

If the test market is successful, the chance of a first-year profit is 60%. We can also work out what the chance of a first-year profit would be if the test market was not successful by changing two numbers in this calculation. The probability that a profitable product would be successful in the test market was, as we showed, 80%. So the chance that a profitable product would have had an unsuccessful test market is 20%. We would write this as

P($\sim$S|FYP)=20%. Likewise, if the probability of a successful test for all products (profitable or not) is 40%, then the overall chance of a test failure must be 60% or P($\sim$S)=60%. If we substitute P($\sim$S|FYP) and P($\sim$S) for P(S|FYP) and P(S) above we get:

$$P(FYP|\sim S) = P(FYP) \times P(\sim S|FYP)/P(\sim S) = 30\% \times 20\%/60\% = 10\%$$

That is, the chance of a first-year profit is only 10% if the test market is judged to be a failure.

Sometimes we don't know the probability of a given result but can estimate the probabilities of other things that we can use to compute it. Suppose we didn't have a history of success rates for test markets—this might be our first test market. We can compute this value from some others. A calibrated estimator has already given us the probability of getting a successful test for a product that is actually going to be profitable the first year: P(S|FYP)=80%. Now, suppose a calibrated expert gave us the probability of a successful test where the product would eventually fail (New Coke being the classic example) or P(S|$\sim$FYP)=23%. As before, we knew that the chance of a product being profitable in the first year, P(FYP), is 30%, so the chance of it not being profitable, P($\sim$FYP), is 70% (1-P(FYP)). If we can add up the products of each of the conditional probabilities and the chance of that condition, we can get the total chance of the event occurring. In this case:

$$P(S) = P(S|FYP) \times P(FYP) + P(S|\sim FYP) \times P(\sim FYP)$$
$$= 80\% \times 30\% + 23\% \times 70\% = 40\%$$

This step can be very useful because, in some cases, computing the odds of certain results given certain conditions is simple and obvious. Most of the charts I made for Chapter 9 started with a questions like "If there really was just 10% of the population in this group, what is the chance that a random sample of 12 would get 5 in that group?" or "If the median time spent on a customer complaint is more than 1 hour, what is the chance that a random sample of 20 will produce 10 samples that were less than 1 hour?"

In each of these cases, we can work out the chance of A given B from the knowledge of the chance of A, the chance of B, and the chance of B given A. This type of algebraic maneuver is called a Bayesian inversion, and someone who begins to use Bayesian inversions in one area will soon find many other areas where it applies. It becomes a very handy calculation for the person who sees measurement problems as easily as Emily, Enrico, and Eratosthenes. We'll deal with the more technical issues involved a little later, but first, let's work on a more intuitive understanding of the inversion. As a matter of fact, you may have been doing this all along without really knowing it. You might have a "Bayesian instinct."

USING YOUR NATURAL BAYESIAN INSTINCT

Even these more advanced methods don't deal with other qualitative knowledge you have about your samples. In our earlier advertising campaign example, you may have been working with the individuals on the sales team for a long period of time. You have qualitative knowledge about how Bob is always too optimistic, how thoughtful and considered Manuel tends to be, and how cautious Monica usually is. Naturally, you have different degrees of respect for the opinion of a person whom you know very well and a younger, newer salesperson. How does statistics take this knowledge into account? The short answer is that it doesn't, at least not in the introductory statistics courses that many people have taken.

Fortunately, there is a way to deal with this information in a way that is much simpler than any chapter in even the first semester of statistics. We will call this the instinctive Bayesian approach:

1. Start with your calibrated estimate.

2. Gather additional information (polling, reading other studies, etc.).

3. Update your calibrated estimate subjectively, without doing any additional math.

I call this an instinctive Bayesian approach because when people update their prior uncertainties with new information, there is evidence to believe that those people update their knowledge in a way that is mostly Bayesian. In 1995 Caltech behavioral psychologists Mahmoud A. El-Gamal and David M. Grether studied how people consider prior information and new information when they assess odds.[1] They asked 257 students to guess from which of two bingo-like rolling cages balls were drawn. Each cage had balls marked either N or G but one cage had more N's than G's and the other had an equal number of each. Students were told how many balls of each type were drawn after six draws.

The students' job was to determine which of the two cages the balls were drawn from. For example, if a student saw a sample of 6 balls where 5 were N and only 1 was G, the student might be inclined to think it was probably from the cage with more N's than G's. However, prior to each draw of 6 balls, the students were told that the cages themselves were randomly selected with a one-third, one-half, or two-thirds probability. In their answers, the students' seemed to be intuitively computing the Bayesian answer with a slight tendency to overvalue the new information and undervalue the prior information. In other words, they were not quite ideally Bayesian but were more Bayesian than not.

I also find that calibrated estimators were even better at being Bayesian. The students in the study would have been overconfident on most estimating problems if they were like most people. But a calibrated estimator should still have this basic Bayesian instinct while not being as overconfident.

Several of the models I've built include conditional probabilities from calibrated estimators on a variety of subjects. In 2006, I went back to several of my calibrated estimators in a particular government agency and asked them these five questions:

A. What is the chance a Democrat will be president four years from now?

B. What is the chance your budget will be higher four years from now, assuming a Democrat will be president?

C. What is the chance your budget will be higher four years from now, assuming a Republican will be president?

D. What is the chance your budget will be higher four years from now?

E. Imagine you could somehow see your budget four years from now. If it were higher, what then is the chance that a Democrat is the president?

Now, a person who is instinctively Bayesian would answer these questions in a way that would be consistent with Bayes' theorem. If a person said her answers to questions A through C were 55%, 60%, and 40%, then the answers to questions D and E must be 51% and 64.7%, respectively, to be consistent. The answer to D must be $A \times B + (1 - A) \times C$ not, strictly speaking, because of Bayes, but because the conditional probabilities need to add up correctly. In other words, the chance of something happening is equal to the chance of some condition times the chance of the event occurring under that condition plus the chance that condition won't occur times the chance of the event without the condition. Now, to be Bayesian, a person would have to answer A, B, D, and E such that $B = D/A \times E$.

This might not seem intuitive at first glance, but, apparently, most calibrated decision makers instinctively give answers that are surprisingly close to these relationships. Take the last example where a calibrated expert gave the answers to A, B, and C were 55%, 70%, and 40%. But the calibrated expert also gave 50% and 75% for questions D and E. The answers to A, B, and C logically require that the answers to D and E be 56.5% and 68.1%, not 50% and 75%. In Exhibit 10.2 we show how the subjective estimates for these questions compare to the computed Bayesian values.

Notice that a couple of the Bayesian values would have to be less than zero or greater than 100% to be consistent with the other subjective answers given. This would obviously be illogical, but, in those cases, when calibrated experts gave their subjective values, they did not realize they were logically inconsistent. However, most of the time the answers were closer to "proper Bayesian" than even the calibrated experts expected. (See Exhibit 10.2.)

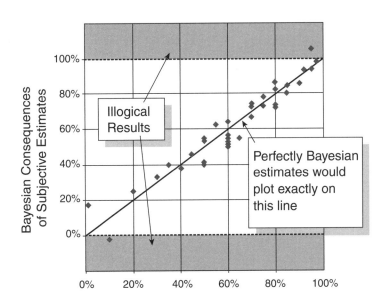

Calibrated Expert Subjective Probabilities

EXHIBIT 10.2   Calibrated Subjective Probabilities vs. Bayesian

In practice, I use a method I call Bayesian correction to make subjective calibrated estimates of conditional probabilities internally consistent. I show calibrated estimators what the Bayesian answers would be for some questions given their answers to other questions. They then change their answers until all their subjective calibrated probabilities are at least consistent with each other.

Interestingly, humans seem to be mostly logical when considering new information in relation to old information. This fact is extremely useful because a human can consider qualitative information that does not fit in standard statistics. For example, if you were giving a forecast for how a new policy might change "public image"— measured in part by a reduction in customer complaints, increased revenue, and the like—a calibrated expert should be able to update current knowledge with "qualitative" information about how the policy worked for other companies, feedback from focus groups, and similar details. Even with sampling information, the calibrated estimator—who has a Bayesian instinct—can consider qualitative information on samples that most textbooks don't cover.

Try it yourself by considering this: Will your company's revenue be higher next year? State your calibrated probability. Now ask two or three people you consider as knowledgeable on the topic. Don't just ask them if they think revenue will be higher; ask them to explain why they believe it. Have them go into some detail. Now give another subjective probability for the chance that revenue will be higher. This new answer will, more often than not, be a rational reflection of the new information even though the new information was mostly qualitative.

Exhibit 10.3 shows how the calibrated expert (who is both instinctively Bayesian and not over- or underconfident) compares to three other groups: the traditional non-Bayesian sampling methods such as t-statistics, uncalibrated estimators, and pure Bayesian estimators. This conceptual map tells you how different people and approaches stand relative to each other on their Bayesianness. One axis is how confident they are relative to their actual chance of being right, and the other axis is how much they emphasize or ignore prior information.

This method might cause anxiety among those who see themselves as sticklers for "objective" measurement, but such anxiety would be unwarranted. First, I've already shown that the subjective estimates of calibrated experts are usually closer to rational than irrational. Second, this

EXHIBIT 10.3   Confidence vs. Information Emphasis

method applies where first-semester "objective" statistics offer no help whatsoever and, therefore, the only alternative would be to do nothing. Third, those same people use this method all the time for personal decisions without realizing it. Say they read an article about the possible softening of the housing market that affected their decision to buy or sell a house; was their decision affected because they ran an extensive simulation against a table of data offered in the article? More likely they didn't, and the article did not offer that detail. Rather, they made a qualitative reassessment about a quantity (e.g., a list price).

Some controls could be used to offset some of the more legitimate concerns about this method. As a method that relies on human judgment, this approach is subject to several types of previously discussed bias. Here are some controls you could use in the instinctive Bayesian approach.

- *Use impartial judges if possible.* If a department head's budget will be affected by the outcome of the study, don't rely on that person to assess new information qualitatively.

- *Use blinds when possible.* It is sometimes possible to provide useful information to judges while keeping them in the dark about what specific problem they are assessing. If a marketing report provides transcripts from a focus group for a new product, references to the product can be deleted and judges can still determine if the reaction is positive or negative.

- *Use separation of duties.* This can be useful in conjunction with blinds. Get one set of judges to evaluate qualitative information, and give a synopsis to another judge who may be unaware of the specific product, department, technology project, and so on, involved. The second judge can give the final Bayesian response.

- *Precommit to Bayesian consequences.* Get judges to say in advance how certain findings would affect their judgments and apply Bayesian correction until they are internally consistent. This way, when the actual data are available, only the Bayesian formula is used and no further references to subjective judgment is required.

HETEROGENEOUS BENCHMARKING: A "BRAND DAMAGE" APPLICATION

> *Anything you need to quantify can be measured in some way that is superior to not measuring it at all.*
>
> —GILB'S LAW

In Chapter 9's jelly bean sampling problem, part of the uncertainty of the estimators in estimating the weight of a jelly bean was a lack of context for the measurement scale involved. One estimator said, "I'm just not sure I can picture exactly how much a gram of candy looks like." Another said, "I don't have any feel for the weights of small things."

Imagine I had told you that a business card weighs about 1 gram, a dime weighs 2.3 grams, and a large paper clip weighs 1 gram. Would that have reduced your range much? It did for some of the people I surveyed, especially those with the widest ranges. One person who had an upper bound of 20 grams immediately reduced it to 3 grams after hearing this information. Providing this information works because, as we now know, people are instinctively Bayesian, especially calibrated estimators. They tend to update prior knowledge with new information in a fairly rational way even when the new information is qualitative or only somewhat related to the estimated quantity.

I'm calling this method of updating prior knowledge based on dissimilar but somewhat related examples the "heterogeneous benchmark" method. When people feel they have no idea what a quantity might be, just knowing a context of scale, even for unlike items, can be a huge help. If you need to estimate the size of the market for your product in a new city, it helps to know what the size of the market is in other cities. It even helps just to know the relative sizes of the economies of the different cities.

GETTING A SENSE OF SCALE

Heterogeneous benchmark: A method where calibrated estimators are given other quantities as benchmarks to estimate an uncertain quantity, even when those quantities seem only remotely related.

Example: Estimating the sales of a new product by knowing the sales of other products or similar products by competitors.

One intriguing example of the heterogeneous benchmark shows up in information technology (IT) security. In the VA IT security example used throughout Chapters 4 through 6, I showed how we can model various security risks in a quantitative way using ranges and probabilities. But the IT security industry seems to be a bottomless pit of both curious attitudes about things that can't be measured and the number and type of "intangibles." One of these supposedly impossible measurements is the "softer costs" of certain catastrophic events.

A person who has a lot of experience with the resistance to measurement in IT security is Peter Tippett of Cybertrust. He applied his MD and PhD in biochemistry in a way that none of his classmates probably imagined: He wrote the first antivirus software. His innovation later became Norton Antivirus. Since then, Tippett has conducted major quantitative studies involving hundreds of organizations to measure the relative risks of different security threats. With these credentials, you might think that his claim that security can be measured would be accepted at face value. Yet many in the IT security industry seem to have a deeply rooted disposition against the very idea that security is measurable at all.

Tippett has a name for what he finds to be a predominant mode of thinking about the problem. He calls it the "Wouldn't it be horrible if. . ." approach. In this framework, IT security specialists imagine a particularly catastrophic event occurring. Regardless of its likelihood, it must be avoided at all costs. Tippett observes: "Since every area has a 'wouldn't it be horrible if. . .' all things need to be done. There is no sense of prioritization." He recalls a specific example. "A Fortune 20 said we are going to spend $100M on 35 projects. The CIO wanted to know which projects are more important. His people said nobody knows."

One particular "wouldn't it be horrible if. . ." that Tippett encounters is brand damage, a marred public image. It is possible, imagines the security expert, that something sensitive—like private medical records from a health maintenance organization or the loss of credit card data—could be breached by hackers and exploited. The security expert further imagines that the public embarrassment would so tarnish the brand name of the firm that it should be avoided, whatever the cost and however likely or unlikely it may be. Since the true cost of brand damage or the probability cannot be measured, so this "expert" insists, protection here is just as important as investments guarding against every other catastrophe—which also need to be funded without question.

But Tippett did not accept that the magnitude of the brand damage problem was completely indistinguishable from the magnitude of other problems. He devised a method that paired hypothetical examples of brand damage with real events where losses were known. He asked, for example, how much it hurts to have a company's e-mail go down for an hour, along with other benchmarks. He also asked how much more or less it hurt (e.g. "about the same," "half as much," "10 times as much," etc).

Cybertrust already had some idea of the relative scale of the cost of these events from a larger study of 150 "forensic investigations" of loss of customer data. This study included most of the losses of customer data from MasterCard and Visa.

Cybertrust surveyed chief executives as well as the general public about perceptions of brand damage. The company also compared the actual losses in stock prices of companies after such events. Through these surveys and comparisons, Tippett was able to confirm that the brand damage due to customer data stolen by hackers was worse than the damage caused by misplacing a backup tape.

By making several such comparisons with other benchmarks, it was possible to get an understanding of the difference in scale of the different types of catastrophes. Some amount of brand damage was worse than some things but not as bad as others. Furthermore, the relative level of loss could be taken into account along with the probability of that type of loss to compute "expected" loss.

I can't overstate the prior amount of uncertainty regarding this problem. The organizations weren't just uncertain about how bad brand damage could be. Until Tippett's study, they had no idea of the order of magnitude of the problem at all. Now they finally have at least a sense of scale of the problem and can differentiate the value of reducing different security risks.

At first, Tippett observed a high degree of skepticism in these results at one client, but he notes: "A year later one person is a bit skeptical and the rest are on board." Perhaps the holdout still insisted that no observation could have reduced his uncertainty. Again, with examples like brand damage, uncertainty is so high that almost any sense of scale is a reduction in uncertainty—therefore, a measurement.

Your organization, of course, will probably not set out to conduct a vast survey of over 100 organizations to conduct a measurement. But it is helpful to realize that such studies already exist. (Cybertrust sells this research.) Also, applying this method even internally can reduce uncertainty, whether your organization purchases external research or not.

APPLICATIONS FOR HETEROGENEOUS BENCHMARKS

Heterogeneous benchmarks are ideal for a simple measurement of the "soft costs" of many types of catastrophic events, especially where initial uncertainty is extremely high. Consider these examples:

- Hackers stealing customer credit card and Social Security information
- Inadvertent release of private medical data to the public
- Major product recalls
- Major industrial catastrophes at a chemical plant
- Corporate scandal

It might seem that we are focusing too much on IT security, but think about how broadly applicable this concept is. It is not just an approach for measuring brand damage from a security breach. It might be how we deal with the priority of investments meant to avoid a major product recall, corporate scandal, a catastrophic accident at a chemical plant, and the like. In fact, we can imagine how this method could apply to the positive side of these same issues. What is the value of being perceived as the "quality product" in the industry? Benchmarks are a practical way to bring some sense of scale to the problem whenever uncertainty is so high that it seems unmanageable.

If this use of benchmarks seems "too subjective," consider the objective of measurement in this case. What *is* brand damage but perception? We are not measuring some physical phenomenon but human opinions. The beginning of this measurement is understanding that something like "brand damage" is, by definition, one of public perception. And you assess public perception by, of course, asking the public. Alternatively, you can indirectly watch what the public does with its money by observing how the unfortunate event affected sales or stock price. Either way, it's been measured.

GETTING A BIT MORE TECHNICAL: BAYESIAN INVERSION FOR RANGES

As mentioned earlier, many of the other charts and tables I created for this book were done with a type of Bayesian inversion. For most problems in statistics and measurement, we are asking "What is the chance the truth is X, given what I've seen?" But it's actually easier to answer the question "If the truth was X, what is the chance of seeing what I did?" Bayesian inversion allows us to answer the first question by answering the second. Often the second question is much easier to answer.

Caution: This is going to get a little more technical. If you would like to skip this description, please refer to the spreadsheet for Bayesian inversion, which includes the example that follows, in the supplementary Web site at www.howtomeasureanything.com under the "Bayesian Inversion" link. I'll try to keep this description as simple as possible. The procedure will seem detailed, but I will minimize the math by, skipping straight to Excel functions when possible.

Suppose we have an automotive parts store and we want to measure our customer retention. We suspect we are having a problem with customer satisfaction. Our calibrated estimate for the number of customers who will shop at our auto parts store again after the first experience is 75% to 90% (a normal 90% CI). We want it to be as high as possible, of course, but unless it is at least 80%, we must undertake some costly corrective actions. We computed the information value at well over $500,000, but wisely, we want to minimize the burden on customers with customer surveys. Keeping in mind that we want to measure incrementally, we see how much information we can get from sampling just 20 customers. If we sample just 20 customers and 14 of them said they would shop here again, how can we change this range? Remember, typical parametric, non-Bayesian methods can't consider our prior range in the calculation.

Let's start with a much simpler question: If 90% of all customers would say they will shop again at the automotive parts store, what is the expected number of customers out of 20 that would say the same? Simple: 90% of 20, or 18. If it was 80%, then we would expect to get 16. Of course, we know that, by chance alone, a random sample of 20 could get us 15 or maybe even 20 customers who would say they will shop here again. So we need to know not just the expected outcome, but the chance of each of these specific results.

We use a special distribution mentioned earlier called the binomial distribution to help with this. To review, the binomial distribution allows us to compute the chance of a certain number of "hits" given a certain number of "trials," and given the probability of a single hit in one trial. For example, if you were flipping a coin, you could call getting heads a "hit," the number of flips would be the "trials," and the chance of a hit is 50%. Suppose, for example, we wanted to know the chance of getting exactly 4 heads out of 10 flips if the chances of getting heads is 50%. Instead of explaining the entire formula and the theory behind the field of combinatorics, I'm going to skip straight to the Excel formula. In Excel, we simply write

= binomdist (number of hits, number of trials, probability of a hit,0)

With the numbers in our coin-flipping example, we write binomdist(4,10,.5,0), and Excel returns the value of 20.5%. (The zero at the end tells Excel that we want only the chance of that particular result. Using a "1" will produce the cumulative probability, that is, the chance that the stated number of hits *or less* will occur.) This result means that there is a 20.5% chance that 10 coin flips will produce exactly 4 heads.

In our automotive parts chain example, a customer who says "Yes, I will shop here again" is a hit. And the sample size is the number of trials. Using the binomial distribution, a manager can work out the chance of a specific result, such as the chance that 14 out of a random sample of 20 customers will say they will shop here again if, in reality, 90% of the total population of customers would shop here again. Again, in Excel we write =binomdist (14,20,.9,0) which gives us a 0.887% chance that we would have gotten exactly 14 hits out of 20 randomly sampled customers if, in fact, 90% of the entire population of customers would have said they would shop here again. Already, we can see that the upper part of our original range is looking very unlikely.

Now, suppose we computed this chance for a population where 75% would be repeat shoppers, then 76%, 77%, and so on for every possible 1%-wide increment in our initial range of 75% to 90%. Setting up some tables in an Excel spreadsheet, we can quickly compute the chance of a specific result, given each of the "true" population proportions. In each little increment, we get the probability of getting exactly 14 out of 20 customers saying "yes" to our repeat-shopping question given a specific population proportion. I would compute this in 1% increment starting at, say, 60% (which, given our 90% CI, is unlikely but possible) and going up to 100%. For each increment, we conduct a calculation with Bayes' theorem. We can put it all together like this:

$$P(Prop = X | Hits = 14/20) = P(Prop = X)$$
$$\times\, P(Hits = 14/20 | Prop = X)/P(Hits = 14/20)$$

Where:

P(Prop=X | Hits=14/20) is the probability of a given population proportion X given that 14 of 20 random samples were hits.

P(Prop=X) is the probability that a particular proportion of the population will shop here again (e.g., X=90% of the population of customers really would say they will shop here again).

P(Hits=14/20 | Prop=X) is the probability of 14 hits out of a random sample of 20, given a particular population proportion is equal to X.

P(Hits=14/20) is the probability that a we would get 14 hits out of 20, given all the possible underlying populating proportions in our initial range.

We know how to compute P(Hits=14/20|Prop=90%) in Excel: (=binomdist(14,20,.9,1). Now we have to figure out how to compute P(Prop=X) and P(Hits=14/20). We can work out the probability of each 1% increment in our range by going back to the =normdist() function in Excel and using the calibrated estimate. For instance, to get the probability that between 78% and 79% of our customers are repeat customers (or at least say they are on a survey), we can write the Excel formula:

$$=\text{normdist}(.79, .825, .0456, 1) - \text{normdist}(.78, .825, .0456, 1)$$

The .825 is the mean of our calibrated range: (75% + 90%)/2. The .0456 is the standard deviation (remember there are 3.29 standard deviations in a 90% CI): (90%−75%)/3.29. The normdist formula gives us the difference between the probability of getting less than 79% and the probability of getting less than 78%, resulting in a value of 5.95%. We can compute this for each 1% increment in our range so we can compute the probability the population proportion is X (i.e., P(Prop=X) for every remotely likely value of X in our range.

Computing the value of P(Hits=14/20) builds on everything we've done so far. To compute P(Y) when we know P(Y|X) and P(X) for every value of X, we add up the product of P(Y|X) × P(X) for every value of X. Since we know how to compute P(Hits=14/20|Prop=X) and P(Prop=X) for any value of X, we just multiply these two values for each X and add them all up to get P(Hits=14/20)=8.56%.

Now, for each value in our range (and a little outside of the range to get the tails in the equation), we compute the P(Prop=X), P(Hits=14/20|Prop=X), and P(Prop=X|Hits=14/20) for each increment in the population proportion (P(Hits=14/20) is the same for all of them at 8.56%)). (See Exhibit 10.4.)

The value of each row in the last column is the chance of that particular population proportion. If we add up the cumulative values in the last column (the sum of all the rows up to that point), we find that the values add up to about 5% by the time we get to a population proportion of 79% and cumulative value increases to 95% by the time we get to 85%. This means our new 90% CI is about 73% to 85%. This seems like only a slight reduction from our original range of 75% to 90%, but it is not uninformative. The chance we are under our key threshold of 80% is now 61%, according to the

EXHIBIT 10.4 **EXAMPLE ROWS FROM BAYESIAN INVERSION SPREADSHEET TABLE**

P(Hits=14/20)=sumproduct(column A, column B)=.0856

(X) Population Proportion	(A) =normdist(X+.01,.825,.0446,1)- normdist(X,.825,.0446,1)	(B) =binomdist(14,20,X,0)	=A × B/.0856
60%	8.04E-07	0.1244	1.169
61%	2.25E-06	0.1347	3.545E-06
62%	6.01E-06	0.1447	1.017E-05
⬇	⬇	⬇	⬇
0.98	0.000189	1.869E-06	4.139E-09
0.99	8.59E-05	3.367E-08	3.381E-11

Detailed worksheet at www.howtomeasureanything.com.

cumulative values in the last column. This entire spreadsheet is available on www.howtomeasureanything.com.

Customer retention is looking bleak. But we recalculate the information value, and, while it has decreased, there is still a value to more measurements. We sample another 40 customers for a total of 60. In total, only 39 out of the 60 said they would shop there again. Our new 90% CI is 69% to 80%. Our latest upper bound is now equal to our original critical threshold of 80%, making it 95% certain that our stated repeat business from customers is low enough to require us to make some serious, expensive changes.

This has been a somewhat dense procedure. But remember, you have example spreadsheets at your disposal at the supplementary Web site. And it's quite possible that the subjective Bayesian approach discussed earlier could have worked here with calibrated estimators. Perhaps the customer survey process could have revealed some qualitative factors that our calibrated estimators could take into account. However, the information value for this critical business measurement was high enough that the extra effort was easily worth it.

We could also have used the population proportion chart used in Chapter 4 (although we would be looking up the range for customers who *didn't* say they would shop again, since the subgroup sizes are all less than 50% of the sample size). But we couldn't take into account this stated initial range. The chart in Chapter 9 was, by the way, also derived with a Bayesian inversion, except I started with the widest possible uncertainty that any population proportion can possibly have: a uniform distribution of 0% to 100% population proportion. Using such a wide range in the example in this chapter, we would have gotten a wider range with a lower bound even worse than what we got with the approach presented here. In this case, we started with the knowledge that results as potentially bad as the assumptions in Chapter 9 (even considering our disappointing results) were unlikely. Whether it is good or bad, the Bayesian range takes this prior knowledge into account. As the number of samples increase, however, the effect of the initial range diminishes. After getting to 60 samples or more, the answer will begin to get closer to what the parametric population proportion method would produce.

If you can master this type of analysis, you can take it further and see how to analyze problems where the initial distribution was some other kind of shape instead of normal. For example, the distribution could be uniform, or it could be normal truncated, so that it is not implied that more than 100% of the customers could be repeat shoppers. (The upper tail of or normal 90% CI gives a small chance of that being the case.) Again, see the supplementary Web site for examples of both of these distributions.

AVOID "OBSERVATION INVERSION" PROBLEMS

Many people focus on the question "What can I conclude from this observation?" But Bayes showed us that the question "What should I observe if X were true?" is often more straightforward. When this question is answered, it can be converted into the answer for the former question.

Although it may seem cumbersome at first, Bayesian inversion is one of the most powerful measurement tools at our disposal. If you can think of the question "What is the chance of seeing X if the truth was really Y?" and invert it to "What is the chance the truth is Y if I see X?" you've solved a wide variety of measurement problems. In effect, this is exactly how most scientific inquiry progresses. If a proposed hypothesis was true, what should we see?

In contrast, many managers seem to treat all measurement as answering the question "What can I conclude from what I do see?" If they imagine any error in the observation, they conclude only that they can conclude nothing from the observation, regardless of how likely that error may be. A Bayesian analysis might show, however, that the errors they are imagining are extremely unlikely and that the measurement will still be a significant uncertainty reduction. In other words, the lack of at least a conceptual understanding of Bayesian inversion leads to getting the question backward and believing unlikely errors neutralize measurement—an unfortunate kind of "observation inversion."

ENDNOTES

1. David M. Grether and Mahmoud A. El-Gamal, "Are People Bayesian?: Uncovering Behavioral Strategies," *Social Science Working Paper 919,* California Institute of Technology, 1995.
2. Tom DeMarco and Timothy Lister, *Peopleware,* 2nd ed. (New York: Dorset House Publishing, 1999).

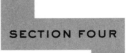

Beyond The Basics

## CHAPTER 11

Preference and Attitudes: The Softer Side of Measurement

The brand damage example in Chapter 10 is one instance of a large set of subjective valuation problems. The term "subjective valuation" can be considered redundant because, when it comes to value, what does "objective" really mean? Is the value of a pound of gold "objective" just because that is the market value? Not really. The market value itself is the result of a large number of people making subjective valuations.

It's not uncommon for managers to feel that concepts such as "quality," "image," or "value" are immeasurable. In some cases, this is because they can't find what they feel to be "objective" estimates of these quantities. But that is simply a mistake of expectations. All quality assessment problems—public image, brand value, and the like—are about human preferences. In that sense, human preferences are the only source of measurement. If that means such a measurement is subjective, then that is simply the nature of the measurement. It's not a physical feature of any object. It is only how humans make choices about that thing. Once we accept this class of measurements as measurements of human choices alone, then our only question is how to observe these choices.

OBSERVING OPINIONS, VALUES, AND THE PURSUIT OF HAPPINESS

Broadly, there are two ways to observe preferences: what people say and what people do. *Stated* preferences are those that individuals will say they prefer. *Revealed* preferences are those that individuals display by their actual behaviors. Either type of preference can significantly reduce uncertainty, but revealed preferences are usually, as you might expect, more revealing.

If we ask people what they think, believe, or prefer, then we are making an observation where the statistical analysis is no different from how we analyze "objective" physical features of the universe (which are just as likely to fool us as humans; the controls are just different). We simply sample a group of people and ask them some specific questions. The form of these questions fall in one of a few major categories. Professionals in the field of survey design use an even more detailed and finely differentiated set of categories, but four types are good enough for beginners:

- *The Likert scale.* Respondents are asked to choose where they fall on a range of possible feelings about a thing, generally in the form of "strongly dislike," "dislike," "strongly like," "strongly disagree," and "strongly agree."

- *Multiple choice.* Respondents are asked to pick from mutually exclusive sets, such as "Republican, Democrat, Independent, other."

- *Ordinal.* Respondents are asked to rank order several things. Example: "Rank the following 8 activities from least preferred (1) to most preferred (8)."

- *Open ended.* Respondents are asked to simply write out a response in any way they like. Example: "Was there anything you were dissatisfied with about our customer service?"

Those who specialize in designing surveys often refer to the survey itself as an *instrument.* Survey instruments are designed to minimize or control for a class of biases called response bias, a problem unique to this type of measurement instrument.

Response bias occurs when a survey, intentionally or not, affects respondents' answers in a way that does not reflect their true attitudes. If the bias is done deliberately, the survey designer is angling for specific response (e.g., "Do you oppose the criminal negligence of Governor. . .?"), but surveys can be biased unintentionally. Here are five simple strategies for avoiding response bias:

1. *Keep the question precise and short.* Wordy questions are more likely to confuse.

2. *Avoid loaded terms.* A loaded term is a word with a positive or negative connotation, which the survey designer may not even be aware of, that affects answers. Asking people if they support the "liberal" policies of a particular politician is an example of a question with a loaded term. (It's also a good example of a highly imprecise question if it mention no specific policies.)

3. *Avoid leading questions.* A leading question is worded in such a way that it tells the respondent which particular answer is expected. Example: "Should the underpaid, overworked sanitation workers of Cleveland get pay raises?" Sometimes leading questions are not deliberate. Like loaded terms, the easiest safeguard against unintended leading questions is having a second or third person look the questions over. The use of intentional leading questions leads me to wonder why anyone is even taking the survey. If they know what answer they want, what "uncertainty reduction" are they expecting from a survey?

4. *Avoid compound questions.* Example: "Do you prefer the seat, steering wheel, and controls of car A or car B?" The respondent doesn't know which question to answer. Break the question into multiple questions.

5. *Reverse questions to avoid response set bias.* A response set bias is the tendency of respondents to answer questions (i.e., scales) in a particular direction regardless of content. If you have a series of scales that ask for responses ranging from 1 to 5, make sure 5 is not always the "positive" response (or vice versa). You want to encourage respondents to read and respond to each question and not fall into a pattern of just checking every box in one column.

Of course, directly asking respondents what they prefer, choose, desire, and feel is not the only way to learn about those things. We can also infer a great deal about preferences from observing what people do. In fact, this is generally considered to be a much more reliable measure of people's real opinions and values than just asking them.

If people say they would prefer to spend $20 on charity for orphans instead of the movies but, in reality, they've been to the movies many times in the last year without giving to an orphanage once, then they've revealed a preference different from the preference they've stated. Two good indicators of revealed preferences are things people tend to value a lot: time and money. If you look at how they spend their time and how they spend their money, you can infer quite a lot about their real preferences.

Now, it seems like we've deviated from measuring true "quantities" when survey respondents say they "strongly agree" with statements like "Christmas decorations go up too early in retail stores." But the concepts we've introduced in earlier chapters haven't changed. You have a current state of uncertainty about this variable (e.g., the percentage of shoppers who think Christmas decorations go up too early is 50% to 90%), and you have a point where it begins to change some decision (if more than 70% of shoppers strongly agree that decorations go up too early, then the mall should curtail plans to put them up even earlier). Based on that information, you compute the value of additional information and you devise a sampling method or some other measurement appropriate to that question at that information value.

Yes, we have departed from the type of unit-of-measure-oriented quantities we've focused on up to this point. Whenever we assessed exactly why we cared about a quantity, we generally were able to identify pretty clear units, not Likert scales. But we do have another step we can introduce. We can correlate opinion survey results to other quantities that are unambiguous and much more useful. If you want to measure customer satisfaction, isn't it because you want to stay in business by keeping repeat customers and getting word-of-mouth advertising?

Actually, you can correlate subjective responses to objective measures, and such analysis is done routinely. Some have even applied it to measuring happiness (see "Measuring Happiness" box). If you can correlate two things to each other, and then if you can correlate one of them to money, you can express both of them in terms of money. And if that seems too difficult, you can even ask them directly "What are you willing to pay?"

MEASURING HAPPINESS

Andrew Oswald, professor of economics at the University of Warwick, produced a method for measuring the value of happiness.[1] He didn't exactly ask people directly how much they were willing to pay for happiness. Instead, he asked them how happy they *are* according to a

Likert scale and then asked them to state their income and a number of other life events, such as recent family deaths, marriages, children born, and so on.

This allowed Oswald to see the change in happiness that would be due to specific life events. He saw how a recent family death decreased happiness or how a promotion increased it. Furthermore, since he was also correlating the effect of income on happiness, he could compute equivalent-income happiness for other life events. He found that a lasting marriage, for example, makes a person just as happy as earning another $100,000 per year. (Since my wife and I just had our 10-year anniversary, I'm about as happy as I would be if I had earned an extra $1 million in that same 10-year period without being married. Of course, this is an average, and individuals would vary a lot. So I tell my wife it's probably a low estimate for me, and we can continue to have a happy marriage.)

A Willingness to Pay: Measuring Value via Trade-offs

To reiterate, valuation, by its nature, is a subjective assessment. Even the market value of a stock or real estate is just the result of some subjective judgments of market participants. If people compute the net equity of a company to get an "objective" measure of its value, they have to add up things like the market value of real estate holdings (how much they think someone else would be willing to pay for it), the value of a brand (at best, how much more consumers are willing to pay for a product with said brand), the value of used equipment (again, how much someone else would pay for it), and the like. No matter how "objective" they believe their calculation is, the fundamental unit of measure they deal in—the dollar—is a measure of value.

This is why one way to value most things is to ask people how much they are willing to pay for it or, better yet, to determine how much they *have been* paying for it by looking at past behaviors. The willingness to pay (WTP) method is usually conducted as a random sample survey where people are asked how much they would pay for certain things—usually things that can't be valued in any other way. The method has been used to value avoiding the loss of an endangered species, improvements in public health, and the environment, among others.

In 1988 I had my first consulting project with Coopers & Lybrand. We were evaluating the printing operations of a financial company to determine whether the company should outsource more printing to a large local printer. The board of directors of the company felt there was an "innate value" on working with businesses in the local community. Plus, the president of the local printer had friends of the board. He asked, "I'm not in the financial services business, why are you in the printing business?" and he was lobbying to get more of the printing outsourced to his firm.

A few skeptics on the board engaged Coopers & Lybrand to evaluate the business sense of this. I was the junior analyst who did all the numbers on this project. I found that not only did it make no business sense to outsource more printing, but that, instead, the company should in-source more of it. The company was large enough that it could compete well for skilled printing professionals, it could keep all of its equipment at a high usage rate, and it could negotiate good deals with suppliers. The company already had a highly skilled staff who knew quite a lot about the printing business.

Whether printing should be part of the "core business" of such a company could be argued either way, but the cost benefit was clearly in favor of keeping what the company did in house and doing even more. There was no doubt the company would have paid more to have this large volume of printing done externally, even after taking into account all employee benefits, equipment maintenance, office space, and everything else. The proposed outsourcing would have cost this company several million dollars per year more than it spent to get the same service and product. Some argued the company may even get lower-quality service by outsourcing since this large printing staff the insurance company hired doesn't have any other customer priorities to worry about. The net present value of the proposed outsourcing would have been a worse than *negative* $15 million over five years.

So the choice came down to this: Did the company value this printer's friendship and its sense of community support of small businesses by more or less than $15 million? As the junior analyst, I didn't see my role as one of telling the board members how much they should value it, I simply honestly reported the cost of their decision, whatever they chose. If they valued this community friendship (in this particular limited case, anyway) more than $15 million, then the financial loss would have been acceptable. If they valued it less, then the financial loss would have been unacceptable. In the end, they decided that the gain in this particular friendship and this specific type of "community support" wasn't worth *that* much. They didn't outsource more and even decided to outsource less.

At the time, I referred to this as a type of "art buying" problem. You might think it would be impossible to value a "priceless" piece of art, but if I at least make sure you know the true price of the art, you can decide the value for yourself. If someone said something Picasso created was "priceless" but nobody could be enticed to spend $10 million for it, then clearly its value is less than that. We didn't attempt to value the friendship exactly, we just made sure the company knew how much it would be paying for it; and then it could make the choice.

A modification of WTP is the "Value of a Statistical Life" (VSL) method. With the VSL, people are not directly asked how much they value life but rather how much they are willing to pay for incremental reduction in the risk of death. People routinely make decisions where they, in effect, make a choice between money and a slight reduction in the chance of an early death. You could have spent more on a slightly safer car. Let's say it amounts to an extra $5,000 for a 20% reduction in dying from an automobile collision, which only has, say, a 0.5% chance of causing your death anyway (given how much you drive, where you drive, your driving habits, etc.), resulting in an overall reduction of mortal risk of one-tenth of 1%. If you opted against that choice, you were saying the equivalent of "I prefer keeping $5,000 to a 0.1% lower chance of premature death." In that case you were valuing your VSL at something less than $5,000/.001, or $5 million (because you declined the expenditure). You could also have spent $1,000 on your deductible for a medical scan that has a 1% chance of picking up a fatal condition that, if detected early, can be prevented. In that case you opted to take it, implying your VSL was at least $500/.01, or $100,000. We can continue to look at your purchasing decisions for or against a variety of other safety-related products or services and we can infer how much you value a given reduction of life-threatening risk and, by extrapolation, how much you value your life.

There are some problems with this approach. First, people are pretty bad at assessing their own risk on all sorts of issues, so their own choices might not be all that enlightening. Dr. James Hammitt and the Harvard Center for Risk Analysis observed:

> People are notoriously poor at understanding probabilities, especially the small ones that are relevant to health choices. In a general-population survey, only about 60 percent of respondents correctly answered the question "Which is a larger chance, 5 in 100,000 or 1 in 10,000?" This "innumeracy" can confound people's thinking about their preferences.[2]

If people are really that mathematically illiterate, it would be fair to be skeptical about valuations gathered from public surveys. Undeterred by the limited mathematical capacity of some people, Hammitt simply adjusts for it. Respondents who answer questions like these correctly are assessed separately from those who didn't understand these basic concepts of probability and risk.

In addition to the mathematical illiteracy of at least some respondents, those of us who measure such things have to face a misplaced sense of righteous indignation. Some studies have shown that about 25% of people in environmental value surveys refused to answer on the grounds that "the environment has an absolute right to be protected" regardless of cost.[3] The net effect, of course, is that those very individuals who would probably bring up the average WTP for the environment are abstaining and making the valuation smaller than it otherwise would be. But I wonder if this sense of indignation is really a facade. Those same individuals have a choice right now to forgo any luxury, no matter how minor, to give charitable donations on behalf of protecting the environment. Right now, they could quit their jobs and work full time as volunteers for Greenpeace. And yet they do not. Their behaviors often don't coincide with their claim of incensed morality at the very idea of the question. Some are equally resistant to the idea of placing a monetary value on a human life, but, again, they don't give up every luxury to donate to charities related to public health.

There may be explanation for this disconnect between their claim that certain things are beyond monetary valuation while making personal choices that appear to put a higher value on personal luxuries, even minor ones. As Hammitt's study (and many others) has shown, a surprisingly large share of the population is so mathematically illiterate that resistance to valuing a human life may be part of a fear of numbers in general.

Perhaps for them, a show of righteous indignation is part of a defense mechanism. Perhaps they feel their "innumeracy" doesn't matter as much if quantification itself is unimportant, especially on issues like these.

Measuring the values related to human happiness, health, and life is a particularly touchy topic. An Internet search of the phrase "being reduced to a number" will produce hundreds or thousands of hits, most of which are an objection to some form of measurement applied in any way to a human being. Even though modeling the world mathematically is as uniquely a human trait as language or art, you would rarely find anyone complaining of being "reduced to a poem" or "reduced to a painting."

I've done several risk/return analyses of federal government projects where one component of the benefit of the proposed investment was increased public health risk. In every one we simply used wide ranges gathered from a variety of VSL or WTP studies. Rarely did that range, as wide as it was, turn out to be what required further measurement. For those who would get anxious at the idea of using any monetary value at all for such things, they should think of the alternative: Ignoring the factor effectively treats the value as zero in a business case, which causes an irrational undervaluation of (and lack of sufficient priority for) the effort the business case was trying to argue for. With only one exception in the many cases I worked on did the value of information even guide us to measuring such variables any further. In most cases the real uncertainty was, surprisingly, *not* the value of public safety or welfare. The initial ranges (as wide as they were) turned out to be sufficient, and measurement focused on other uncertain variables.

By the way, the range many government agencies used, based on a variety of VSL and WTP studies, was $2 million to $20 million to avoid one premature death randomly chosen from the population. If you think that's too low, look at how you spend your own money on your own safety. Also look at how you choose to spend money on some luxury in your life—no matter how modest—instead of giving more to AIDS or cancer research. If you really thought each and every human life was worth far, far more than that range, then you would already be acting differently. When we examine our own behaviors closely, its easy to see that only a hypocrite says "life is priceless."

PUTTING IT ALL ON THE LINE:
QUANTIFYING RISK TOLERANCE

One common area where these sorts of internal trade-offs have to be made to evaluate something is the tolerance for risk. No one can compute for you how much risk you or your firm should tolerate, but you can measure it. Like the VSL approach, it is simply a matter of examining a list of trade-offs—real or hypothetical—between more reward or lower risk.

For managing financial portfolios, some portfolio managers do exactly that. In 1990 the Nobel Prize in Economics was given to Harry Markowitz for Modern Portfolio Theory (MPT). First developed by Markowitz in the 1950s, the theory has since become the basis for most portfolio optimization methods. Perhaps the simplest component of MPT is a chart that shows how much risk investors are willing to accept for a given return. If they are given an investment with a higher potential return, investors are usually willing to accept a little more risk. If they are given an investment with much more certainty, they are willing to accept a lower return. This is expressed as a curve on a chart where risk and return are just barely acceptable. Exhibit 11.1 shows what someone's investment boundary might look like.

This is a little different from the chart Markowitz used. His risk axis was really historical volatility of the return on a particular stock (capital gains or losses as well as dividends). But investments like IT projects or

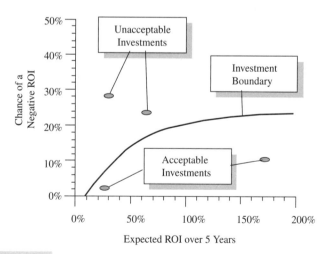

EXHIBIT 11.1   The Investment Boundary

new product development don't typically have "historical volatility." They do, however, share another characteristic of risk that is more fundamental than Markowitz's measure: They have a chance of a loss.

You can quickly construct your own investment boundary or one for your firm. Imagine a large investment for your portfolio. What would a "large" — but not uncommon—investment be: $1 million? $100 million? Whatever it is, pick a size and state it explicitly for the rest of this example.

Now imagine you computed, using a Monte Carlo simulation, the return from thousands of scenarios. The average of all the possible returns is an annual return on investment (ROI) of 50% for 5 years. But there is enough uncertainty about the ROI that there is a chance it actually will be negative— let's say a 10% chance of a negative ROI. Would you accept this investment? If so, let's raise the risk to 20%; if not, lower it to 5%. Would you accept it now? Repeat the previous step, raising or lowering the risk, until the return and risk are just barely acceptable. This point is on your "investment boundary." Now increase the ROI to 100%. What would the risk have to be to make it just barely acceptable? That would be another point on your investment boundary. Finally, suppose you could make an investment that had no chance of a negative return. How low of an average ROI are you willing to accept if there were no chance of a negative return?

Each of these three points is a point on your investment boundary. If you need to, you can fill in the boundary curve with a few more points at higher or lower ROIs. But at some point the curve that connects these points will become obvious to you.

It's worth mentioning a few additional caveats for those sticklers for MPT. First, you have to have a different investment boundary for investments of different sizes. Markowitz originally meant the investment curve to be for the entire portfolio, not for individual fixed investments. But I just make three curves—one for a small investment, another for an average-size investment, and one for the largest investment I'm likely to assess—and the interpolation is fairly obvious. (I wrote a simple spreadsheet that interpolates the curve for me, but you can get just as close by visualizing it.)

I often use this simple component to evaluate each investment independently for a number of reasons. Opportunities for new projects can come at any time in the year while several other projects are in progress. There is rarely an opportunity to "optimize" the entire portfolio as if we could opt in or out of any project at any point.

In 1997 and 1998 I wrote articles in *Information Week*[3] and *CIO Magazine*[4] on the investment boundary approach I've been using in the Applied Information Economics method.[4] I've taken many executives through this exercise, and I've collected dozens of investment boundaries for many different types of organizations. In each case the investment boundary took between 40 and 60 minutes to create from scratch, regardless of whether there was one decision maker in the room or 20 members of an investment steering committee.

Of all the people who ever participated in those sessions—all policy makers for their organization—not one failed to catch on quickly to the point of the exercise.

I noticed something else, too. Even when the participants were a steering committee consisting of over a dozen people, the exercise was thoroughly consensus building. Whatever their disagreements were about which project should be of higher priority, they seemed to reach agreement quickly on just how risk averse their organization really was.

The result of using investment boundaries like this to evaluate investments is that we find the risk-adjusted ROI requirements to be considerably higher than the typical "hurdle rates"—required minimum ROI's—sometimes used by IT decision makers (hurdle rates are often in the range of 15% to 30%). This effect increases rapidly as the size of proposed projects increase. The typical IT decision maker in the average development environment should require a return *of well over 100%* for the largest projects in the IT portfolio. The risk of cancellation, the uncertainties of benefits, the risk of interference with operations, all contribute to the risk and, therefore, the required return for IT projects. These findings have many consequences for IT decision makers, and I will present some of them here.

It is not too bold a statement to say that the software development project is one of the riskiest investments a business makes. For example, the chance of a large software project being canceled increases with project duration. In the 1990's, those projects that exceeded two years of elapsed calendar time in development have a default rate that exceeded the worst-rated junk bonds (something over 25%).

Yet most companies that use ROI analysis do not account for this risk. The typical hurdle rates are not adjusted for differences in the risk of IT projects, even though risk should be a huge factor in the decision. If the decision makers looked at the software development investment from a risk/return point of view, they would probably make some very different decisions from those that would be made with fixed hurdle rates.

QUANTIFYING SUBJECTIVE TRADE-OFFS: DEALING WITH MULTIPLE CONFLICTING PREFERENCES

The investment boundary is just one example of the "utility curves" business managers learn about in first-semester economics. Unfortunately, most managers probably finished such classes thinking they were purely theoretical discussions with no practical application. But these curves are a perfect tool for defining how much of one thing a manager is willing to trade for another thing. A variety of other types of curves allows decision makers to explicitly define acceptable trade-offs.

"Performance" and "quality" are examples where such explicitly defined trade-offs are useful in the measurement of preferences and value. Terms like "performance" and "quality" are often used with such ambiguity that it is virtually impossible to tell anything more than that more "performance" or "quality" is good, less is bad. As we've seen before, there is no reason for this ambiguity to persist; these terms can be clarified just as easily as any other "intangible."

When clients say they need help measuring performance, I always ask, "What do you mean by 'performance'?" Generally, they provide a list of separate observations they associate with performance, such as "This person gets things done on time" or "She gets lots of positive accolades from our clients." They may also mention factors such as a low error rate in work or a productivity-related measure, such as "error-free modules completed per month." In other words, they don't really have an issue with how to observe performance at all. As one client put it: "I know what to look for, but how do I total all these things? Does someone who gets work done on time with fewer errors get a higher performance rating than someone who gets more positive feedback from clients?"

This is not really a problem with measurement, then, but a problem with documenting subjective trade-offs. It is a problem with how to tally up lots of different observations into a total "index" of some kind. This is where we can use utility curves to make such tallies consistent. Using them, we can show how we want to make trade-offs similar to these:

- Is a programmer who gets 99% of assignments done on time and 95% error free better than one who gets only 92% done on time but with a 99% error-free rate?

- Is total product quality higher if the defect rate is 15% lower but customer returns are 10% higher?

- Is "strategic alignment" higher if the profit went up by 10% but the "total quality index" went down by 5%?

For each of these examples, we can imagine a chart that shows these trade-offs similar to how we charted trade-off preferences for risk and return. Each point on the same curve is considered equally valuable to every other point on that curve. In the investment boundary example, each point on the curve has the identical value of zero. That is, the risk is just barely acceptable given the return, and the decision maker would be indifferent to the options of acceptance versus rejection of the proposed investment.

We could define multiple other utility curves on the same chart for investments of greater value than zero, each with a constant utility. Sometimes economists refer to utility curves as "iso-utility" curves, meaning "constant or fixed utility." Because a person would be indifferent to any two points on the same utility curve, it is also accepted convention in economics to refer to a utility curve as an indifference curve. In the same way that the elevation lines on a relief map show points of equal altitude, a utility curve is made of points that are all considered to be equally valuable.

Exhibit 11.2 shows a chart with multiple utility curves. It is a hypothetical example of how management might value trade-offs between quality of work and punctuality. This could be used to clarify the requirements for job performance for a programmer, engineer, copy editor, and so on. It is easy to see that if workers A and B had the same amount of on-time work, but A had a higher error-free work rate, A would be considered preferable. The curve clarifies preferences when the choice is not that clear—such as when worker A has better work quality but B has better punctuality.

The curves are drawn by management such that any two points on the same curve are considered equally valuable. For example, management drew the top curve in a way that indicates it considers a worker who has 96% error-free work and a 96% on-time completion rate to be equal to one who has

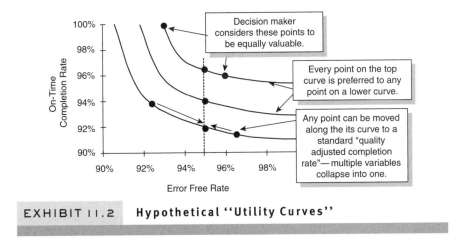

EXHIBIT 11.2   Hypothetical "Utility Curves"

93% error-free work and a 100% on-time completion rate. Keep in mind that this is just the hypothetical valuation of some particular manager, not a fixed, standard trade-off. Your preferences would probably be at least a little different.

A series of similar curves was drawn where any point on one curve is considered preferable to any point on a curve below it. Although only a few curves need to be drawn for reference, there are really an infinite number of curves between each of those shown. Management simply draws enough curves to interpolate as necessary.

The utility curve between any two things (e.g., quality and timeliness or risk and return) provides for an interesting way to simplify how we express the value of any point on the chart. Since every point can be moved along its curve without changing its value, all points can be considered equivalent to a position on a single standardized line. In this case, we standardize quality and express the relative value of any point on the chart in terms of quality-adjusted, on-time rate. We collapsed two variables into one by answering the question "A worker with error-free rate X and on-time completion Y is just as good as a 95% error-free rate and _____ on-time completion rate."

The same is routinely done with risk and return. Using a series of risk/return curves, we can take the risk and return of any investment and express it simply as risk-adjusted return. This method of collapsing two different factors can be done no matter how many attributes there are. If, for example, I created utility curves for factors X versus Y and then I create utility curves for Y versus Z, then anyone should be able to infer my utility curve for X versus Z. In this manner several different factors affecting such topics as job performance, evaluating new office locations, choosing a new product line, or anything else can be collapsed into a single standardized measure.

Furthermore, if any of the trade-offs I defined include a trade-off for money, then I can monetize the entire set of factors. In the case of evaluating different investments with different risks (e.g., the chance of a negative return, worst-case return, etc.) and different measures of return (e.g., seven-year internal rate of return, first year return, etc.), it is sometimes useful to collapse all these different considerations into a certain monetary equivalent (CME). The CME of an investment is the fixed and certain dollar amount that the investor considers just as good as the investment.

Suppose, for example, I had to buy you out as a partner in a real estate development firm. I give you the option of buying a vacant lot in the Chicago suburbs for $200,000 to do with as you please *or* I give you $100,000 cash right now. If you were truly indifferent between these choices, then you consider the CME of the vacant lot investment to be $100,000. If you thought buying the lot at that price was was a fantastically good deal, your CME for the investment might be, say, $300,000. This means you would consider the option of making this investment—with all its uncertainties and risks—to be just as good as being given $300,000 cash in hand. You might have defined trade-offs for dozens of variables to come to this conclusion, but the result couldn't be simpler. No matter how complicated the variables and their trade-offs get, you will always prefer a $300,000 CME to a $100,000 cash.

This is exactly how I've helped many clients prioritize IT investments where there are a variety of risks and ways of looking at the return. We collapse all the variables into one CME by defining trade-offs between each of the variables and a certain monetary value of some kind. This is a very powerful tool in general for deciding whether 12 different parameters describing, for example, quality could be combined into one monetary quality value. Even though your choices may be subjective, you still can be entirely quantitative about the trade-offs.

Next we'll turn to situations where the trade-offs aren't necessarily just subjective values of decision makers.

KEEPING THE BIG PICTURE IN MIND: PROFIT MAXIMIZATION VERSUS SUBJECTIVE TRADE-OFFS

Very often, such trade-offs between different factors do not have to be purely subjective. Sometimes it makes more sense to reduce them to a profit or shareholder value maximization problem. A clever analyst should be able to set up a statistically valid spreadsheet model that shows how error rates, punctuality, and the like affect profit. These solutions all boil down to an argument that there is only one important preference—like profit—and that the importance of factors like productivity and quality are entirely related to how they affect profit. If this is the case, then there is no need to make subjective trade-offs between things like performance and customer satisfaction, quality and quantity, or brand image and revenue.

This is really what all business cases should be about. They use several variables of costs and benefits to compute some ultimate measure like net present value or return on investment. There is still a subjective choice, but it's a simpler and more fundamental choice—it's the choice of what the ultimate goal to strive for should really be. If you can get agreement on what the ultimate goal should be, then the trade-offs between different indicators of performance (or, for that matter, quality, value, effectiveness, etc.) might not be subjective at all. For example, the fact that $1 million cost reduction in one area is just as preferable as a $1 million reduction in another is not really a subjective trade-off, because they both affect profit identically. Here are three more examples of how people in some very different industries defined some form of "performance" as a quantifiable contribution to some ultimate goal.

1. Tom Bakewell of St. Louis, Missouri, is a management consultant who specializes in measuring performance in colleges and universities. In this environment, Bakewell notes, "People have said for decades that you can't measure performance." Bakewell argues that the financial health of the institution—or, at least, the avoidance of financial ruin—is the ultimate measure struggling colleges should stay focused on. He computes a type of financial ratio for each program, department, or professor, compares them to other institutions, and ranks them in this manner. Some would argue that this calculation misses the subtle "qualitative" performance issues of a professor's

performance, but Bakewell sees his measurement philosophy as a matter of necessity: "When I get called in, they've played all the games and the place is in a financial crisis. They explain why they can't change. They've cut everywhere but their main cost, which is labor." This pragmatic view is inevitably enlightening. Bakewell observes: "Generally, they usually know who isn't productive, but sometimes they are surprised."

2. Paul Strassmann, the guru of chief information officers, computes a "return on management" by dividing "management value added" by the salaries, bonuses, and benefits of management.[6] He computes management value added by subtracting from revenue the costs of purchases, taxes, cost of money, and a few other items he believes to be outside of what management controls. Strassmann argues, that management value added ends up as a number (expressed in dollars per year) that, management policy directly affects. Even if you take issue with precisely what Strassman subtracts to get management value added from revenue, the philosophy is sound: The value of management must show up in the financial performance of the firm.

3. Billy Bean, the manager of the Oakland A's baseball team, decided to throw out traditional measures of performance for baseball players. The most important offensive measure of a player was simply the chance of not getting an out. Likewise, defensive measures were a sort of "out-production." Each of these contributed to the ultimate measure, which was the contribution a player made to the chance of the team winning a game relative to his salary. At a team level, this converts into a simple cost per win. The Oakland A's were spending only $500,000 per win, while some teams were spending over $3 million per win.[5]

In each of these cases, the decision makers probably had to change their thinking about what performance really means. The methods proposed by Bakewell, Strassmann, and Bean probably met resistance from those who want performance to be a more qualitative measure. Detractors would insist that some methods are too simple and leave out too many important factors. But what does performance mean if not a quantifiable contribution to the ultimate goals of the organization? How can performance be high if value contributed relative to cost is low? As we've seen many times already, clarification of what is being measured turns out to be key. So, whatever you mean by "performance," any thorough clarification of its real meaning might guide you to something more like these three examples.

■ ENDNOTES

1. Andrew Oswald, "Happiness and Economic Performance," *Economic Journal* 107 (1997): 1815–1831..
2. James Hammitt, "Valuing Health: Quality-Adjusted Life Years or Willingness to Pay?" *Risk in Perspective,* Harvard Center for Risk Analysis; J. K. Hammitt and J. D. Graham, "Willingness to Pay for Health Protection: Inadequate Sensitivity to Probability?" *Journal of Risk and Uncertainty* 18, no.1 (1999): 33–62.
3. Douglas Hubbard, "Risk vs. Return," *InformationWeek,* June 30, 1997.
4. Douglas Hubbard, "Hurdling Risk," *CIO Magazine,* June 15, 1998.
5. Michael Lewis, *MoneyBall,* (New York: W.W. Norton & Company, 2003).
6. Strassmann, Paul A. "The Business Value of Computers: An Executive Guide," 1990.

## CHAPTER 12

The Ultimate Measurement Instrument: Human Judges

The human mind does have some remarkable advantages over the typical mechanical measurement instrument. It has a unique ability to assess complex and ambiguous situations where other measurement instruments would be useless. Tasks such as recognizing one face or voice in a crowd is a great challenge for software developers (although progress has been made) but trivial for a five-year-old. And we are a very long way from developing an artificial intelligence that can write a critical review of a movie or business plan. In fact, the human mind is a great tool for genuinely objective measurement. Or, rather, it would be if it weren't for a daunting list of common human biases and fallacies.

It's no revelation that the human mind is not a purely rational calculating machine. It is a complex system that seems to comprehend and adapt to its environment with a prosaic array of simplifying rules. Nearly all of these rules prefer simplicity over rationality, and many even contradict each other. Those that are not quite rational but perhaps not a bad rule of thumb are called heuristics. Those that utterly fly in the face of reason are called fallacies.

If we have any hope of using the human mind as a measurement instrument, we need to find a way to exploit its strengths while adjusting for its errors. In the same way that calibration of probabilities can offset the human tendency for overconfidence, there are methods that can offset other types of human judgment errors and biases. These methods work particularly well on any estimation problem where humans are required to make a large number of judgments on similar issues. Examples include estimating costs of new IT projects, the market potential for new products, and employee evaluations. It might be very difficult to consider all the qualitative factors in these measurements without using human judgment, but the humans need a little help.

HOMO ABSURDUS: THE WEIRD REASONS BEHIND OUR DECISIONS

The types of biases mentioned in Chapter 8 are just one broad category of measurement errors. They deal with errors in observations in an attempt to do a random sample or controlled experiment. But if we are attempting to measure a thing by asking a human expert to estimate it, then we have to deal with another category of problems: cognitive biases. We already discussed one such example regarding the issue of statistical overconfidence, but there are more. Some of the more striking biases in human judgment follow.

- *Anchoring.* Anchoring is a cognitive bias that was discussed in Chapter 5 on calibration, but it's worth going into a little further. It turns out that simply thinking of one number affects the value of a subsequent estimate even *on a completely unrelated issue.* In one experiment, Amos Tversky and 2002 Economics Nobel Prize winner Daniel Kahneman asked subjects about the percentage of member nations in the United Nations that were African. One group of subjects was asked whether it was more than 10%, and a second group was asked whether it was more than 65%. Both groups were told that the percentage in the "Is it more than. . .?" question was randomly generated. (In fact, it was not.) Then each group was asked to estimate how much it thought the percentage was. The group that was first asked if it was more than 10% gave an average answer of 25%. The group that was asked if it was more than 65% gave an average answer of 45%. Even though the subjects believed that the percentage in the previous question was randomly selected, the percentage affected their answers. In a later experiment, Kahneman showed that the number subjects anchor on didn't even have to be related to the same topic. He asked subjects to write down the last four digits of their Social Security number and to estimate the number of physicians in New York City. Remarkably, Kahneman found a correlation of 0.4 between the subjects' estimate of the number of physicians and the last four digits of their Social Security number. Although this is a modest correlation, it is much higher than can be attributed to pure chance.

- *Halo/horns effect.* If people first see one attribute that predisposes them to favor or disfavor one alternative, they are more likely to interpret additional subsequent information in a way that supports their conclusion, regardless of what the additional information is. For example, if you initially have a positive impression of a person, you are likely to interpret additional information about that person in a positive light (the halo effect). Likewise, an initially negative impression has the opposite effect (the horns effect). This effect occurs even when the initially perceived positive or negative attribute should be unrelated to subsequent evaluations. An experiment conducted by Robert Kaplan of San Diego State University shows how physical attractiveness causes graders to give essay writers better evaluations on their essays.[1] Subjects were asked to grade an essay written by a student. A photograph of the student was provided with the essay. The grade given for the essay correlated strongly with a subjective attractiveness scale evaluated by other judges. What is interesting is that all the subjects received the exact same essay, and the photograph attached to it was randomly assigned.

- *Bandwagon bias.* If you need something measured, can you just ask a group of people in a room what they think instead of asking them each separately? Additional errors seem to be introduced with that approach. In 1951 a psychologist named Solomon Asch told a group of test subjects (students) that he was giving them an eye exam (see Exhibit 12.1). When asked which line was closest in length to the test line, 99% correctly chose C. But Asch also ran tests where there were several students in the room who were each asked, in turn, to pick the line closest in length. What the test subjects didn't know is that the first few students were part of the experiment and were secretly instructed to choose A, after which the real test subject would pick an answer. When there was one other person in the room who picked the wrong answer, the next person was only 97% likely to choose the right

Test   A   B   C

Subjects were told they were getting an eye exam and asked whether line A, B, or C is the same length as the test line.

EXHIBIT 12.1   **The Asch Conformity Experiment**

answer. When there were two or three persons choosing the wrong answer before the test subject answered, only 87% and 67%, respectively, chose the right answer. When there was a group reward offered if everyone in the group got it right (adding pressure to conform), then *only 53%* of subjects gave the right answer.

- *Emerging preferences.* Once people begin to prefer one alternative, they will actually change their preferences about additional information in a way that supports the earlier decision. This sounds similar to the halo/horns effect, but it involves actually changing one's preferences midcourse in the analysis of a decision in a way that supports a forming opinion. For example, if managers prefer project A over project B and, after they made this choice, you then tell them that project A is less risky but much longer than project B, they are more likely to tell you that they always preferred less risk to faster completion times. But if you told them that B is the less risky and longer option, they are more likely to respond that they always preferred faster completion and realization of benefits to a lower risk.

Fortunately, there is something we can do about every one of these irrational effects on the human ability to estimate. Jay Edward Russo at Cornell is a leading researcher in cognitive bias who is developing some solutions. To alleviate the effect of emerging preferences, for example, Russo proposes a simple form of a blind. He has experts explicitly rank the order of preferences before they begin evaluation of individual alternatives. This prevents them from later claiming "I always preferred this feature to that feature" to support their initial decision.

As with the previously discussed experimental and sampling biases, the first level of protection is acknowledging the problem. Imagine how the effects listed here can change expert estimates on project costs, sales, productivity benefits, and the like. Experts may feel as if their estimate could not be affected by unrelated information, but, then again, people are rarely ever aware of the fact that they are guilty of bias. We each might like to think we are less intellectually malleable than the subjects in these studies, but I find the most gullible people are the ones who insist they are impervious to these effects.

GETTING ORGANIZED: A PERFORMANCE EVALUATION EXAMPLE

You might think that the head of the Information and Decision Sciences Department at the University of Illinois at Chicago (UIC) might come up with a fairly elaborate quantitative method for just about everything. But when Dr. Arkalgud Ramaprasad needed to measure faculty productivity, he came up with an approach that was much more basic than you might suspect. "Previously they had the 'stack of paper' approach," says Dr. Ram (as he prefers to be called). "The advisory committee would sit around a table covered with files on the faculty and discuss their performance." In no particular order, they would discuss the publications, grants awarded, proposals written, professional awards, and the like of each faculty member and rate them on a scale of 1 to 5. Based on this unstructured approach, they were making important determinations on such things as faculty pay raises.

Dr. Ram felt the error being introduced into the evaluation process was, at this point, mostly one of inconsistently presented data. Almost any improvement in simply organizing and presenting the data in an orderly format, he felt, would be a benefit. To improve on this situation, he simply organized all the relevant data on faculty performance and presented it in a large matrix. Each row is a faculty member, and each column is a particular category of professional accomplishments (awards, publications, etc.).

Dr. Ram does not attempt to formalize the analysis of these data any further, and he still uses a 1 to 5 score. Evaluations are based on a consensus of the advisory committee, and this approach simply ensures they are looking at the same data. It seemed too simple. When I suggested that the columns of data could at least be part of some index or scoring scheme, he replied, "When data is presented this way, they see the difference between them and other faculty instead of focusing on the arbitrary codification. There is a discussion about what the points should be, but there is no discussion about the data." Because previously they were looking at different data, there would have been more error in the evaluations.

This is another useful example of a very productive perspective regarding measurement. Some would (and, no doubt, have) shoot down any attempt to measure faculty productivity because the new method would introduce new errors and would not handle a variety of exceptions. Or, at least, that's what they would claim. (It is just as likely that the concerns were entirely about how some would fare poorly if their performance was measured.) But Dr. Ram realizes that whatever the flaws of the new measurement method might be, it is still superior to what they were doing before. It is, by any fair assessment, a reduction in uncertainty and therefore a measurement. As Stevens' taxonomy (Chapter 3) allows, Dr. Ram is at least able to say, with some confidence, that person A has better performance than person B. Given the nature of the decisions this evaluation supports (who gets a promotion or raise), that is all that is needed.

My only objection to this approach is that it probably would not be difficult to use a more analytical technique and improve the evaluation process even further. Dr. Ram has not addressed any of the cognitive biases we discussed; he has only corrected for the potential noise and error of considering inconsistent data on each faculty member. For this reason, I consider the step of "getting organized" to merely be a necessary precursor to the rest of the methods we can consider.

SURPRISINGLY SIMPLE LINEAR MODELS

Another approach exists which is not the most theoretically sound or even the most effective solution, but it is simple. If you have to make estimates for a list of similar items, some kind of weighted score is one way to go. If you are trying to estimate the relative "business opportunity" of, say, a list of real estate investments, you could identify a few major factors you consider important, evaluate these factors for each investment, and combine them somehow into an aggregate score. You might identify factors such as location desirability, cost, market growth for that type of real estate, liens, and so on. You might then weight each factor by multiplying it times some number and adding them all up to get a total value.

While I used to categorically dismiss the value of weighted scores in general as something not better than astrology, subsequent research has convinced me that they may offer some benefit after all. Unfortunately, the methods that seem to have some benefits are not usually the ones businesses typically employ.

According to the decision science researcher and author Jay Edward Russo, the efficacy of weighted scores "depends on what you are doing now. People usually have so far to go that even simple methods are a big improvement." Indeed, even the simplest weighted scores seem to improve on human decision making. Robyn Dawes of the University of Michigan wrote a paper in 1979 titled "The Robust Beauty of Improper Linear Models."[2] Remarkably, he claims: "The weights on these models often don't matter. What you have to know is what to measure, then add."

There are just two clarifications worth making about their claims. First, Dr. Ram's experience with faculty evaluation is consistent with what Russo and Dawes seem to be saying. The previous methods were so riddled with error that organization itself seemed to be a benefit in measurement. Furthermore, when Dawes is talking about a score, he is actually talking about a normalized z-score, not an arbitrary scale. He takes the values for one attribute among all of the evaluated options and creates a normalized distribution for it so that the average is zero and each value is converted to a number of standard deviations above or below the mean (e.g., -1.7, $+.5$, etc.). He might, for example, take all the publication rankings from Dr. Ram's faculty rating table and go through these five steps:

1. For each attribute column in a table of evaluated options, evaluate them on some ordinal or cardinal scale. Note: Cardinal scales with real units (e.g., cost in dollars, duration in months) are preferred when available for the type of problem being considered.

2. Compute the mean for all of the values in each column.

3. Use the Excel population standard deviation formula =stdevp(..) to compute a standard deviation for each column.

4. For each value in a column, compute the z-score as
$$z = (\text{value} - \text{mean})/\text{standard deviation}$$

5. This will result in a score with a mean of 0, a lower bound as low as -2 or -3, and an upper bound as high as $+2$ or $+3$.

The reason this might work is that it takes care of inadvertent weighting. In a scheme where the score is not converted to z-score, you may happen to use a higher range of values for one attribute than another, effectively changing the weight. For example, suppose the real estate investments are evaluated on each factor on an arbitrary scale of 1 to 10. But one criterion, location desirability, varies a lot, and you tend to give out 7s and 8s frequently while on the criterion of market growth, you tend to give very consistent scores around 4 or 5. The net effect is that even if you think market growth is more important, you end up weighting location higher. Dawes' method of converting this to a z-score handles this type of inadvertent-weighting error.

Although this simple method doesn't directly address any of the cognitive biases we listed, the research by Dawes and Russo seems to indicate that there is a benefit to decision making, if only a minimal one. Just thinking about the problem this way seems to cause at least a slight uncertainty reduction and improvement in the decisions. However, for big and risky decisions, where the value of information is very high, we can and should get much more sophisticated than merely getting organized and using a weighted score.

How to Standardize Any Evaluation: Rasch Models

As I surveyed the wide landscape of statistical methods for this book, I made a point of looking outside of areas I've dealt with before. One of the areas that were new to me was the methods used in educational testing, which included some methods almost unheard of in other fields of measurement. It was in this field where I found a book with the inclusive-sounding title *Objective Measurement*. The title might lead you to believe such a book would be a comprehensive treatment of the issues of measurement that might be interesting to any astronomer, chemical engineer, or economist. However, it is only about human performance and education testing. It's as if you saw an old map titled "Map of the World" that was really a map of a single, remote Pacific island, made by people unaware that they were on just one part of a larger planet. One expert in the educational testing field told me about something he called "invariant comparison"—a feature of measurement he considered so basic that it was simply "measurement fundamentals, statistics 101 stuff." Another said, "It is the backbone of what physicists do." All but one of the several physicists and statisticians I asked later about it said they haven't even heard of it. Apparently, what those in the educational measurement field consider "fundamental" to everyone is just fundamental to themselves. To be fair, I'm sure some will think the same of a book claiming it teaches how to measure anything.

There is, actually, something very interesting to be learned from the educational testing area. The experts in this field deal with all the issues of judging the performance of humans—a large category of measurement problems where businesses can find many examples they labeled "immeasurable." The concept of invariant comparison deals with a key problem central to many human performance tests, such as the IQ test. Invariant comparison is a principle that says if one measurement instrument says A is more than B, then another measurement instrument should give the same answer. The comparison of A and B, in other words, does not vary with the type of measurement instrument used. This might seem so obvious to a physicist that it hardly seems worth mentioning. You would think that if one weight scale says A weighs more than B, then another instrument should give the same answer regardless of whether the first instrument is a spring scale and the second is a balance or digital scale. Yet this is exactly what could happen with an IQ test or any other test of human performance. It is possible for one IQ test, having different questions, to give a very different result from another type of IQ test. Therefore, it is possible for Bob to score higher than Sherry on one test and lower on another.

Another version of this problem arises when different human judges have to evaluate a large number of individuals. Perhaps there are too many individuals for each judge to evaluate, so the individuals are divided up among the judges and each person may get a different set of judges. Perhaps one judge evaluates only one aspect of a subject while evaluating different aspects of another person, or different people have to be evaluated on problems with different levels of difficulty. For example, suppose you wanted to evaluate the proficiency of project managers based on their performance when assigned to various projects. If you have a large number of project managers, you probably have to have more than one judge of their performance. The judges, in fact, might be the project managers' immediate superiors, (as others are not familiar with the project). The assigned projects, also, probably vary greatly in difficulty. But now suppose all project managers, regardless of their project or who they reported to, had to compete for the same limited pool of promotions or bonuses. Those assigned to a "hard grader" or a difficult project would be at a disadvantage that had nothing to do with their performance. The comparison of different project managers would not be invariant (i.e., independent) of who judged them or the conditions they were judged on. In fact, the overriding determinant of their relative standing among project managers may be related entirely to factors they did not control.

In 1961 a statistician named Georg Rasch developed a solution to this problem.[3] He proposed a method for predicting the chance that a subject would correctly answer a true/false question based on (1) the percentage of other subjects in the population who answered that particular item correctly and (2) the percentage of other questions that the subject answered correctly. Even if test subjects were taking different tests, the performance on a test by a subject who never took it could be predicted with a computable error.

First, Rasch computed the chance that a randomly selected person from the population of test subjects would answer a question correctly. This is simply the percentage of people who answered correctly from those who were given the opportunity to answer the question. This is called the "item difficulty." Rasch then computed the "log-odds" for that probability. Log-odds are simply the natural logarithm of the ratio of the chance of getting the answer right to the chance of getting it wrong. If the item difficulty was 65%, that meant that 35% of people got the answer right and 65% got it wrong. The ratio of getting it right to getting it wrong is .548, and the natural log of this is −0.619. If you like you can write the Excel formula as:

$$= ln(A1/(1 - A1))$$

where A1 is the chance of getting it right. Rasch then did the same with the chance of that person getting any question right. Since this particular person was getting 82% of the answers right, the subject's log-odds would be ln(.82/.18), or 1.52. Finally, Rasch added these two log-odds together, giving −.619 + 1.52 = .9. To convert this back to a probability, you can write a formula in Excel as:

$$=1/(1/\exp(.9) + 1)$$

The calculation produces a value of 71%. This means that this subject has a 71% chance of answering that question correctly, given the difficulty of the question and the subject's performance on other questions. Over a large number of questions and/or a large number of test subjects, we would find that when the subject/item chance of being correct is 70%, about 70% of those people got that item correct. Likewise for 90%, 80%, and so on. In a way, Rasch models are just another form of calibration of probabilities.

Mary Lunz of Measurement Research Associates, Inc. in Chicago applied Rasch models to an important public health issue for the American Society of Clinical Pathology. Their previous pathologist certification process had a large amount of error, and they needed to reduce it. Each candidate is assigned one or more cases, and one or more judges evaluates each of their case responses. It is not practical to have each judge evaluate every case, nor can cases be guaranteed to be of equal difficulty. Previously, the best predictor of who was given certification was simply the judge and the cases the candidates were assigned to, not, as we might hope, the proficiency of the candidate. In other words, lenient examiners were very likely to pass incompetent candidates. Lunz computed standard Rasch scores for each judge, case, and candidate for each skill category. Using this approach, it was possible to predict whether a candidate would have passed with an average judge with an average case even if the candidate had a lenient judge and an easy case (or a hard judge and a hard case). Now variance due to judges or case difficulty can be completely removed from consideration in the certification process. None too soon for the general public, I'm sure.

MEASURING READING WITH RASCH

A fascinating application of Rasch statistics is measuring the difficulty of reading text. Jack Stenner, PhD, is president and founder of MetaMetrics, Inc. and used Rasch models to develop the Lexile Framework for assessing reading and writing difficulty and proficiency. This framework integrates the measurement of reading, writing, over tests, texts, and students, making universal comparisons in common languages possible in these areas for the first time. With a staff of 65, MetaMetrics has done more in this area than perhaps any other institution, public or private, including:

- All major reading tests report measures in Lexiles. About 20 million U.S. students have reading ability measures in Lexiles.

- The reading difficulty of about 100,000 books and tens of millions of magazine articles is measured in Lexiles.
- The reading curricula of several textbook publishers are structured in Lexiles.
- State and local education institutions are adopting Lexiles rapidly.

A text of 100 Lexiles is first grade, while 1700 Lexile text is found in Supreme Court decisions, scientific journals, and the like. MetaMetrics can predict that a 600 Lexile reader will have a average 75% comprehension of a 600 Lexile text.

REMOVING HUMAN INCONSISTENCY: THE LENS MODEL

In the 1950s a decision psychology researcher named Egon Brunswik wanted to measure expert decisions statistically.[4] Most of his colleagues were interested in the hidden decision-making process that experts went through. Brunswik was more interested in describing the decisions they actually made. He said of decision psychologists: "We should be less like geologists and more like cartographers." In other words, they should simply map what can be observed externally and should not be concerned with what he considered hidden internal processes. With this end in mind, Brunswik began to run experiments where experts would make an estimate of something (say, the admission of a graduate school applicant or the status of a cancerous tumor) based on some data provided to the expert. Brunswik would then take a large number of these expert assessments and find a best-fit regression model. (This is done easily now using the regression tool in Excel, as shown in Chapter 9.) The result he would find would be a formula with a set of implicit weights used by the decision maker, consciously or unconsciously, to determine what the estimate should be.

Amazingly, he also found that the formula, while simply based on expert judgments and no objective historical data, was better than the expert at making these judgments. For example, the formula would predict better

Student ratings of teaching effectiveness
Cancer patient life expectancy
Failures of IT investments
Psychology course grades
Graduate students grades
Changes in stock prices
IQ scores using Rorschach tests
Mental illness using personality tests
Business failures using financial ratios
Life-insurance sales-rep performance

0%   10%   20%   30%

% Reduction in the Judgment Errors of Experts

EXHIBIT I2.2   **Effect of Lens Model on Improving Various Types of Decision**

than the expert who would do well in graduate school or which tumor was malignant. This became known as the Lens Model.

The Lens Model has been applied in a wide variety of situations including medical prognosis, aircraft identification by naval radar operators, and the chance of business failure based on financial ratios. In each case the model was just as good as human experts and in most cases it was a significant improvement. (See Exhibit 12.2.)

The Lens Model does this by removing the error of judge inconsistency from the evaluations. The evaluations of experts usually vary even in identical situations. The linear model of the expert's evaluation, however, gives perfectly consistent valuations.

Furthermore, since the Lens Model is a mathematical expression based on known data inputs, it can be automated and applied to much larger data sets that would be entirely impractical for human judges to assess one by one.

The seven-step process is simple enough. I've modified it somewhat from Brunswik's original approach to account for some other methods (e.g., calibration of probabilities) we've learned about since Brunswik first developed this approach. (See Exhibit 12.3.)

1. Identify the experts who will participate.

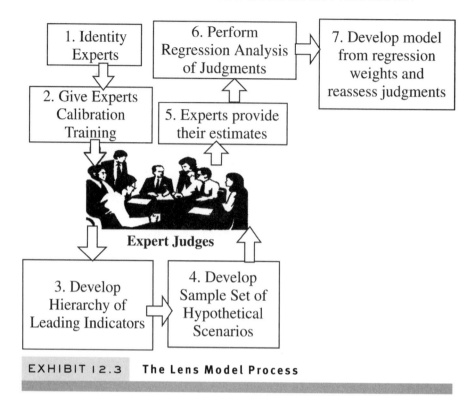

EXHIBIT 12.3   The Lens Model Process

2. If they will be assessing a probability or range, calibrate them.

3. Ask them to identify a list of factors relevant to the particular item they will be estimating (e.g., the duration of a software project affects the risk of failure or the income of a loan applicant affects the chance he will repay), but keep it down to 10 or less.

4. Generate a set of scenarios using a combination of values for each of the factors just identified—they can be based on real examples or purely hypothetical. Make 30 to 50 scenarios for each of the judges you are surveying.

5. Ask the experts to provide the relevant estimate for each scenario described.

6. Perform a regression analysis as described in chapter 9. The independent "X" variables are those given to the judges for consideration. The dependent "Y" variable is the estimate the judge was asked to produce.

7. For each of the columns of data in your scenarios, there will be a coefficient displayed in the output table created by Excel. Pair up each variable with its coefficient, multiply them, and then add them up all the results for each of the coefficient/variable pairs. This is the quantity you are trying to estimate.

This process will produce a table with a series of weights for each of the variables in our model. Since the model has no inconsistency whatsoever, we know that at least some error has been reduced.

We can quickly estimate how much less uncertainty we have with this model by estimating the inconsistency of judges. We can estimate inconsistency by using some duplicate scenarios unknown to the judges. In other words, the seventh scenario in the list may be identical to the twenty-ninth scenario in the list. After looking at a couple of dozen scenarios, the experts will forget that they already answered the same situation and often will give a slightly different answer. Thoughtful experts are fairly consistent in their evaluation of scenarios. Still, inconsistency accounts for 10% to 20% of the error in most expert estimates. This error is completely removed by the Lens Method.

Robyn Dawes, the proponent of simple, nonoptimized linear models, agrees that Brunswik shows a significant improvement over unaided human judgment but argues that it might not be due to the "optimization" of weights from regression. In published research of four examples, Dawes showed that the Lens Model is only a slight improvement on what he has called "improper" models, where weights are not derived from regression but are all equal or, remarkably, *randomly* assigned.[5]

Dawes concluded that this is the case because, perhaps, the value of experts is simply in identifying factors and whether each factor is "good" or "bad" (affecting whether they would be positive or negative weights) and that the exact magnitude of the weights do not have to be optimized with regression.

Dawes's examples may not be representative of Lens Models applied to estimating problems in business,[6] but his findings are still useful. First, Dawes's own data do show some advantage for optimal linear models over improper models, even if it is only slight. Second, his findings give even further support to the conclusion that some consistent Model—with or without optimized weights—is better than human judgment alone. Still, I find the effort to create optimal models, especially for really big decisions, is easily justified by an even slight improvement over simpler models.

But I find we can often do better than even "optimal" linear models. The regression models I use for business tend to have a few conditional rules, such as "The duration of a project is a differentiating factor only if it is more than a year—all projects less than a year are equally risky." In that sense, the models are not strictly linear, but they get much better correlations than purely linear Lens Models. All of the studies Dawes refers to in his original paper are strictly linear and generally lower correlations than I get with nonlinear models.

I find these conditional rules from two sources, the experts' explicit statements and the patterns in their responses. For example, if an expert evaluating the chance the scope of a software project will be significantly expanded tells me that she doesn't make any distinction among projects less than 12 months long, then I won't just use the original "project duration" as a variable. Instead, I might change the variable so that any value less than 12 months is a 1, 13 months is a 2, 14 a 3, and so on. Or, even if the expert didn't tell me that, it might be apparent by looking at her judgments. Suppose we plotted the expert's judgments on "chance of change in requirements" (something significant, say, more than a 25% increase in effort) as a function of "project duration in months," and we saw the chart shown in Exhibit 12.4.

EXHIBIT 12.4   A Non-linear Example of a Lens Model Variable

If you see something other than a straight line in these data, you would not be alone. A project that takes longer than one year introduces a different set of factors. Perhaps some of the variables matter to the expert more or less depending on the length of the project. A Lens Model that allows for such nonlinear conditions not only fits the expert's opinions better; more important, it can fit actual project outcomes better.

I also sometimes find that a variable is a better fit if I use even more elaborate rules. Perhaps the correlation with a variable is best with the variables' logarithm, its inverse or by making part of a product of other variables. Experimentation is encouraged. I generally try several versions of nonlinear variables on the same data, and I usually find one version that stands out as a clear winner.

It turns out that you can use weighted decision models at many different levels of complexity. If you feel confident in experimenting with nonlinear methods, that's your best shot. If you can't do that but can handle linear regression, do that. If you don't feel comfortable using regression at all, then stick with Dawes's equally weighted z-scores. Each method is an improvement on the simpler method, and all improve on unaided experts.

PANACEA OR PLACEBO?: QUESTIONABLE METHODS OF MEASUREMENT

THE BIG MEASUREMENT "DON'T"

Above all else, don't use a method that *adds* more error to the initial estimate.

Some readers might think that, so far, my approach has been to lower the bar for what counts as measurement so much that this change in standards alone makes everything "measurable." I've stated, after all, that in order to count as a measurement, any reduction in uncertainty would suffice. The existence of all sorts of errors in an observation is not an obstacle to measurement as long as the uncertainty is less than it was before. Even methods that analyze what would normally be thought of as "subjective" still count as measurement (e.g., Rasch and Lens models) if there is overwhelming evidence that such methods really do result in more accurate estimates. But there are methods that, even under these apparently relaxed constraints, I do not count as proper measurements. At this point, it is time to offer a few caveats and to judiciously apply some brakes as we speed off into several new measurement methods.

The "uncertainty reduction" definition of measurement we have been using definitely makes measurement more feasible on just about everything (since we don't have to worry now about exactitudes). But that definition is also a hard constraint. If a method doesn't actually result in reduced uncertainty or, worse yet, *adds* uncertainty to a quantity, then it does not suffice as a measurement and has absolutely no economic value to a decision maker. In the spirit of some perhaps overdue measurement skepticism, we should discuss two common measurement methods: the typical cost/benefit analysis and the subjective weighted score.

As I began writing this book, I put out a general solicitation to a large number of my contacts for interesting measurement solutions I could use as case studies. I said I was looking for "interesting examples of difficult or impossible-sounding measurement problems which had clever solutions and, preferably, surprising results that had changed a major decision." There was no shortage of ideas, and I conducted many more phone interviews for case studies than what I eventually included in this book. I did notice, however, that many analysts, consultants, and businesspeople seemed to equate "measure" with "business case." They didn't provide examples of resourceful uses of observations to reduce uncertainty about an unknown quantity. Instead, they were explaining how they made a business-case justification for a pet project.

To be fair, I believe the cost/benefit analysis (CBA) certainly does count as the type of decomposition mentioned in Chapter 8, and it may, by itself, reduce uncertainty without further measurement. Just as Fermi did with his questions, a business case breaks the problem down and, without technically being a measurement based on new observations, reveals something about what you already knew. But I also pointed out that in the cases I've assessed in the last decade, decomposition alone was sufficient to reduce uncertainty in only 25% of the high-information-value variables. In most cases where an effort was justified to reduce uncertainty, some empirical observation still was necessary.

In contrast, the examples of measurements so many businesses seem to produce are *only* the decomposition types (i.e., the business case) without any attempt at empirical methods. Every variable was simply the initial estimate—either from a single expert or agreed to by "committee"—and was always a point value with no range to express any uncertainty about the variable. No survey, experiment, or even methods to improve subjective judgments were ever applied or even considered. The same people who enthusiastically submitted a business case as an example of measurement could not, no matter how much I pressed them, think of a single quantity in their CBA that was arrived at after some kind of real-world observation.

A very different behavior occurs when the task is to generate exact values for a business case, especially one where the estimator has a stake in the outcome, as opposed to a calibrated estimator providing an initial 90% confidence interval (CI). Sitting in a room, one or more people working on the business case will play a game with each estimate. Forced to choose exact values, no matter how uncertain or arbitrary, the estimators ask: "How much should this value be to be agreeable to others and still be sufficient to prove my (predetermined) point?" It is almost as if the terms "consensus" and "fact" are used as synonyms. The previously discussed Asch experiment on the bandwagon bias is only one problem with this approach.

A different and disturbing trend in management decision making is to develop a type of weighted score where the score and the weight are both subjective scales with arbitrary point values, not z-scores like those Dawes used. Like the simple linear models discussed previously, these methods might ask a project portfolio manager to rate a proposed project in categories such as "strategic alignment," "organizational risk," and so on.

Most of these methods have between 4 and 12 categories of evaluation, but some have over 100. The proposed project is typically given a score of, say, 1 to 5 in each of these categories. The scores in each category are then multiplied by a weighting factor —perhaps also a scale of 1 to 5—which is meant to account for the relative importance of each of the scores categorized. The weighting factors are usually standardized for a given company so that all projects are evaluated by comparable criteria. The adjusted scores are then totaled to give an overall score for the proposed project.

Scores are methods of attempting to express relative worth, preference, and so on, without employing a real unit of measure. Although scoring is fairly called one type of ordinal measurement system we discussed in Chapter 3, I've always considered an arbitrary score to be a sort of measurement wannabe. It introduces additional errors for four reasons.

1. Scores are often used for situations where proper quantitative measures are feasible and would be much more enlightening (e.g., converting a perfectly good return on investment (ROI) to a score or computing risk as a score instead of treating it like an actuary or financial analyst would).

2. Scores add their own type of error to the evaluation process since the relative value of different scores is ambiguous and/or inconsistent. Consider the number of stars a movie critic might give to a movie or a restaurant critic might give to a restaurant (the first is often a four-star scale, the latter a five-star scale). In that situation, two stars aren't exactly twice as good as one star, and four one-star movies does not equate to seeing one four-star movie.

3. Scores can be revealing if they are part of a survey of a large group (e.g., customer satisfaction surveys), but they are much less enlightening when individuals use them to "evaluate" options, strategies, investments, and the like. People are rarely surprised in some way by a set of scores they applied themselves.

4. Scores are merely ordinal but many users add error when they treat these ordinal scores as a real quantity. As previously explained, a higher ordinal score means "more" but doesn't say how much more. Multiplying and adding ordinal scores to other ordinal scores has consequences users are often not fully aware of. Therefore, the method is likely to have unintended consequences.

It's worth getting a little deeper into how this scoring is different from the z-scores Robyn Dawes used and the weights generated from the Lens Model. First, Dawes' "improper" linear models and Brunswik's optimized Lens Models use objective unit-of-measure inputs, such as "project duration in months" for an IT project or "grade point average" for a graduate-school applicant. None of the inputs was an arbitrary scale of 1 to 5 set by the experts. Second, the weights Dawes and Brunswik used were also not arbitrary point scales. The psychology of how people use such scales is more complicated than it looks. When experts select weights on a scale of 1 to 5, it's not necessarily clear they interpret a 4 to mean twice as important as a 2. The 5-point scale (or 7-point or whatever) adds additional error to the process because of these ambiguities.

The only positive observation we can make about arbitrarily weighted point-scale systems is that apparently managers often have the sense to ignore the results. I found that decision makers were overriding the results from weighted scoring models so often that there was apparently no evidence that the scores even *changed decisions*, much less improved decisions. This is strange since, in many cases, the managers spent quite a lot of time and effort developing and applying their scoring method.

One of these methods is sometimes used in IT and is misleadingly referred to as Information Economics.[7] It is represented as objective, structured, and formal, but, in fact, the method is not based on any kind of accepted economic model and cannot truly be called economics at all. Upon closer examination, the name turns out to be entirely a misnomer. The method is more accurately called subjective and unadjusted weighted scores for IT.

The total score this method produces for a proposed IT system has no meaning in financial terms. The definitions of the different scores in a category and the weight of a category are not tied to any scientific approach, either theoretical or empirical. The method is actually nothing more than another entirely subjective evaluation process without the error-correcting methods of Rasch and Lens models. Many users of IT weighted scores claim they see a benefit, but there is no demonstrated measurable value to this process.

Curiously, the "Information Economics" method takes useful and financially meaningful quantities, such as an ROI, and converts it to a score. The conversion goes like this: An ROI of 0 or less is a score of 0, 1% to 299% is a score of 1, 300% to 499% is a 2, and so on. In other words, a modest ROI of 5% gets the same score as an ROI of 200%. In more quantitative portfolio prioritization methods, such a difference would put a huge distance between the priorities of two projects. The user of this approach began with a meaningful and significant differentiation between two projects; now they are both a "1" in the ROI category. This has the net effect of "destroying" information.

A report by IT management author Barbara McNurlin agrees with this assessment. McNurlin analyzed 25 different benefit estimation techniques, including various weighted scoring methods.[8] She characterizes those methods, none of which she considers as based in theory, as "useless."

Paul Gray, a book reviewer for the *Journal of Information Systems Management*, may have summed it up best. In his review of a book titled *Information Economics: Linking Business Performance to Information Technology*, one of the definitive books about the "Information Economics" method, Gray wrote: "Don't be put off by the word 'economics' in the title: the only textbook economics discussed is in an appendix on cost curves."[9] Meant as an accolade, Gray's words also sum up the key weakness of the approach: This version of information economics contains no actual economics.

Another popular version of arbitrary weighted scores is called the Analytic Hierarchy Process (AHP). AHP is different from other weighted scores in two ways. First, it is based on a series of pair-wise comparisons instead of directly scored attributes. That is, the experts are asked if one attribute is "strongly preferred," "slightly preferred," and so on over another attribute, and different choices are compared within the same attribute in the same manner. For example, subjects would be asked if they preferred the "strategic benefits" of new product A over new product B. They would then be asked if they preferred the "development risk" of A over B. They would also be asked if "strategic benefit" was more important than "development risk." They would continue comparing every possible choice within each attribute, then every attribute to each other. Pair-wise comparisons avoid the issue of developing arbitrary scoring scales, so that could be an advantage to this method. However, strangely enough, the data on the comparisons is converted by AHP to an arbitrary score.

The second difference between AHP and other arbitrary weighted scoring methods is that a "consistency coefficient" is computed. This is a method for determining how internally consistent the answers are. For example, if you prefer strategic benefit to low development risk and prefer low development risk to exploiting existing distribution channels, then you should not prefer exploiting existing distribution channels to strategic benefit. If this sort of circularly inconsistent result happens a lot, then the consistency calculation will have a low value. A perfectly consistent set of answers earns a consistency value of 1.

The consistency calculation is based on a method from matrix algebra called Eigenvalues, used to solve a variety of mathematical problems.

Because AHP utilizes this method, it is often called "theoretically sound" or "mathematically proven." If the criteria for theoretical soundness were simply, at some point in a procedure, using a mathematical tool (even one as powerful as Eigenvalues), then proving a new theory or procedure would be much easier than it actually is. Someone could find a way to use Eigenvalues in astrology or differential equations in palm readings. In neither case will the method become more valid merely because a mathematical method that is proven in another context has been applied.

The fact is that AHP is simply another weighted scoring method that has the one noise-reducing method for recognizing inconsistent answers. But that hardly makes the outputs "proven," as is often claimed. The problem is that comparing attributes like strategic alignment and development risk is usually meaningless. If I asked you whether you prefer a new car or money, you should ask me, first, what kind of car and how much money I'm talking about. If the car was a 15-year-old subcompact and the money was $1 million, you would obviously give a different answer than if the car was a new Rolls-Royce and the money was $100. Yet, I've witnessed that when groups of people engage in this process with an AHP tool, no one stops to ask "How much development risk versus how much manufacturing costs are we talking about?" Amazingly, they simply answer as if the comparison were clearly defined. Doing this introduces the danger that they simply imagine a completely different trade-off from someone else. It merely adds another unnecessary level of noise.

A final, particularly bizarre flaw in AHP is rank reversal.[10] Suppose you used AHP to rank alternatives A, B, and C in that order, A being the most preferred. Suppose then that you delete C; should it change the rank of A and B so that A is second best and B is best? As nonsensical as that is, AHP can result in exactly that.

There is one "showstopper" criterion for whether cost/benefit analyses or various weighted scores could count as a measurement: The result has to be an improvement on your previous state of knowledge. If the method adds more error than you had before, then it's not a measurement. If it is held up as a "formal, structured" method but has no scientific evidence of reducing error and improving decisions, then it's not a measurement. In some cases, organizations spent more time and effort on faux measurements than they would have spent on methods that are proven to reduce uncertainty. So, why even consider anything short of real uncertainty reduction?

COMPARING THE METHODS

Human judgment is not a bad measurement instrument after all. If you have a large number of similar, recurring decisions, Rasch and Lens models can definitely reduce uncertainty by removing certain types of errors from human judgment. Even Dawes' simple z-score seems to be a slight improvement on human judgment.

As a benchmark for comparison, it is worth introducing another approach that appears to improve on all of these methods: the objective, optimized, linear model. Unlike the other methods discussed in this chapter, it does not depend on human judgment in any way and, consequently, typically performs much better. Usually we'd prefer to use this sort of method, but in many cases where we need to quantify "immeasurables," these detailed, objective, historical data are harder to come by. Hence the need for the other methods like Lens, Rasch, and so on.

In Chapter 9 we discussed how to perform regression analysis to isolate and measure the effects of multiple variables. If we have lots of historical data on a particular recurring problem, complete documentation on each of the factors, and the factors are based on objective measures (not subjective scales), *and* we have recorded the actual results, then we can create an "objective" linear model.

While the Lens Model correlates input variables to expert estimates, the objective model correlates input variables to actual historical results. On each of the Lens Model studies mentioned in Exhibit 12.2, a regression model also was completed on historical data. The study shown about cancer patient life expectancy, for example, involved giving the doctors medical chart data on cancer patients and then building a Lens Model on their estimates for life expectancy. The study also kept track of *actual* life expectancy by continuing to track the patients. While the Lens Model of the physicians' prognoses had just 2% less error than human judges, the objective model had fully 12% less error. For all the studies listed in the exhibit, the Lens Model had on average 5% less error than a human estimator of a measurement, while objective linear models had on average 30% less error than the human experts. Of course, even objective linear models are not the ultimate answer. More elaborate decomposition of the problem, as we discussed in previous chapters, usually can reduce uncertainty even further. If we were to arrange these methods on a spectrum ranging from unaided and

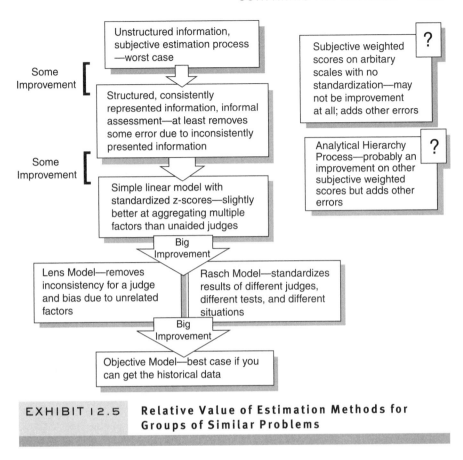

EXHIBIT 12.5   Relative Value of Estimation Methods for
Groups of Similar Problems

unorganized human intuition to the objective linear model, it would look something like Exhibit 12.5.

No matter their shortcomings, these estimation methods are consistently a significant improvement on the estimates of unaided humans. Methods such as Rasch and Lens models help to remove some startling errors from human judgment and make it possible to turn the human expert into a very flexible, calibrated, and powerful instrument of measurement. For many researchers in the decision sciences, debating the effectiveness of these methods is beating a dead horse. Paul Meehl, professor of psychology at the University of Minnesota, summarized it best:

> There is no controversy in social science which shows such a large body
> of qualitatively diverse studies coming out so uniformly in the same

direction as this one. When you're pushing 90 investigations [now closer to 150], predicting everything from the outcome of football games to the diagnosis of liver disease and when you can hardly come up with a half dozen studies showing even a weak tendency in favor of the [human expert], it is time to draw a practical conclusion.[11]

ENDNOTES

1. Robert Kaplan, "Is Beauty Talent? Sex Interaction in the Attractiveness Halo Effect," Paper presented at the Annual Meeting of the Western Psychological Association, Los Angeles, California, April 8–11, 1976.
2. Robyn M. Dawes, "The Robust Beauty of Improper Linear Models in Decision Making," *American Psychologist* 34 (1979): 571–582.
3. G. Rasch, "On General Laws and the Meaning of Measurement in Psychology," *Proceedings of the Fourth Berkeley Symposium on Mathematical Statistics and Probability* (Berkeley: University of California Press, 1980), pp. 321–334.
4. Egon Brunswik, "Representative Design and Probabilistic Theory in a Functional Psychology," *Psychological Review* 62 (1955):193–217.
5. Robyn M. Dawes and Bernard Corrigan, "Linear Models in Decision Making" *Psychological Bulletin* 81, no. 2 (1974): 93–106.
6. In at least one of the four examples, the "experts" were students. In two of the remaining examples, the experts were predicting the opinions of other experts (clinical psychologists predicting diagnoses by other clinicians and faculty predicting the evaluations given by the admissions committee). Also, most of the experts I model appear to be at least slightly better at predicting outcomes than the experts Dawes's research discusses.
7. M. Parker, R. Benson, and H. E. Trainor, *Information Economics: Linking Business Performance to Information Technology* (Englewood Cliffs, NJ: Prentice-Hall, 1988).
8. Barbara McNurlin *Uncovering the Information Technology Payoff*, United Communications Group, Rockville, MD, 1992.
9. Paul Gray, book review of *Information Economics: Linking Business Performance to Information Technology, Journal of Information Systems Management* (Fall 1989).
10. A. Stam and A. Silva, "Stochastic Judgments in the AHP: The Measurement of Rank Reversal Probabilities," *Decision Sciences Journal* 28, no. 3 (Summer 1997).
11. P. E. Meehl, *Clinical versus Statistical Prediction* (Minneapolis: University of Minnesota Press, 1954), pp. 372–373.

## CHAPTER 13

New Measurement Instruments for Management

I wonder what minds like Eratosthenes, Enrico, and Emily might have been able to measure if they only had used some of the measurement instruments mentioned in this book. No doubt, a lot. But, unfortunately, these instruments are not nearly as widely utilized as they could be, and big, risky decisions have probably suffered because of it.

Again, when I talk about measurement instruments, I'm not just talking about tabletop devices used in some scientific observation. I'm talking about things you are already aware of but may not have thought of as types of measurement instruments. This includes some new wireless devices and even the entire Internet.

THE TWENTY-FIRST-CENTURY TRACKER: KEEPING TABS WITH TECHNOLOGY

One of the methods of observation we discussed was using instrumentation to track a phenomenon that, up until that point, was not being tracked. By inserting something into the phenomenon itself, you make it easier to observe. To measure the motion of the upper atmosphere, my father, as an employee of the National Weather Service, would release balloons into the wind carrying a radio transponder and basic meteorological measurement devices. In the fish population example we discussed, the much simpler tag is introduced into the fish population so that its size could be measured with the release and re-catch method. If something is difficult to observe as it is, there are multiple ways to insert tags, probes, or tracers into the process.

It's not just what the instruments do, but their cost that creates so many possibilities. The simple Radio Frequency ID (RFID), for example, has revolutionized the measurement of certain activities in business but could be used on so much more. The RFID is a small strip of material that reflects a radio signal and sends a unique identifier along in the reflected radio signal. RFIDs currently are produced for just 10 to 20 cents each and are used mostly for inventory tracking.

When I asked the renowned physicist and author Freeman Dyson what he thought to be the most important, most clever, and most inspiring measurement, he responded without hesitation, "GPS [Global Positioning System] is the most spectacular example. It has changed everything." Actually, I was expecting a different kind of response, perhaps something from his days in operations research for the Royal Air Force during World War II, but GPS made sense as both a truly revolutionary measurement instrument as well as a measurement in its own right. GPS is economically available for just about anyone and comes with a variety of software support tools and services. Yet many people may not think of GPS when they think of a new measurement instrument for business, partly because GPS is already so ubiquitous. But when a mind like Dyson's believes it's the most spectacular example of a measurement, we should listen.

Most vehicle-based industries benefit from the measurement capabilities GPS technology provides. One firm that is helping transportation companies to fully exploit GPS is GPS Insight, based in Scottsdale, Arizona. GPSI provides vehicle-mounted GPS units on a wireless network that can be accessed through the company's Web site. GPSI overlays the locations of the vehicles against maps and data accessible with Google Earth. As anyone familiar with Google Earth knows, it takes satellite photos of Earth, as well as information about roads, businesses, and countless other custom Geographic Information System (GIS) data layers, and patches them together in software. Anyone can download Google Earth for free and see satellite images of their neighborhood or anywhere else they want to look.

The images on Google Earth are not real time and are sometimes over two years old; however, the road and other data are usually more current. (The image of my neighborhood used to show a construction project that has been completed over two years earlier.) And some areas are not as well covered as others. In many locations you can easily make out cars but in my tiny boyhood hometown of Yale, South Dakota, the resolution is so low that you can barely make out any of the roads in the picture. No doubt coverage, resolution, and timeliness of the images will improve over time.

Third-party high-quality aerial photographs are available on the Internet, however, and GPS Insight typically provides them for customers by adding them to Google Earth as an overlay. The cost is trivial, ranging between $1 and $10 per square mile.

A clever person could use each of these tools as a measurement instrument in its own right. But by combining GPS, wireless networks, Internet access, and Google Earth, GPS Insight is able to produce detailed reports of vehicle locations, driver activities, and driving habits that were not previously practical to track. These reports succinctly show trip times, stop times, as well as their averages and variances, which help to determine where to "drill down." By drilling down, exact locations, times, and activity can be determined, such as a two-hour stop at a building at 43rd and Central. By turning on "bars and restaurants" in Google Earth, even the exact restaurant may be determined.

Other types of reports quantify who is speeding, how long various vehicles are used throughout the day versus payroll hours, when vehicles are used outside of normal business hours, whether the prescribed route is taken, and how many miles/hours are spent driving in each state, for simplified fuel tax reporting purposes. Because this tool reduces uncertainty on many quantities in an economical fashion, it qualifies as a very useful measurement instrument.

Another clever use of technology is in the field of measuring human interactions and relationships in business. George Eberstadt is a cofounder of nTAG, a company that developed a name tag that can track who is interacting with whom. Weighing under 5 ounces, the tags use peer-to-peer radio technology to identify each other as their wearers come within talking distance. For attendance tracking at a speaking session, the nTAG system uses an infrared strobe to "ping" everyone in a room. The tags track who is talking to whom and for how long. The data are transmitted wirelessly to a network of radio access points, then to a central database.

The name-tag approach addresses a key issue of acceptance. Eberstadt says, "While most people don't like to wear electronic tracking devices, the name tag is the credential. We get 100% acceptance rates." He calls it a type of "reciprocity device"—a device you are willing to use because of the benefits to you. "People are willing to give up information about themselves if you give them value in return."

If you wanted to measure the "level of communication" in different venues, these data would probably be revealing. If you are running a conference and notice that several groups interact a lot within themselves but not much with others, you might find ways to facilitate better communication. nTAG has focused primarily on the conference industry but has plans for broader use in mind. Eberstadt says, "People usually think of networking, education, and motivation as the key goals of any meeting. If you want to measure the value of the meeting, you have to measure those goals." nTAGs tracks who talks to whom and for how long so the company can measure how well an event meets networking goals.

If Eratosthenes could measure the circumference of Earth by looking at shadows, I wonder what sorts of economic, political, and behavioral phenomenon he could measure with Web-based GPS. If Enrico Fermi could measure the yield of an atom bomb with a handful of confetti, I wonder what he could have done with a handful of RFID chips. If Emily could debunk therapeutic touch with a simple experiment with a cardboard screen, I wonder what she can measure now with a slightly bigger budget and a few new tools.

MEASURING THE WORLD: THE INTERNET AS AN INSTRUMENT

The author William Gibson wrote several novels in a genre of science fiction for which he can take large credit for creating. He coined the term "cyberspace" as a future version of the Internet where users did not just use a keyboard and mouse but, instead, "jacked in" and entered a virtual reality. Some of the characters specialized in flying around a type of data landscape looking for patterns, trying to identify such things as market inefficiencies that might allow them to turn a quick buck.

As science fiction writers often are, Gibson was unrealistic in some respects. While it sounds like fun, I personally see limited research value in flying over data landscapes in cyberspace. I think I get more useful data faster by using good old-fashioned Google and Yahoo on a monitor. But the idea of Gibson's cyberspace being not just a repository of data but a kind of real-time pulse of everything that goes on in the whole planet is not far from reality. We really do have an instantly accessible vast landscape of data. Even without flying over it in virtual reality, we can see patterns that can affect important decisions.

There is nothing novel in touting the wondrous possibilities of the Internet—nothing could be more cliché. But a particular use of the Internet seems to be underexploited. The Internet itself may be the most important new instrument of measurement most of us will see in our lifetimes. It is simple enough to use the Internet with some search engines to dig up research on something you are trying to measure. But there are several other implications for the Internet as a measurement instrument, and it is quickly becoming the answer to the question of how to measure anything.

A couple of general emerging technologies on the Web need to be pointed out. One is a method for collecting data from the Internet itself, and the other is using the Internet to collect data from others.

There is quite a lot of information on the Internet, and it changes fast. If you use a standard search engine, you get a list of Web sites, but that's it. Suppose, instead, you need to measure the number of times your firm's name comes up in certain news sites or the blog traffic about a new product. You might even need to use this information in concert with other specific data reported in structured formats on other sites, such as economic data from government agencies.

Internet "screen-scrapers" are a way to gather all this information on a regular basis without hiring a 24×7 staff of interns to do it. Todd Wilson, president and founder of www.screen-scraper.com says, "There are certain sites that change every three or four seconds. Our tool is very good at watching changes over time on the Web." You could use a screen-scraper to track used-market versions of your product on www.ebay.com, correlate your store's sales in different cities to the local weather, or even check the number of hits on your firm's name on various search engines hour by hour (although if you simply want to be alerted to new entries and aren't concerned with building a database, try signing up for "Google Alerts").

As a search on the Internet will reveal, several "mashups" exist where data are pulled from multiple sources and presented in a way that provides new insight. A common angle with mashups now is to plot information about business, real estate, traffic, and so on against a map site like MapQuest or Google Earth. I've found a mashup of Google Earth and real estate data on www.housingmaps.com that allows you to see recently sold home prices on a map. Another mashup on www.socaltech.com shows a map that plots locations of businesses that recently received venture capital. At first glance, you might think these sites are just for looking to buy a house or find a job with a new company. But how about research for a construction business or forecasting business growth in a new industry? We are limited only by our resourcefulness.

You can imagine almost limitless combinations of analysis by creating mashups of sites like MySpace and/or YouTube to measure cultural trends or public opinion. EBay gives us tons of free data about the behavior of sellers and buyers and what is being bought and sold, and several powerful analytical tools exist to summarize all the data on the site. Comments and reviews of individual products on the sites of Sears, Wal-Mart, Target, and Overstock.com are a source of free information from consumers if we are clever enough to exploit them. The mind reels.

Or, instead of "mining" the Web for information with screen-scapers and mashups, you could use the Web to facilitate direct surveys of clients, employees, and others. Key Survey is one such Web-based survey firm (www.keysurvey.com). These firms offer a variety of statistical analysis capabilities; some have an "intelligent" or adaptive survey approach where the survey dynamically asks different questions depending on how respondents answer earlier questions. Although these capabilities can be very valuable, many clients of Web-based survey services find that the cost reduction alone is reason enough to use these methods of measurement.

Consider these statistics. It used to cost *Farm Journal*, a client of Key Survey, an average of $4 to $5 per respondent for a 40- to 50-question survey of farmers. Now, using Key Survey, it costs *Farm Journal* 25 cents per survey, and it is able to survey half a million people.

NATIONAL LEISURE GROUP

Another client of Key Survey is National Leisure Group (NLG), a major leisure cruise that generates about $700 million in annual revenue.

Jullianna Hale is the director of human resources (HR) and internal communications for the National Leisure Group. She originally brought the Key Survey tool in for HR use, specifically employee satisfaction, performance coach assessments, and training evaluations, but later saw its potential for measuring customer satisfaction. She says, "When you are in the travel industry, every penny is hard to come by. It's a very small profit margin." Given these constraints, it was still important to measure how positive NLG's image was with customers. "We had a lot of great closers [salespeople] but low repeat rates," Hale explains. "So we created a customer experience department and started measuring customer satisfaction. It took us a while to buy into the measurement. It was a big battle."

Every six to eight months, Key Survey put together a customer survey across departments. Being sensitive to the use of customers' time, the company had to do it efficiently. Hale recounts: "There were several iterations of the customer survey but everyone eventually signed off on it." A "postbooking" survey sent in an automated e-mail right after a reservation is made, and another was sent in a "welcome home" e-mail after the customer returned from the cruise. Hale says: "We just wanted to see what kind of results we would get. We were getting a 4% to 5% response rate initially, but with the welcome-home e-mail we were getting an 11.5% response rate." By survey standards, that is very high. In a clever use of a simple control, NLG compares responses to questions like "Will you refer us to a friend?" before and after customers take the trip to see if scores are higher after the vacation.

When they found that clients weren't as happy after the trip, NLG decided to launch a whole new program with the sales team. Hale says, "We had to retrain the sales team to sell in a different way and get the customer to the right vacation." Simply discovering the problem was a measurement success. Now they need to measure the effect of the new program.

Prediction Markets: Wall Street Efficiency Applied to Measurements

The Internet has also made possible a new, dynamic way to make measurements by aggregating opinions with a mechanism similar to what the stock market uses. When an economist talks about the stock market being "efficient," he or she means that it is very hard to beat the market consistently. For any given stock at any given point in time, its price is just about as likely to move up as move down in the very short term. If this was not true, then market participants would bid up or sell off the stock accordingly until that "equilibrium" was achieved.

This process of aggregating the opinions is better at forecasting than almost any of the individual participants in the market are. Far better than an opinion poll, participants have an incentive not only to carefully consider the questions but even, especially when a lot of money is involved, to expend their own resources to get new information to analyze about the investment. People who place bids irrationally tend to run out of money faster and get out of the market. Irrational people also tend to be "random noise" that cancels out in a large market since irrational people are just as likely to overvalue a stock as undervalue it. And because of the active participation the market encourages, news about the value of the company is quickly reflected in its stock price.

This is exactly the type of mechanism the new "prediction markets" are trying to summon. Although they've been researched at least as far back as the early 1990s, they were introduced to a much wider audience in 2004 by the popular book *The Wisdom of the Crowds* by James Surowiecki. Several software tools and public Web sites have created "markets" for such things as who will win the Oscar for Best Actress or who will be nominated as the GOP nominee for president. Exhibit 13.1 shows some examples of various prediction market tools.

Participants in this market buy or sell shares of "claims" about a particular prediction, let's say who will be the GOP nominee for U.S. president. The claims usually states that one share is worth a given amount if it turns out to be true, often $1. You can bet for the claim by buying a "Yes" share and against it by buying a "No" share. That is, you make money if the claim comes true if you own a "Yes" share, and you make money if the claim turns out to be false if you buy a "No" share. A "retired" share is one that has already been judged true or false and the rewards have been paid.

If you are holding 100 "Yes" shares that a particular person becomes the nominee and, in fact, that person becomes the nominee, you would win $100. But when you first bought those shares, it was far from certain that the claim would turn out to be true. You might have paid only 5 cents each for the claims when you bought them a few months prior to the candidate's announcement; the cost may have gone up when the candidacy was announced, down a bit when another popular candidate made an

EXHIBIT 13.1	SUMMARY OF AVAILABLE PREDICTION MARKETS
Consensus Point www.consensuspoint.com	A service for businesses that want to set up prediction markets for internal use. Developed by some of the same people who created Foresight Exchange, the business has a lot of flexibility in how to set up and create reward systems for good forecasters, including monetary incentives.
Foresight Exchange www.ideosphere.com	A free Web site available to the public and one of the earliest experiments on the concept of prediction markets. All bets are "play money." Claims are proposed by the public and reviewed by volunteers. It is an active market with a large number of players, and a good way to get introduced to prediction markets.
NewsFutures www.newsfutures.com	A direct competitor for Consensus Point, it offers businesses services to set up prediction markets.
TradeSports www.tradesports.com	This prediction market started as a type of sports betting Web site then into politics, economics, world events, and other areas. Anyone can create an account but real money is at stake. Anyone can propose a claim but that also takes money. All non-sports trading has now been spun off to Intrade.

announcement to run, and generally went up each time another candidate dropped out. You can make money by holding the shares to the end or by selling at any point you think the market is overpricing the claim.

But the claims examined in prediction markets don't have to be political victories, Oscars, or who wins *American Idol.* They can be any forecast you are tying to measure, including whether two competitors will merge, the sales of a new product, the outcome of some critical litigation, or even whether the company will still be in business. Exhibit 13.2 shows the price on Foresight Exchanges Web site, www.ideosphere.com, for the retired claim "Apple Computer dies by 2005." This claim would have paid $1 for each "Yes" share a player owned if Apple ceased to exist as a viable corporate entity by January 1, 2005. The exact meaning of the claim—how it is judged if Apple is bought or merged into another firm, restructured in bankruptcy, and so on—is spelled out in a detailed description and judge's notes written by the person who will be judging if the claim is true or false. As we know now, Apple did not go out of business, and anyone who owned "Yes" shares would find they were worth nothing. But people who bet against the claim by buying "No" shares would have made $1 per "No" share owned. Like

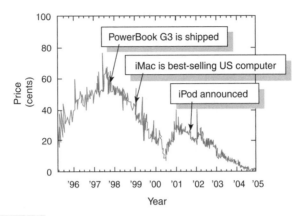

Share Price for "Apple Computer dies by 2005" on Foresight Exchange

stock prices, the price at various times reflects news available in the market (the chart shows some key events in Apple history before the claim retired). Unlike stock prices, however, the price of a "Yes" share is immediately convertible to the chance the company would go out of business. In January 1999, the price of the "Yes" shares was about 30 cents, meaning that the market was saying that there was a 30% chance that Apple computer would no longer be in business by January 1, 2005. By 2004, the price of "Yes" shares dropped below 5 cents per share as it was becoming more obvious that Apple would still be in business at the beginning of the next year.

What is interesting about prediction markets is how well the prices seem to match with the probability of the claim coming true. When large numbers of retired claims are examined, we can see how well prediction markets work. Just like calibrated experts, we determine if a calculated probability is a good one by looking at a large number of old predictions historically and seeing what actually happened. If a method for producing a probability is a good one, then when it tells us each of a set of events is 80% likely, about 80% should actually be correct. Likewise, of all the claims that sell at 40 cents, about 40% should eventually become true. Exhibit 13.3 shows how well this test holds up for TradeSports, NewsFutures, and Foresight Exchange.

The chart shows prices for TradeSports and NewsFutures on the same set of 208 National Football League (NFL) games collected in research

EXHIBIT 13.3   **Performance of Prediction Markets:**
Price vs. Reality

published in *Electronic Markets.*[1] I overlaid on these data my findings from analysis of 353 Foresight Exchange claims collected from all Foresight Exchange data (not just NFL games) but was limited to only those claims that had a significant number of transactions.

We can see that as the price increases, so does the probability that the event will come true. TradeSports, a real-money gambling site, is a well-calibrated fit (i.e., the probability of an event is very close to its price). NewsFutures fits just as well even though players use play money, not real money. (The best players are allowed to use their "money" to bid on prizes like an iPod.)

Foresight Exchange is very different from the other two sites. The exchange uses only play money and does not offer players the chance to buy a prize. Players simply get a $50 allowance of play money every week. There is nothing to spend the money on but claim shares, and there is no reward but bragging rights for the best forecasters. This may be why almost everything in this market is overpriced (i.e., prices are higher than the probability of the event coming true would justify). Another reason might be related to the fact that the claims in Foresight Exchange are submitted by the general public. Most of the claims in this exchange are long shots—many of them fairly bizarre; only 23% of all claims ever come true. It is interesting, though, how *consistent* the overpricing is. It is so consistent that we could simply apply an adjustment factor to the market price to convert it to a probability that is just about as good as TradeSports or NewsFutures. Since this study TradeSports has spun off its non-sports-related trading to a new company called Intrade (www .intrade.com).

Some companies, such as General Electric (GE) and Dow Chemical, are beginning to examine prediction markets as a useful tool for measuring the chance of specific future events. GE, for example, used it to measure the probability that different innovations proposed by employees would be marketable. One useful way to apply prediction markets for a measurement is to bet on the threshold. If a new product is a good investment only if the first-year revenue is $25 million, then the company can set up a claim "Product X will generate more than $25 million revenue in the first 12 months after going to market."

Prediction markets are definitely a powerful new tool for measuring things that might seem impossible to measure. Proponents of prediction markets are almost evangelical in their zeal, believing these tools are the end-all and be-all of measuring virtually anything. I've heard some proponents state that to create a business case, you simply create a claim for every single variable in the business case and open it up to the market. After Surowiecki's book came out, the fervor only increased.

With that in mind, some cautions are in order. Prediction markets are not magic. They are just a way to aggregate the knowledge of a group of people and, especially if real money is used, to provide people with incentives to do research on their trades. Other methods we discussed also work well and may preferable, depending on your needs. Exhibit 13.4 summarizes the judgment-improving methods we have discussed so far.

A LESSON LEARNED: THE DARPA "TERRORISM MARKET" AFFAIR

In 2001 the Defense Advanced Research Projects Agency (DARPA) Information Awareness Office (IAO) decided to research the possibility of using prediction markets in policy analysis, based on studies that showed such markets outpredict individual experts on a variety of topics. This experiment would blow up into a public controversy.

In 2002 demonstration markets were created to predict the spread of SARS and security threat levels. These markets were planned to be run only within government agencies, but concerns that there would not be enough traders and legal problems with conditional transfers of money between agencies led to trading being opened to the general public.

One report showed a mocked-up screen with possible miscellaneous predictions such as assassination of Yasir Arafat and a missile attack from North Korea. The example did not go unnoticed. On July 28, 2003, U.S. Senators Ron Wyden (D-Ore.) and Byron Dorgan (D-N.D.) wrote to the director of the IAO, John Poindexter: "The example that you provide in your report would let participants gamble on the question, 'Will terrorists attack Israel with bioweapons in the next year?' Surely, such a threat should be met with intelligence gathering of the highest quality—not by putting the question to individuals betting on an Internet website, spending taxpayer dollars to create terrorism betting parlors is as wasteful as it is repugnant." A media firestorm ensued.

Within two days, the program was canceled and Poindexter resigned. Robin Hansen of George Mason University, a team member and widely recognized as the conceptual leader of prediction markets, stated: "No one from Congress asked us if the accusations were correct, or if the more offending aspects could be cut from the project. DARPA said nothing."

The senators framed the issue as a moral one and assumed that the program would not be effective. They also implied it would somehow displace other intelligence-gathering methods, when, of course, intelligence agencies have always used multiple methods in concert. If their indignation was based on the idea that terrorists could get rich by exploiting this market, again, their indignation is misplaced. Their position ignored the fact that market participants could have won only trivial amounts, since there was a $100 limit on any trade. Hansen summarized the entire affair: "They had to take a position on a project they knew little about. As a million-dollar project in a trillion-dollar budget, it was an easy target." The net effect of the moral and political posturing was that a very cost-effective tool that may have been a significant improvement on intelligence analysis was taken away.

EXHIBIT 13.4	COMPARISON OF OTHER SUBJECTIVE ASSESSMENT METHODS TO PREDICTION MARKETS
Calibration training	Best when lots of, quick, low-cost estimates are needed. Requires only one expert to work and an answer is immediate. Should be the first estimating method in most cases—more elaborate methods can be used if the VIA justifies it.
Lens Model	Use when there are a large number of repeated estimates of the same type (eg. assessment of investments in a big portfolio, etc.) and when the same type of data can be gathered on each. Once created, the Lens model will generate instant answers for this class of problems regardless of the availability of the original expert(s). Could be created using only hypothetical scenarios.
Rasch Model	Used to standardize different estimates/assessments from different experts or tests on different problems. Unlike Lens, it requires a large set of real evaluations (not hypothetical) and then all are taken into consideration for standardization.
Prediction Markets	Best for forecasts especially where it is useful to track changes in probabilities over time. Requires at least two market players for even the first transaction to occur. Not ideal if you need fast answers for a large number of quantities, homogeneous or not. If the number of claims exceeds the number of transactions in a market, many claims will simply have no estimate.

▓ ENDNOTE

1. Emile Servan-Schreiber, et. al., "Prediction Markets: Does Money Matter?" *Electronic Markets,* 14–3, Sep 2004.

CHAPTER 14

A Universal Measurement Method: Applied Information Economics

I n 1984 the consulting firm The Diebold Group assembled the chief executive officers (CEOs) and chief financial officers (CFO) of 10 major companies in a room at the prestigious Chicago Club to give presentations to their peers in 30 of Chicago's biggest firms. The companies, including IBM, Mobile, AT&T, and Citibank, gave presentations on the process they used when making big investment decisions. The presentations were consistent and simple: If an investment was considered strategic, it received funding. No attempt at computing a return on investment (ROI) was made. This came as a surprise to some of the 30 Chicago companies represented in the room.

Ray Epich, currently with RiverPoint Group LLC, is a venerable sage of IT wisdom and former consultant for The Diebold Group who was in the room during the presentation. Skeptical of the CEOs' rule of automatic acceptance of "strategic" projects, Epich had plenty of counterexamples for the "success rate" of this decision-making approach. "Mead Paper tried to put sap in the paper and blew $100 million," was one example he related.

Epich also mentioned a conversation with Bob Pritzker, of The Marmon Group, the third richest family in the world at the time. "I asked him how he did capital budgeting. He said my guys call me on the phone and I say 'yes or no.' He said he couldn't afford guys to do the ROI." Since then a new appreciation for doing a few simple calculations may have combined with some healthy skepticism about executive gut feelings. Perhaps not.

Such was the world I entered when I first began as a management consultant with Coopers & Lybrand in 1988. I was working on several interesting quantitative problems. Even if they didn't start out as quantitative problems, I tended to define them in that way. That was and is just my world outlook. Through no deliberate career planning of my own, however, I was getting assigned more often as an analyst in large software development projects and, eventually, as a project manager.

Around this time, I first noticed that the quantitative methods routinely used in other parts of business and government were rare or even unheard of in IT management. Things I saw measured in one part of business were frequently dismissed as immeasurable in IT. This is when I decided that someone needed to develop a method for introducing proven quantitative methods to IT.

By then I was employed by DHS & Associates in Rosemont, Illinois. This firm later became RiverPoint, where Ray Epich now works. The management at DHS & Associates also saw the need for a more quantitative solutions in IT, and the company culture afforded consultants a lot of leeway in developing new ideas.

The same year, I began to assemble a method I called Applied Information Economics (AIE). Although I developed it for IT, it turned out to address some fundamental measurement challenges in any field.

BRINGING THE PIECES TOGETHER

The methods discussed in Section II for measuring uncertainty, risk, and the value of information are all key components of AIE. In short, the AIE method addresses four things:

1. How to model a current state of uncertainty
2. How to compute what else should be measured
3. How to measure those things in a way that is economically justified
4. How to make a decision

To get just a little deeper into the AIE process, refer to Exhibit 14.1. You can see that AIE is really nothing more than just a summary of everything we've discussed so far.

The Applied Information Economics Approach

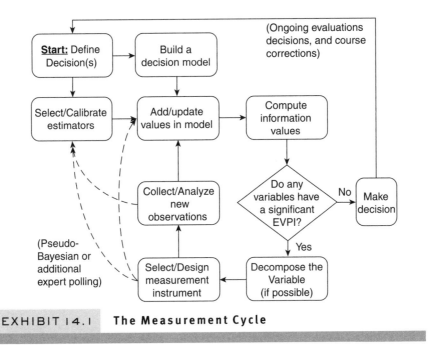

EXHIBIT 14.1   The Measurement Cycle

Applied Information Economics Approach

Since 1995, I've been using AIE to measure all sorts of things that initially seemed difficult or impossible to measure. The name, while unwieldy, was meant to be descriptive. By constantly computing the value of information in every uncertain variable in a decision and recomputing it after each new measurement, we are able to reduce uncertainty on just the right things.

As the necessary precursor to measuring the value of information, the AIE method also emphasizes the quantification of uncertainty and risk at the beginning of the problem definition. And when measurements are justified, AIE would use only methods with a track record of reducing error. The trick was putting this all together into a cohesive method. After the first few projects, the activities tended to settle into these distinct phases:

Phase 0: Project Preparation

- *Initial research.* Interviews, secondary research and prior reports are studied so the AIE analyst can get up to speed on the nature of the problem.
- *Expert identification.* Four or five experts who provide estimates is typical, but I've included as many as 20 (not recommended).
- *Workshop planning.* Four to six half-day workshops are scheduled with the identified experts.

Phase 1: Decision Model

- *Decision problem definition.* In the first workshop, the experts identify what specific problem they are really trying to analyze. For example, are they really deciding whether to proceed with a particular investment, or is the dilemma just about how to modify the investment? If the decision is an investment, project, commitment, or other initiative, then we need to have a meeting with decision makers to develop an investment boundary for the organization.
- *Decision model detail.* By the second workshop, using an Excel spreadsheet, we list all of the factors that matter in the decision being analyzed and show how they add up. If it is a decision to approve a particular major project, then we need to list all of the benefits and costs, add them into a cash flow, and compute a return on investment (as in any simple business case).
- *Initial calibrated estimates.* In the remaining workshops, we calibrate the experts and fill in the values for the variables in the decision model. These values are not fixed points (unless you really know the values exactly). They are the calibrated expert estimates. All quantities are expressed as 90% confidence interval (CI) or other probability distributions.

Phase 2: Preliminary Measurements

- *Value of information analysis (VIA).* At this point we run a VIA on every variable in the model. This tells us the information values and thresholds for every uncertain variable in the decision. A macro I wrote for Excel does this very quickly and accurately, but the methods discussed earlier in the book are a good estimate.

- *Preliminary measurement method designs.* From the VIA, we realize that most of the variables have sufficient certainty and require no further measurement beyond the initial calibrated estimate. Usually only a couple of variables have a high information value (and often they are somewhat of a surprise). Based on this information, we choose measurement methods that, while being significantly less than the Expected Value of Perfect Information (EVPI), should reduce uncertainty. The VIA also shows us the threshold of the measurement—that is, where it begins to make a difference to the decision. The measurement method is focused on reducing uncertainty about that relevant threshold.
- *Measurements methods.* Decomposition, random sampling, subjective-Bayesian, controlled experiments, Lens models (and so on) or some combination thereof are all possible measurement methods used to reduce the uncertainty on the variables identified in the previous step.
- *Updated decision model.* We use the findings from the measurements to change the values in the decision model. Decomposed variables are shown explicitly in their decision model (e.g., an uncertain cost component may be decomposed into smaller components and each of its 90% CIs is shown).
- *Final value of information analysis.* VIAs and measurements (the previous four steps) may go through more than one iteration. As long as the VIA shows a significant information value that is much greater than the cost of a measurement, measurement will continue. Usually, however, one or two iterations is all that is needed before the VIA indicates that no further measurements are economically justified.

Phase 3: Metrics Design and Final Deliverable
- *Completed risk/return analysis.* A final Monte Carlo simulation shows the probabilities of possible outcomes. If the decision is about some major investment, project, commitment, or other initiative (it's usually one of them), then compare the risk and return to the investment boundary for the organization.
- *Identified metrics procedures.* There are often residual VIAs (variables with some information value that were not practical or

economical to measure completely but would become obvious later on). Often these are variables about project progress or external factors about the business or economy. These are values that need to be tracked because knowing them can cause mid-course corrections. Procedures need to be put in place to measure them continually.

- *Decision optimization.* The real decision is rarely a simple "yes/no" approval process. Even if it were, there are multiple ways to improve a decision. Now that a detailed model of risk and return has been developed, risk mitigation strategies can be devised and the investment can be modified to increase return by using what-if analysis.

- *Final report and presentation.* The final report includes an overview of the decision model, VIA results, the measurements used, the position on the investment boundary, and any proposed ongoing metrics or decision optimization methods.

This seems like a lot to digest, but it is really just the culmination of everything covered in the book so far. Now let's turn to a couple of examples in areas that many of the participants in my study presumed to be partly or entirely immeasurable.

CASE: THE VALUE OF THE SYSTEM THAT MONITORS YOUR DRINKING WATER

The Safe Drinking Waters Information System (SDWIS) at the Environmental Protection Agency (EPA) is the central system for tracking drinking water safety in the United States and ensuring quick response to health hazards. When the branch chief for the SDWIS program, Jeff Bryan, needed more money, he had to make a convincing business case. His concern, however, was that the benefits for SDWIS were ultimately about public health, which he didn't know how to quantify economically.

Mark Day, deputy chief information officer and chief technology officer for the Office of Environmental Information, suggested that Bryan conduct an AIE analysis to measure the value. Day, who had spearheaded most of the AIE projects at the EPA to date, even said his office would split the cost.

Phase 0

In Phase 0, the planning phase, we identified 12 persons who would represent the expertise of the EPA on SDWIS and its value. We scheduled five half-day workshops to take place within a three-week period. Jeff Bryan was considered a "core team" person—one who we would rely on to identify other experts and be available for other questions.

Phase 1

In the very first workshop (when the decision is defined), it became apparent that they were really not analyzing SDWIS as a whole, even though that had been my initial assumption. The system had been in place for years, and terminating it or replacing it was not seriously considered. The real dilemma was simply about the justification of three specific improvements to SDWIS: reengineering an exception tracking system, Web-enabling the application for access by states, and modernizing the database. These three initiatives required initial commitments of about $1 million, $2 million, and $500,000, respectively, plus ongoing maintenance. We had to answer which of these improvements was really justified and, of those that were justified, the best priority.

The spreadsheet had to show three separate business cases, one for each of the proposed system modifications, each with its own benefits. The problem was how to compare the cost to health benefits. The Office of Management and Budget (OMB) already required the EPA to produce economic arguments for any proposed environmental policy. The EPA had to compute costs of compliance and benefits to the public for each policy it wanted to enforce. Several such studies showed the economic impact of different types of the most common drinking water contamination. The EPA often resorted to a willingness to pay (WTP) argument, but sometimes only used workdays lost in calculating the cost of contamination. By focusing on how SDWIS is supposed to help public health in the next two workshops, we were able to define a spreadsheet model that tied in the SDWIS modifications to an economic valuation of health benefits. The model had a total of 99 separate variables identified, structured as shown in Exhibit 14.2.

Each of the boxes in the exhibit represents a handful of variables in the spreadsheet business case. For example, for Web-enabled access for states, we were estimating how much time is spent in certain activities, how much

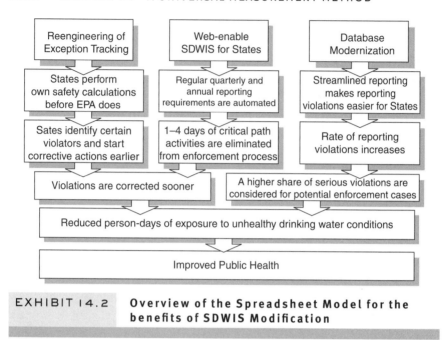

EXHIBIT 14.2   **Overview of the Spreadsheet Model for the benefits of SDWIS Modification**

those activities would be reduced, and the impact on how much sooner violations of water safety regulations could be corrected.

In the last two workshops of Phase 1, we took all the experts through calibration training and asked for initial estimates of every variable in the model. The results from the calibration training showed that the experts were very well calibrated (i.e., 90% of real answers were within the stated 90% CI). Every variable in the model had some level of uncertainty, and some of them were very wide ranges. For example, one of the proposed benefits included an expected increase in the reporting rate of violations—not all water contamination gets reported. The increase was highly uncertain, so experts put a 90% CI of 5% to 55% on the reporting rate increase.

The spreadsheet computed a return on investment for each of the three modifications to SDWIS. At this point, we had a detailed model that showed the experts' current state of uncertainty.

Phase 2

In Phase 2, we ran a VIA. Even though the ranges in all the variables expressed a lot of uncertainty, only one variable merited measurement: the average health effects of new safe drinking water policies. The entire purpose of SDWIS was to track contaminations better and to make corrections more quickly and efficiently. While the upper bound of potential health benefits for a single policy was on the order of $1 billion per year, there was also a chance the benefits could be lower than the cost of compliance for the policy. In other words, the economic benefits of these policies were so uncertain that they actually allowed for the possibility that the net benefits were negative.

If there is no net value to enforcing water regulations (that is, value of the health impacts minus the cost of compliance), then there is no benefit in enforcing the regulations better and faster. All of the uncertainties about state adoption rates of the technology, efficiency improvements, improved reporting rates, and the like turned out to have an information value of zero. All we had to do was reduce our uncertainty about the net economic benefits of drinking water policies. But the potential health benefits (i.e., the upper bounds) were very large compared to the small cost of the SDWIS upgrades. This put the threshold for the economic benefit measurement just barely above zero. In other words, what we really had to reduce uncertainty about was whether the net economic benefits of the drinking water policies were positive at all. We set out to reduce our uncertainty about that and that alone.

Since many of the previous water policy economic analyses varied somewhat in the methods they used, we decided to start with a simple instinctive-Bayesian approach based on a more detailed review of all the economic analysis done to date.

The reason calibrated experts included the possibility of a negative net benefit for water policies was that, out of several economic analyses, one of them showed a negative economic impact for one particular water policy. On further review, it turns out that this particular economic analysis looked only at extremely conservative economic impacts of water contamination—basically, just workdays lost and the economic impact of the loss. However, most people would agree that being sick is worse than just losing a couple of days of wages. The other economic analyses included WTP values for avoiding illness in addition to lost wages. Every analysis that included WTP values for avoiding illness had, as a worst case, a slightly positive net benefit.

As a result, we created a more detailed breakdown of the individual benefits of each water policy. Then we showed a calibrated 90% CI for what the real benefits of the least beneficial policy would be if it included all the same benefits as all the other policies. It became obvious that there was virtually no chance that the net economic impact of water policies would be negative. We updated the model to show this information. The next VIA showed that no further measurement was required to justify any of the SDWIS modifications.

Phase 3

In Phase 3, we ran a final Monte Carlo simulation on each of the three investments. With the reduced uncertainty about the economic benefits of the water policies, each one turned out to be a highly desirable investment. There was, however, a way to improve on their previously planned implementation schedule. The improved exception reporting had a very high potential return (the average ratio of benefits to costs was about 3 to 1), but there was enough uncertainty that there was still a 12% chance of a negative return. The other two modifications had less than a 1% chance of a negative return.

The need for some ongoing metrics was also identified. Adoption rates by state users and how quickly the new system could be implemented were two of the more uncertain items. Therefore, they had "residual" VIAs (that is, they still had some value to measurement, but it was low). We recommended that the EPA should accelerate the other two investments and defer the reengineering of exception reporting. The adoption rates experienced in the other two investments would be considered before beginning development for the exception reporting, in case they were low enough to cancel development (unlikely, but possible).

Epilogue

Mark Day got what he came to expect from an AIE analysis. He said, "Translating software to environmental and health impacts was amazing. The fact that software modules could be traced through a chain of events to some benefit to the public was assumed but never quantified. I think people were frankly stunned anyone could make that connection." He also notes the impact that quantitative analysis has on the decision process. "The result I found striking was the level of agreement of people with disparate views of what should be done. From my view, where consensus is difficult to achieve, the agreement was striking." To Mark Day, the benefit of the VIA was another important part of the process. "Until then, nobody understood the concept of the value of the information and what to look for. They had to try to measure everything, couldn't afford it, and so opted for nothing. The number of variables quickly overwhelmed the ability to measure because they don't know what really matters."

Unlike Day, Jeff Bryan had no exposure to the AIE process before this project. He says: "I was the guy kicking and screaming coming into this AIE analysis. I didn't want to pull people away from what they were doing to do a study like this. But it turned out to be valuable." He was also initially skeptical about calibration, "but after going through the process, and seeing people respond to estimates, I could see the value of calibration." To Bryan, perhaps the most useful step was simply visualizing the connection between an information system and the goals of the program. "The chart [Exhibit 13.2] showed how SDWIS connected to public health and how to compute the benefits. I didn't think that just defining the problem quantitatively would result in something that eloquent. I wasn't getting my point across, and the AIE approach communicated the benefits much better. I can't tell you how many times I used the chart." Finally, and most important, Bryan followed through. "We followed every last recommendation—including the content and timing of recommendations."

I have presented this example for two reasons. First, it is an example of how an "intangible" like public health is quantified for an IT project. I've seen many IT projects dismiss much more easily measured benefits as "immeasurable" and exclude them from the ROI calculation. Second, this example is about what *didn't* have to be measured. Only one variable out of 99 turned out to require uncertainty reduction. The initial calibrated estimates were sufficient for the other 98. As usual, the measurements that would have been considered without doing the VIA probably would have been some of the much lower value measurements such as costs and productivity improvement and the bigger uncertainties, such as public health.

CASE: FORECASTING FUEL FOR THE MARINE CORPS

In the fall of 2004, I was asked to apply AIE on a very different type of problem from what I was used to in business and government. A highly regarded consulting firm was the contractor on a project with the Office of Naval Research (ONR) and the U.S. Marine Corps (USMC) to examine ways logistics planners could better forecast fuel requirements for the battlefield. For operations in Iraq, the USMC used hundreds of thousands of gallons of fuel per day just for ground units alone. (Aviation used about three times as much.) Running out of fuel was an unacceptable scenario for operational success and for the safety of the Marines on the ground.

For planning and logistics purposes, however, they had to start making preparations 60 days in advance in order to have to have sufficient fuel in place when needed. Unfortunately, it is impossible to predict with precision what the battlefield requirements will be that far out. Because uncertainty was so high and the risk of running out was unacceptable, the natural reaction is to plan on delivering three or four times as much fuel as best estimates say would be needed.

Chief Warrant Officer 5 (CWO5) Terry Kunneman, a 27-year USMC veteran, oversaw policy and procedures for bulk fuel planning at Headquarters Marine Corps. "We knew we were working off of older and less reliable consumption factors. In OIF [Operation Iraqi Freedom], we found that all of the traditional systems we had were not working well. It was garbage in, garbage out." Luis Torres, the head of the fuel study at the Office of Naval Research, saw the same problems. "This was all part of an overall directive to reduce the consumption of fuel. The problem was brought up to us that the method we were using had inherent errors in the estimating process."

This amount of additional fuel needed for a safety margin was an enormous logistics burden. Fuel depots dotted the landscape. Daily convoys pushed the fuel from one depot to the next depot farther inland. The depots and, especially, the convoys were security risks; Marines had to put themselves in harm's way to protect the fuel.

If the USMC could reduce their uncertainty about fuel requirements, they would not have to have so much fuel on hand and they still would not increase the chance of running out. At the time, the USMC used a fairly simple forecasting model. First, they counted up all the equipment of different types in the deployed units, then subtracted equipment that was missing due to maintenance, transfer, combat losses, and the like. Then they identified which units would be in "assault" mode and which would be in a "administrative/defensive" mode for approximate periods of time during the next 60 days. Generally, if a unit is in the assault mode, it is moving around more and burning more fuel. Each piece of equipment has a different average consumption measured in gallons per hour and also hours of operation per day. The hours of operation usually increased when the equipment was in a unit that was in assault mode. For each unit, they computed a total daily fuel consumption based on the unit's equipment and whether it is in the assault mode. They then added up all the unit fuel consumptions for each day for 60 days.

The accuracy and precision of this approach was not very high. Fuel estimates could easily be off by a factor of two or more (hence the large safety margins). Even though I had never before dealt with forecasting supplies for the battlefield, I approached the problem the same way I did any other big measurement problem: using AIE.

Phase 0

In Phase 0, I reviewed several previously conducted studies on armed forces' fuel requirements. None offered any specific statistical forecasting methods in detail. At best, they talked about potential methods, and only at a high level. Still, they gave me a good background for the nature of the problem. We identified several logistics experts who could participate in the workshops, including CWO5 Kunneman and Luis Torres. Six half-day workshops were scheduled to occur within a three-week period.

Phase 1

The first workshop, in Phase 1, was set on defining the forecasting problem. Only then was it clear that the USMC wanted to focus on the total fuel use of ground forces only and for a 60-day period for a single Marine Expeditionary Force (MEF), a force consisting of tens of thousands of Marines. Using the existing fuel forecasting tables we studied in Phase 0, I constructed a series of "where does all the fuel go?" charts. The charts gave everyone on the team (but especially us analysts who didn't work with this every day) a sense of orders of magnitude about fuel use. It was clear that most of the fuel does not go into tanks or even armored vehicles in general. True, the M-1 Abrams gets a mere third of a mile per gallon, but there are only 58 tanks in a MEF. In contrast, there are over 1,000 trucks and over 1,300 of the now-famous

HMMWVs, or Hummers. Even during combat, trucks were burning eight times as much fuel as the tanks.

Further discussion about what this equipment was actually doing when they burn fuel caused us to make three different types of models. The biggest part of the model was the convoy model. The vast majority of trucks and HMMWVs burned most of their fuel as part of a convoy on specific convoy routes. They traveled in round-trip convoys an average of twice a day. Another part of the model was the "combat model." The armored fighting vehicles, such as the M-1 tank and the Light Armored Vehicles (LAVs), spent less time on convoy routes and tended to burn fuel more as a function of specific combat operations. Finally, all the generators, pumps, and administrative vehicles tended to burn fuel at both a more consistent and a much lower rate. For this group, we just used the existing simple hourly consumption rate model.

In one of the workshops, the experts were calibrated. All showed a finely tuned ability to put odds on unknowns. They estimated ranges for all the quantities that were previously only given point values. For example, where the 7-ton truck was previously assumed to burn exactly 9.9 gallons per hour, they substituted a 90% CI of 7.8 to 12 gallons per hour. For vehicles typically running in convoys, we had to include ranges for the distance of the typical convoy route and how much route conditions might change fuel consumption. For armored vehicles used in combat operations, we had to estimate a range for the percentage of time they spent in the assault over a 60-day period.

These added up to just 52 basic variables describing how much fuel was burned in a 60-day period. Almost all were expressed as 90% CIs. In a way, this was not unlike any business case analysis I had done. But instead of adding up the variables into a cash flow or return on investment, we simply had a total fuel consumption number for the period. A Monte Carlo simulation based on these ranges gave a distribution of possible results that was very similar to the error and distribution of real-life fuel consumption figures.

Phase 2

In Phase 2 we computed the VIA using Excel macros. (In this case, the information value chart in Exhibit 7.3 of this book would have worked, too.) Since the decision was not expressed in monetary gains or losses, the VIA produced results that meant, in effect, change in error of gallons forecast per day. The biggest information values then were details about convoy routes, including distances and road conditions. The second highest information value was how combat operations affected fuel consumption on combat vehicles. We designed methods to measure both.

To reduce uncertainty about fuel use in combat operations, we opted for a Lens Model based on estimates of field logistics officers from the First Marine Division. These were mostly battalion staff officers and some unit commanders, all with combat experience in OIF. They identified several factors that they felt would change their estimate of fuel use by combat vehicles, including chance of enemy contact (as reported in the operations plan), familiarity with the area, whether terrain was urban or desert, and the like. I gave them each calibration training, then created a list of 40 hypothetical combat scenarios for each officer and gave them data on each of these parameters. For each of these scenarios they provided a 90% CI for fuel use for the type of vehicle they commanded (tanks, LAVs, etc.). After compiling all of their answers, I ran regression models in Excel to come up with a fuel use formula for each vehicle type.

For the road condition variables in the convoy model, we decided we needed to conduct a series of road experiments in Twenty-Nine Palms, California. The other contractors on the project procured GPS equipment and fuel flow meters that would be attached to the trucks' fuel lines. Prior to this study, no one on the team knew anything about fuel flow meters. I just told these consultants: "Somebody does stuff like this all the time. Let's get resourceful and find out who does this and how." In short order, they found a supplier of digital fuel flow meters on Google, and they briefed us on how to use them. They also figured out how to dump the data to a spreadsheet and synchronize the GPS and fuel flow data sources. Including travel time, it took three people a couple of weeks to do both the road tests and the Lens Model, including the setup and development of the Excel system.

The GPS units and fuel flow meters were hooked up to three trucks of two different types. Initially there was some concern that larger samples were needed, but, taking the incremental measurement principle to heart, we thought we would first see just how much variance we would measure in these trucks—two of which were identical models, anyway. The GPS units and fuel flow meters recorded location and consumption data several times each second. This information was continuously captured in an onboard laptop computer while the vehicle was driven. We drove the trucks in a variety of conditions, including paved roads, cross-country, different altitudes (parts of the base varied in altitude significantly), level roads, hilly roads, highway speeds, and so on. By the time we were done we had 500,000 rows of fuel consumption data for a variety of conditions.

We ran this data through a huge regression model. There were far more rows than Excel 2003 could handle, but it was much more detail than we really needed. We consolidated the data into six-second increments and ran different regressions for different tests.

By the time we were done with both measurements, we saw several surprising findings. First, the single biggest cause of variation in fuel forecast was simply how much of the convoy routes were paved or unpaved, followed by other simple features of the convoy route. Furthermore, most of these data (other than temperature) are always known well in advance, since the modern battlefield is thoroughly mapped by satellites and unmanned surveillance aircraft. Therefore, uncertainty about road conditions is a completely avoidable error. Exhibit 14.3 summarizes the forecast errors due to other specific variables.

The combat vehicle model was no less of a revelation for the team. The single best predictor of fuel use by combat vehicles was not chance of enemy contact but simply whether the unit had ever been in that area before. When uncertain of their environment, tank commanders leave their fuel-hungry turbine engines running continuously. They have to keep hydraulics pressurized just to be able to turn the turret, and they want to avoid the risk —however small—of not being able to start the engine in a pinch. Other

EXHIBIT 14.3   **SUMMARY OF AVERAGE EFFECTS OF CHANGING SUPPLY ROUTE VARIABLES FOR A MARINE EXPEDITIONARY FORCE**

Change	Change in gallons/days*
Gravel versus Paved	10,303
+5 mph average speed	4,685
+10 meter climb	6,422
+100 meter average altitude	751
+10 degree temperature	1,075
+10 miles of route	8,320
Additional stop on the route	1,980

combat vehicles as well as tanks tend to use a little more fuel by taking longer but more familiar routes or even, sometimes, by getting lost.

The familiarity with the area was, like the route-related measurements, always a factor planners would know in advance. They knew whether a unit had been in an area before. Taking this into account reduced the daily fuel consumption error about 3,000 gallons per day. Putting the chance of enemy contact into the model reduced error by only 2,400 gallons per day—less than all but three of the supply-route-related factors. In fact, it is barely more than the effect that one additional stop on the convoy route would account for.

Phase 3

In Phase 3 we developed a spreadsheet tool for the logistics planners that took all these new factors into account. On average, it would reduce the error of their previous forecasting method by about half. According to the USMC's own cost-of-fuel data (it costs a lot more to deliver fuel in the battlefield than to your local gas station), this would save at least $50 million per year per MEF. There were two MEF's in Iraq at the time this book was written.

Epilogue

This study fundamentally changed how the USMC thought about fuel forecasts. Even the most experienced planners in USMC logistics said they were surprised at the results. CWO5 Kunneman said: "What surprised me was the convoy model that showed most fuel was burned on logistics routes. The study even uncovered that tank operators would not turn tanks off if they didn't think they could get replacement starters. That's something that a logistician in 100 years probably wouldn't have thought of." The more "abstract" benefits of an everything-is-measurable philosophy seemed obvious to CWO5 Kunneman. "You are paying money for fuel. If they tell me it's hard data to get, I say I bet it's not. How much are you paying for being wrong in your forecast?" Luis Torres agreed. "The biggest surprise was that we can save so much fuel. We freed up vehicles because we didn't have to move as much fuel. For a logistics person, that's critical. Now vehicles that moved fuel can move ammunition."

260 CHAPTER 14 A UNIVERSAL MEASUREMENT METHOD

Like the SDWIS case, this is an example of what we didn't have to measure as much as what we did measure. There were many other variables that might otherwise have been examined in much more detail, but we were able to avoid them completely. This is also an example of how much one can do with a hands-on, just-do-it approach to measurement. These bright computer programming consultants on the team, who told me they never change the oil in their own cars themselves, pulled up their sleeves and got greasy under a truck to attach the fuel flow meters and GPS systems. In the end, the fuel consumption measurements turned out to be easy because, in part, we never doubted that it was possible if the team was just resourceful enough. This is a sharp contrast to a previous study done by the Office of Naval Research that was more like typical management consulting: heavy on high-minded concepts and visions, no measurements and no new information.

The final lesson here for measurement skeptics is what such measurement efforts mean for the safety and security of people. We didn't need to explicitly compute the value of the security and safety of Marines for this project (although we could have done so with WTP or other methods), but less fuel being moved means fewer convoys putting Marines in danger of roadside bomb and ambushes. I like to think I could have saved someone's life with the right measurements. I'm glad fear and ignorance of measurements didn't get in the way of that.

IDEAS FOR GETTING STARTED: A FEW FINAL EXAMPLES

In this book we covered several examples of measurement including performance, security, risk, market forecasts, the value of information, and the basic ideas behind valuing health and happiness. I introduced some concepts behind basic empirical measurements, including random sampling, experiments, and regression analysis.

This information might seem overwhelming. But, as with almost everything else in business or life, it's often just a matter of getting started on a few examples, working through a problem, and seeing the results. Here I'm going to introduce some possible measurement problems that we have not already discussed. I'm going just deep enough into each of these to get you going down the right path in thinking through the measurement problem.

For each of these problems, the standard measurement steps still apply, even though I may not mention each step in detail. I suggest a possible clarification for each one, but you will still need to think through your initial uncertainty, the value of information, decomposition, and selecting a measurement instrument. However, I provide enough information to start you off on that path.

Quality

I was once asked by an executive, who said she was a member of a professional quality association, how to measure quality. She added that there is a recurring debate about how to measure quality in the group's monthly meetings. I thought this was odd because the person who is sometimes called the "Father of Quality," Edward Deming, treated quality as a quantity. She seemed familiar with Deming, but she did not know that he was a statistician. He preached that if you don't have a measurement program, you don't have a quality program. To Deming, quality was the consistency with which expectations were met. The lack of meeting defined expectations is a defect. Measuring quality in a manufacturing process was, to Deming, a matter of measuring the frequency of different types of defects and measuring variances from the expected norm.

I consider Deming's view of quality fundamentally necessary to the concept of quality measurement, but perhaps not sufficient by itself. With all due respect to Deming, I think a complete definition of quality would have to include more than this. A very cheaply made product may perfectly fit the expectations of the manufacturer and yet be perceived as low quality by consumers. And if customers don't think the product has quality, why should the producer think it does? Any complete description of quality would have to include a survey of customers.

It might also be helpful to remember the distinction between stated and revealed preferences. In a survey, customers state their preferences. When they are making (or not making) purchases, they reveal their preferences. The ultimate expression of quality is the premium customers are willing to pay for a product. This "premium revenue" can also be compared to advertising dollars spent since—generally—products perceived as high quality have people willing to pay a premium even without the additional advertising that would otherwise be required. Perhaps quality products get more repeat business and more word-of-mouth advertising. Everything mentioned so far lends itself at least to a random survey method and, for the clever analyst, some type of "implied price premium" based on the purchasing behaviors of customers.

Value of a Process, Department, or Function

A question like "what is the value of ___?" is about as loaded as a measurement question gets. Usually, the perceived difficulty in measuring value is really the lack of a clear definition of why it is being measured. I sometimes hear chief information officers (CIOs) ask how to measure the value of information technology. I ask, "Why, are you considering getting rid of it?" All valuation problems in business or government are about a comparison of alternatives. If you were to attempt compute the value of IT for a company, you would presumably have to compare it against the costs and benefits of not having IT. So unless you really are considering doing without IT (or whatever you want to know the value of), the question is irrelevant.

Perhaps, however, the CIO really needs to know whether the value of IT has improved since she took charge. In that case, she should focus on computing the net benefits of specific decisions and initiatives made since she started. This question could also be looked at as the type of performance-as-financial-impacts measurement discussed in previous chapters. If a CIO is asking for the value of IT because she wants to argue against outsourcing her entire department, then she is not really asking about the value of IT itself, just the value of keeping it in-house versus outsourcing it.

No value question will ever be asked that doesn't ultimately imply alternatives. If you have the right alternatives defined and the true decision defined, the value question will be much more obvious.

Innovation

Just like anything else, innovation, if it is real, is observable in some way. Like some other measurement problems, the challenge here is probably more of an issue of defining what decision is being supported. What would you do differently based on possible findings from a measurement of innovation? If you can identify at least some real decision—perhaps evaluating teams or research and development (R&D) efforts for bonuses or termination—then read on. Otherwise, there is no business purpose in measuring it.

If you can identify at least one decision this measurement could actually affect, then I would propose using one of three possible methods. First, there is always the method of leaving it a purely subjective but controlled evaluation. Use independent human judges with Rasch models and controls to adjust for judge biases. Controls would include a blind where the identities of teams or persons are kept from the judges while the judges consider just creative output (e.g., advertisements, logos, research papers, architectural plans, or whatever else the creative teams develop). This might be useful if you are trying to evaluate the quality of research in R&D based on a portfolio of ideas being generated. The Mitre example in Chapter 2 might provide some insight.

Another method might be based on other indicators of innovation that are available when the work has to be published, such as patents or research papers. The field of bibliometrics (the study and measurement of texts, e.g., research papers) uses methods like counting and cross-referencing citations. If a person writes something truly groundbreaking, the work tends to be referenced frequently by other researchers. In this case, counting the number of citations a researcher gets is probably more revealing than just counting the number of papers he or she has written. The same method can be used where patents are produced, since patent applications have to refer to similar existing patents to discuss similarities and differences. An area of research called scientometrics attempts to measure scientific productivity.[1] Although it usually compares entire companies or countries; you might check it out.

A final method worth considering is similar to the performance-as-financials approach discussed in the previous chapter. As the Madison Avenue guru David Ogilvy said, "If it doesn't sell, it isn't creative." Things might seem creative but not actually be creative in a way that is relevant to the business. If the objective was to innovate a solution to a business problem, what was the business (i.e., ultimately financial) impact? How about measuring researchers the way Tom Bakewell measured the performance of academics or the way Billy Bean measured the performance of baseball players (Chapter 12)?

Information Availability

I've modeled information availability at least four different times, and every model ends up with the same variables. Improved availability of information means you spend less time looking for it and lose information less often.

When information is lost, you either do without it or you attempt to re-create it. Looking for a document or attempting to re-create it are simply measured in terms of the cost of effort in these undesirable and avoidable tasks. If the only option is to do without it, then there is a cost of making less informed decisions that are more frequently wrong. To get started, the average duration of document searching, the frequency of document re-creation, and the frequency of going without (per year) are quantities calibrated estimators can put ranges on.

Flexibility

The term "flexibility" itself is so broad and ambiguous it could mean quite a lot of things. Here I'll just focus on how three specific clients defined and measured it. Since they gave such different answers, it will be useful to go into a little detail. In clarifying what "flexibility" meant, these three clients came up with:

> Example 1: Percent reduction in average response time to unexpected network availability problems (e.g., more quickly fixing virus attacks or unexpected growth of demand on the network).
> Example 2: Percent reduction in average development time for new products.
> Example 3: The ability to add new software packages if needed. (The previous IT system had several custom systems that did not integrate with Oracle-based applications.)

All three were related to some proposed IT investment, either infra-structure or software development. As usual, we had to compute the monetary value of each of these for each year in a cash flow so that we could compute a net present value and rate of return for the investment:

Example 1 : Monetary value for each year of a 5-year ROI

= (current downtime hours per year)

× (average cost of one hour of downtime)

× (reduction in downtime from new system)

Example 2 : Monetary value for each year of a 7-year ROI

= ((new product developments per year)

$\times$ (percent of new products that go to market)

$\times$ (current product development time in months)

$\times$ (additional gross profit of new product introduced
one month earlier)

$+$ (cost development)) $\times$ (reduction in time spent)

Example 3 : Monetary value for each year of a 5-year NPV

$=$ (number of new applications per year)

$\times$ (NPV of additional average lifetime maintenance
for custom applications compared to
standardized package)

$+$ (additional near-term cost of custom development
compared to standardized package)

Since these were each large, uncertain decisions, EVPIs were in the hundreds of thousands to millions of dollars. But, as is often the case, in each of these the most important measurement was not what the client might normally have chosen. We applied the methods that follow for these measurement problems.

Example 1. We developed a post-downtime survey for 30 people after each of 5 downtime events. The client was able to determine whether people were affected at all by a downtime or, if so, how much time they actually were unproductive.

Example 2. We decomposed product development time into nine specific activities, used calibrated estimators to estimate time spent in each activity as a percentage of the whole, and used calibrated estimators who were given information about additional studies to estimate the reduction in each activity.

Example 3. We identified specific applications that would be considered in the next couple of years and computed the development and maintenance cost of each relative to an equivalent custom package.

In each example, the measurements cost less than $20,000; the figure ranged from half of 1% to 1% of the computed EVPI. In each case the initial uncertainty was reduced by 40% or more. Additional VIA showed no value to additional measurements. After the measurement, Examples 1 and 3 had clear cases for proceeding with the investment. Example 2 was still very risky and was justified only after a significant reduction in scope and costs as part of a pilot deployment.

Flexibility with Options Theory

In 1997 the Nobel Prize in Economics went to Robert C. Merton and Myron Scholes for developing options theory and, specifically, the Black-Scholes formula for valuing financial options. (The Nobel Prize is given only to living persons; another contributor, Fischer Black, had died before the prize was awarded.) A call option in finance gives its owner the right, but not the obligation, to purchase some other financial instrument (stock, commodity, etc.) at a future point at a given price. Likewise, a put option gives the owner the right to sell it at a given price. If, for example, you have a call option to buy a share of stock at a price of $100 one month from now and, by then, the stock is trading at $130, you can make some money by exercising the option to buy it at $100 and turn it over immediately for a $30 profit. The problem is that you don't know how much the stock will be selling for in one month and whether your option will be of any value. Until the Black-Scholes formula was derived, it was not at all clear how to price such an option.

This theory got more popular buzz in the business press than most economic theories do, and it became fashionable to apply options theory not just to the pricing of put or call options but to how internal business decisions are made. This became known as real options theory, and many managers attempted to formulate a large number of business decisions as a type of options valuation problem. Although this method might make sense in some situations, it was overused. Not every benefit of a new technology, for example, can necessarily be expressed as a type of option valuation problem. In reality, most "real options" don't even boil down to an application of Black-Scholes but a more traditional application of decision theory. If, for example, you run a Monte Carlo simulation for a new IT software platform, and that platform gives you the option to make changes if future conditions make such changes beneficial, then the simulation will show that, on average, there is a value to having the option compared to not having the option. This does not involve Black-Scholes formula, but it is actually what most real option problems are about. Using the same formula that is used to price stock options might be appropriate, but only if you can literally translate the meaning of every variable in Black-Scholes to your problem. Inputs to Black-Scholes formulas include exercise price, strike price, and the price volatility of the stock. If it's not apparent what these items really mean in a given business decision, then Black-Scholes is probably not the solution. (The supplementary Web site has examples of options valuations with and without Black-Scholes.)

SUMMARIZING THE PHILOSOPHY

If you think you are dealing with something "impossible" to measure, keep in mind the examples from SDWIS and the USMC. Meeting such a measurement challenge is really pretty simple when you think about it.

1. If it's really that important, it's something you can define. If it's something you think exists at all, then it's something you've already observed somehow.

2. If it's something important and something uncertain, then you have a cost of being wrong and a chance of being wrong.

3. You can quantify your current uncertainty with calibrated estimates.

4. You can compute the value of additional information by knowing the "threshold" of the measurement where it begins to make a difference compared to your existing uncertainty.

5. Once you know what it's worth to measure something, you can put the measurement effort in context and decide on the effort it should take.

6. Knowing just a few methods for random sampling, controlled experiments, or even just improving on the judgments of experts can lead to a significant reduction in uncertainty.

In retrospect, I wonder if Eratosthenes, Enrico, and Emily would have been deterred by any of the "impossible" measurement problems we have considered. From their actions, it seems clear to me that they at least intuitively grasped almost every major point this book makes about measurement. Perhaps quantifying current uncertainty and computing the value of information itself and how it affects methods would have been new to them. Even though our measurement mentors could not have known some of the methods we discussed, I suspect they would still have found a way to make observations that would have reduced uncertainty.

I hope, if nothing else, that the examples of Eratosthenes, Enrico, and Emily and the practical cases described make you a little more skeptical about claims that something critical to your business cannot be measured.

▪ ENDNOTE

1. Paul Stoneman, et al., *Handbook of the Economics of Innovation and Technological Change*, (Malden, MA: Basil Blackwell Ltd., 1995).

Calibration Tests
(and their answers)

ANSWERS TO CALIBRATION QUESTIONS IN CHAPTER 5:

#	Question	Answer
1	In 1938 a British steam locomotive set a new speed record by going how fast (mph)?	126
2	In what year did Newton publish the universal laws of gravitation?	1685
3	How many inches long is a typical business card?	3.5
4	The Internet (then called "Arpanet") was established as a military communications system in what year?	1969
5	What year was William Shakespeare born?	1564
6	What is the air distance between New York and Los Angeles in miles?	2,451
7	What percentage of a square could be covered by a circle of the same width?	78.5%
8	How old was Charlie Chaplin when he died?	88
9	How many days does it actually take the Moon to orbit Earth?	27.32
10	The TV show *Gilligan's Island* first aired on what date?	Sep 26, 1964
	Statement	**Answer**
1	The ancient Romans were conquered by the ancient Greeks.	FALSE
2	There is no species of three-humped camels.	TRUE
3	A gallon of oil weighs less than a gallon of water.	TRUE
4	Mars is always farther away from Earth than Venus.	FALSE
5	The Boston Red Sox won the first World Series.	TRUE
6	Napoleon was born on the island of Corsica.	TRUE
7	"M" is one of the three most commonly used letters.	FALSE
8	In 2002 the price of the average new desktop computer purchased was under $1,500.	TRUE
9	Lyndon B Johnson was a governor before becoming vice president.	FALSE
10	A kilogram is more than a pound.	TRUE

There are more calibration tests on the following pages.

ADDITIONAL CALIBRATION TESTS

Calibration Survey for Ranges: A

#	Question	Lower Bound (95% chance value is higher)	Upper Bound (95% chance value is lower)
1	How many feet tall is the Hoover Dam?		
2	How many inches long is a 20-dollar bill?		
3	What percentage of aluminum is recycled in the United States?		
4	When was Elvis Presley born?		
5	What percentage of the atmosphere is oxygen by weight?		
6	What is the latitude of New Orleans? Hint: Latitude is 0 degrees at the equator and 90 at the North Pole.		
7	In 1913, the U.S. military owned how many airplanes?		
8	The first European printing press was invented in what year?		
9	What percentage of all electricity consumed in U.S. households was used by kitchen appliances in 2001?		
10	How many miles tall is Mount Everest?		
11	How long is Iraq's border with Iran in kilometers?		
12	How many miles long is the Nile?		
13	In what year was Harvard founded?		
14	What is the wingspan (in feet) of a Boeing 747 jumbo jet?		
15	How many soldiers were in a Roman legion?		
16	What is the average temperature of the abyssal zone (where the oceans are more than 6,500 feet deep) in degrees F?		
17	How many feet long is the Space Shuttle Orbiter (excluding the external tank)?		
18	In what year did Jules Verne publish 20,000 Leagues Under the Sea?		
19	How wide is the goal in field hockey (feet)?		
20	The Roman Coliseum held how many spectators?		

Answers are on page 272.

Answers for Calibration Survey for Ranges: A

#	Answers
1	738
2	63/16ths (6.1875)
3	45%
4	1935
5	21%
6	31
7	23
8	1450
9	26.7%
10	5.5

#	Answers
11	1458
12	4,160
13	1636
14	196
15	6000
16	39°F
17	122
18	1870
19	12
20	50,000

Calibration Survey for Ranges: B

#	Question	Lower Bound (95% chance value is higher)	Upper Bound (95% chance value is lower)
1	The first probe to land on Mars, Viking 1, landed there in what year?		
2	How old was the youngest person to fly into space?		
3	How many meters tall is the Sears Tower?		
4	What was the maximum altitude of the Breitling Orbiter 3, the first balloon to circumnavigate the globe, in miles?		
5	On average, what percentage of the total software development project effort is spent in design?		
6	How many people were permanently evacuated after the Chernobyl nuclear power plant accident?		
7	How many feet long were the largest airships?		
8	How many miles is the flying distance from San Francisco to Honolulu?		
9	The fastest bird, the falcon, can fly at a speed of how many miles per hour in a dive?		
10	In what year was the double helix structure of DNA discovered?		
11	How many yards *wide* is a football field?		
12	What was the percentage growth in Internet hosts from 1996 to 1997?		
13	How many calories are in 8 ounces of orange juice?		
14	How fast would you have to travel at sea level to break the sound barrier (mph)?		
15	How many years was Nelson Mandela in prison?		
16	What is the average daily calorie intake in developed countries?		
17	In 1994, how many nations were members of the United Nations?		
18	The Audubon Society was formed in the United States in what year?		
19	How many feet high is the world's highest waterfall (Angel Falls, Venezuela)?		
20	How deep beneath the sea was the *Titanic* found (miles)?		

Answers are on page 274.
Still not calibrated? Get more calibration tests at www.howtomeasureanything.com.

Answers to Calibration Survey for Ranges: B

#	Answers
1	1976
2	26
3	443
4	6.9
5	20%
6	135,000
7	803
8	2394
9	150
10	1953

#	Answers
11	53.3
12	70%
13	120
14	760
15	26
16	3,300
17	184
18	1905
19	3212
20	2.5 miles

Calibration Survey for Binary: A

	Statement	Answer True/False	Confidence that you are correct (Circle one)
1	The Lincoln Highway was the first paved road in the United States, and it ran from Chicago to San Francisco.		50% 60% 70% 80% 90% 100%
2	The Silk Road joined the two ancient kingdoms of China and Afghanistan.		50% 60% 70% 80% 90% 100%
3	More American homes have microwaves than telephones.		50% 60% 70% 80% 90% 100%
4	"Doric" is an architectural term for a shape of a roof.		50% 60% 70% 80% 90% 100%
5	The World Tourism Organization predicts that Europe will still be the most popular tourist destination in 2020.		50% 60% 70% 80% 90% 100%
6	Germany was the second country to develop atomic weapons.		50% 60% 70% 80% 90% 100%
7	A hockey puck will fit in a golf hole.		50% 60% 70% 80% 90% 100%
8	The Sioux were one of the "Plains" Indian tribes.		50% 60% 70% 80% 90% 100%
9	To a physicist, "plasma" is a type of rock.		50% 60% 70% 80% 90% 100%
10	The Hundred Years' War was actually over a century long.		50% 60% 70% 80% 90% 100%
11	Most of the fresh water on Earth is in the polar ice caps.		50% 60% 70% 80% 90% 100%
12	The Academy Awards (Oscars) began over a century ago.		50% 60% 70% 80% 90% 100%
13	There are fewer than 200 billionaires in the world.		50% 60% 70% 80% 90% 100%
14	In Excel, a " ^ " means "take to the power of."		50% 60% 70% 80% 90% 100%
15	The average annual salary of airline captains is over $150,000.		50% 60% 70% 80% 90% 100%
16	By 1997, Bill Gates was worth more than $10 billion.		50% 60% 70% 80% 90% 100%
17	Cannons were used in European warfare by the eleventh century.		50% 60% 70% 80% 90% 100%
18	Anchorage is the capital of Alaska.		50% 60% 70% 80% 90% 100%
19	Washington, Jefferson, Lincoln, and Grant are the four presidents whose heads are sculpted into Mount Rushmore.		50% 60% 70% 80% 90% 100%
20	John Wiley & Sons is not the largest book publisher.		50% 60% 70% 80% 90% 100%

Answers are on page 276.

Answers for Calibration Survey for Binary: A

#	Answers
11	TRUE
12	FALSE
13	FALSE
14	TRUE
15	FALSE
16	TRUE
17	FALSE
18	FALSE
19	FALSE
20	TRUE

#	Answers
1	FALSE
2	FALSE
3	FALSE
4	FALSE
5	TRUE
6	FALSE
7	TRUE
8	TRUE
9	FALSE
10	TRUE

Calibration Survey for Binary: B

	Statement	Answer True/False	Confidence that you are correct (Circle one)
1	Jupiter's "Great Red Spot" is larger than Earth.		50% 60% 70% 80% 90% 100%
2	The Brooklyn Dodgers' name was an abbreviation for "trolley car dodgers."		50% 60% 70% 80% 90% 100%
3	"Hypersonic" is faster than "subsonic."		50% 60% 70% 80% 90% 100%
4	A "polygon" is three dimensional and a polyhedron is two dimensional.		50% 60% 70% 80% 90% 100%
5	A 1-watt electric motor produces 1 horsepower.		50% 60% 70% 80% 90% 100%
6	Chicago is more populous than Boston.		50% 60% 70% 80% 90% 100%
7	In 2005, Wal-Mart sales dropped below $100 billion.		50% 60% 70% 80% 90% 100%
8	Post-it Notes were invented by 3M.		50% 60% 70% 80% 90% 100%
9	Alfred Nobel, whose fortune endows the Nobel Peace Prize, made his fortune in oil and explosives.		50% 60% 70% 80% 90% 100%
10	A BTU is a measure of heat.		50% 60% 70% 80% 90% 100%
11	The winner of the first Indianapolis 500 clocked an average speed of under 100 mph.		50% 60% 70% 80% 90% 100%
12	Microsoft has more employees than IBM.		50% 60% 70% 80% 90% 100%
13	Romania borders Hungary.		50% 60% 70% 80% 90% 100%
14	Idaho is larger (area) than Iraq.		50% 60% 70% 80% 90% 100%
15	Casablanca is on the African continent.		50% 60% 70% 80% 90% 100%
16	The first man-made plastic was invented in the nineteenth century.		50% 60% 70% 80% 90% 100%
17	A chamois is an alpine animal.		50% 60% 70% 80% 90% 100%
18	The base of pyramid is in the shape of a square.		50% 60% 70% 80% 90% 100%
19	Stonehenge is located on the main British island.		50% 60% 70% 80% 90% 100%
20	Computer processors double in power every three months or less.		50% 60% 70% 80% 90% 100%

Answers are on page 278.

Still not calibrated? Get more calibration tests at www.howtomeasureanything.com.

Answers to Calibration Survey for Binary: B

#	Answers	#	Answers
11	TRUE	1	TRUE
12	FALSE	2	TRUE
13	TRUE	3	TRUE
14	FALSE	4	FALSE
15	TRUE	5	FALSE
16	TRUE	6	TRUE
17	TRUE	7	FALSE
18	TRUE	8	TRUE
19	TRUE	9	TRUE
20	FALSE	10	TRUE

Index